LEARNER VOICES, PERSPECTIVES, AND POSITIONINGS

This book explores the multifaceted concept of learner voice in education, emphasising its significance across various contexts and historical periods. It brings together diverse perspectives from multiple authors, addressing how learner agency can shape educational practices and policies, particularly in contemporary settings.

The chapters delve into critical themes such as the influence of teachers' beliefs on student learning, the impact of polarisation in our current educational discourse and the historical voices of children in Victorian schools. Notable case studies include a narrative approach to understanding higher education students' experiences and the examination of learner voice within prison education. The book also addresses pressing issues such as the representation of marginalised voices and the importance of inclusive practices in school leadership and curriculum design. Groundbreaking content includes discussions on "epistemic violence", highlighting the need for a more nuanced, considered and critically aware approach to learner representation.

This important collection will be essential reading for educational studies students and trainee teachers, as well as educators working in further or higher education. It provides practical insights and theoretical frameworks that constitute a roadmap for strengthening diverse learners' voice and agency, thereby advancing educational equity and inclusion for all.

Simon Taylor is Senior Lecturer and Course Leader at the University of Worcester. He specialises in creativity and cultural education, collaborative research and partnerships. His most recent publication is entitled *Creativity in the Early Years: Engaging Children Aged 0–5*.

Seán Bracken is Doctoral Programme Lead for the College of Education Culture and Society at the University of Worcester and an Adjunct Professor at Curtin University Australia. He is co-founder of the International Collaboratory for Leadership in Universally Designed Education (INCLUDE) and coordinates the Inclusion by Design research group at the University of Worcester (UW).

The Routledge Education Studies Series

Series Editor: Stephen Ward, Bath Spa University, UK

The Routledge Education Studies Series aims to support advanced level study on Education Studies and related degrees by offering in-depth introductions from which students can begin to extend their research and writing in years 2 and 3 of their course. Titles in the series cover a range of classic and up-and-coming topics, developing understanding of key issues through detailed discussion and consideration of conflicting ideas and supporting evidence. With an emphasis on developing critical thinking, allowing students to think for themselves and beyond their own experiences, the titles in the series offer historical, global and comparative perspectives on core issues in education.

Education in Europe
Looking out for what the neighbours do
Edited by Tom Feldges

Pedagogies for the Future
A critical reimagining of education
Gary Beauchamp, Dylan Adams and Kevin Smith

Understanding Education Studies
Critical Issues and New Directions
Edited by Mark Pulsford, Rebecca Morris and Ross Purves

Leadership and Management for Education Studies
Introducing Key Concepts of Theory and Practice
Edited by Catherine A. Simon ad Deborah Outhwaite

New Studies in the History of Education
Connecting the Past to the Present in an Evolving Discipline
Edited by Nicholas Joseph

Understanding the Further Education Sector
History, Challenges, and Achievements
Jim Crawley

Critical Histories in Care and Education
Understanding the Connections Between the English Care and Education Systems from the Nineteenth Century to the Present Day
Kate Brooks

Learner Voices, Perspectives, and Positionings
Providing Agency to Empower Learning
Edited by Simon Taylor and Seán Bracken

For more information about this series, please visit: www.routledge.com/The-Routledge-Education-Studies-Series/book-series/RESS

LEARNER VOICES, PERSPECTIVES, AND POSITIONINGS

PROVIDING AGENCY TO EMPOWER LEARNING

Edited by Simon Taylor and Seán Bracken

LONDON AND NEW YORK

Designed cover image: Getty Images

First edition published 2026
by Routledge
4 Park Square, Milton Park, Abingdon, Oxon, OX14 4RN

and by Routledge
605 Third Avenue, New York, NY 10158

Routledge is an imprint of the Taylor & Francis Group, an informa business

© 2026 selection and editorial matter, Simon Taylor and Seán Bracken; individual chapters, the contributors

The right of Simon Taylor and Seán Bracken to be identified as the authors of the editorial material, and of the authors for their individual chapters, has been asserted in accordance with sections 77 and 78 of the Copyright, Designs and Patents Act 1988.

All rights reserved. No part of this book may be reprinted or reproduced or utilised in any form or by any electronic, mechanical, or other means, now known or hereafter invented, including photocopying and recording, or in any information storage or retrieval system, without permission in writing from the publishers.

Trademark notice: Product or corporate names may be trademarks or registered trademarks, and are used only for identification and explanation without intent to infringe.

British Library Cataloguing-in-Publication Data
A catalogue record for this book is available from the British Library

ISBN: 978-1-032-52372-9 (hbk)
ISBN: 978-1-032-52370-5 (pbk)
ISBN: 978-1-003-40633-4 (ebk)

DOI: 10.4324/9781003406334

Typeset in News Gothic Std
by SPi Technologies India Pvt Ltd (Straive)

Chapter 9 is dedicated to our dear friend and colleague, Rebecca Davidge, whose commitment to education and inclusion was a powerful driving force in realising this work. It is reproduced with kind permission of her husband, Gavin Davidge.

Contents

Preface	ix
Foreword RICHARD WOOLLEY	xii
Contributing Authors	xv
Acknowledgements	xx

1 Education's purpose: Conceptions of teaching, conceptions of learning and learner voice   1
PETER GOSSMAN, ANASTASIA KENNETT AND SHARON SMITH

2 Why don't they teach education at school? Listening to learners' voices and resisting polarisation to restore education as common ground throughout our lifetimes   15
SARA DORNAN, STUART GALLAGHER, LUCY GIBSON, MIA GRIFFIN, NIALL HARRIS AND JESSICA JONES

3 Finding the voice of children past: How do we do it, and what does it tell us?   26
RUTH FELSTEAD

4 Beyond the survey metrics: A narrative approach to higher education student voice   37
PAI USOWICZ AND ELLIE HILL

5 Transitions in education: The importance of learner voice and identity   47
JOANNE SMITH AND ANASTASIA KENNETT

6 Advocating for the learner and their diverse needs   59
SHARON SMITH

7 Examining how academic self-concept and agency shaped a SEND learner's identity across the educational lifespan   69
REBECCA RUSSON AND ALEXANDRA SEWELL

8 Epistemic injustice and the silencing of student voices   80
JEREMIAH ADEBOLAJO OLUSOLA

9 From voice and systemic action: Addressing race and racism in a teacher education programme 91
   ELENA LENGTHORN, REBECCA DAVIDGE AND RACHAEL MOORE

10 Learner voice and the placement experience: Engineering a map of prison-education interactions 102
   EMILY DAVIS AND SIMON TAYLOR

11 Global voices: Empowering students for world-class education 118
   MADELEINE FINDON AND RABIAT MALIK

12 Empowering disabled learners' voices and agency through universal design for learning 130
   SEÁN BRACKEN, ALICE HOPKINS, ANASTASIA KENNETT, HARRIET LAWRENCE, EMMA RICHARDSON, KIRSTY WEDGBURY AND CHRISTIAN T. WILSON

13 The role of learner voice in producing powerful and sustainable educational change 145
   MARIE STEPHENSON

   Index *157*

Preface

Education Studies has become a popular and exciting undergraduate subject in many universities in the United Kingdom. It began in the early 2000s, mainly in the post-1992 universities which had been centres of teacher training. Gaining academic credibility, the subject is now taught and researched in pre-1992 and Russell Group institutions. In 2004, Routledge published one of the first texts for undergraduates, *Education Studies: A Student's Guide* (Ward, 2004), and then its fourth edition (Simon and Ward, 2019). It comprises a series of chapters introducing key topics in Education Studies and has contributed to the development of the subject. Targeted at students and academic staff at levels 5, 6 and 7, the Routledge Education Studies Series offers a sequence of volumes which explore such topics in depth.

It is important to understand that Education Studies is not teacher training or teacher education, although graduates in the subject may well go on to become teachers after a Post Graduate Certificate of Education (PGCE) or school-based training. Education Studies should be regarded as a subject with a variety of career outcomes or, indeed, none: it can be taken as the academic and critical study of education in itself. At the same time, whilst the theoretical elements of teacher training are continually reduced in PGCE courses and school-based training, undergraduate Education Studies provides a critical analysis for future teachers who, in a rapidly changing world, need so much more than simply training to deliver a government-defined school curriculum.

Education Studies is concerned with understanding how people develop and learn throughout their lives, the nature of knowledge and critical engagement with ways of knowing. It demands an intellectually rigorous analysis of educational processes and their cultural, social, political and historical contexts. In a time of rapid change across the planet, education is about how we both make and manage such change. Education Studies, therefore, includes perspectives on international education, economic relationships, globalisation, ecological issues and human rights. It deals with beliefs, values and principles in education and the way that they change over time.

Since its early development at the beginning of the century, the subject has grown in academic depth, drawing explicitly on the disciplines of psychology, sociology, philosophy, history, and economics. It has also broadened its scope to address many social and political questions of globalisation, international education and perceptions of childhood. The list of publications on the early pages gives some idea of the range of topics now embraced by Education Studies.

The International Education Studies Association (TIESA)

Many of the editors and contributors to Education Studies book series are members of The International Education Studies Association (formerly the British Education Studies Association – BESA). Formed in 2005, TIESA provides a network for tutors and students in Education Studies. It holds an annual conference with research papers from staff and students, and funds small-scale research projects.

The website offers information and news about Education Studies and two journals: *Educationalfutures* and *Transformations*, a journal for student publications. Both are available without charge on the website: https://educationstudies.org.uk/.

Learner voice and agency

The University of Worcester was among the first to introduce non-teacher-training Education Studies in the early 2000s and has a long tradition of innovative teaching and research. This book from the Worcester team on learner voice and agency is the first single publication to bring together the many different perspectives on this important subject. Including the views of both lecturers, teachers and students, it will make a lasting impression on all those learning in Education Studies programmes. It is another example of the creative expansion of the Education Studies curriculum and is a welcome addition to the series.

Chapter 1, by **Gossman, Kennett and Smith**, explores how teachers' conceptions of teaching influence learners' conceptions of learning and their voice in their own learning. It examines traditional and discursive teaching methods and their impact on learner agency. In Chapter 2 by **Gallagher et al.**, in collaboration with the student authors, tensions in education are explored in light of the currently hotly contested interfaces between culture, identity and education. The authors advocate for an active listening to learners' voices to find common ground and to promote inclusive, equitable education. It emphasises lifelong learning and collaborative synthesis of educational perspectives. **Felstead's** contribution in Chapter 3 delves into the historical archives to reveal surprising congruence with some current ideas around voice and agency. Using findings from doctoral research, this chapter explores the voices of children in Victorian and Edwardian English primary schools, showing how children exercised agency and initiated change despite limited power.

In Chapter 4, **Usowicz and Hill** take a narrative approach to capturing the student voice is presented. It maps the achievements of a "non-traditional" learner by focusing on a mature student's journey from secondary education to higher education (HE). The account illustrates the strength of narrativity in revealing ways to overcome challenges and celebrates the transformative capacity of access to, and engagement with, education. Continuing the focus on narrativity, **Smith and Kennett** in Chapter 5 examine shifts in learner identity through different educational phases, emphasising the importance of being listened to and the sense of belonging. It discusses the concept of "university-readiness" and the impact of exclusionary HE entry requirements. In Chapter 6, **Smith** explores how lecturers can advocate for diverse learner needs, highlighting the role of the SCALE Project, which developed resources to support lecturers and promote inclusive learning through bespoke provision and Universal Design approaches. In Chapter 7 by **Russon and Sewell**, there is a return to the use of a narrative case report of a student with a declared disability. It explores their educational history and how academic self-concept and agency have helped shape that identity over time with enabling conditions. It emphasises the importance of lived experience perspectives in understanding identity development.

The capacity for contemporary conceptualisations of learner voice to accommodate less enfranchised identity groups is problematised in Chapter 8. Drawing on learning from primary research, **Olusola** advocates for a re-reading of learner voice to democratise student representation and to include a broader range of voices when considering the positioning of Muslim students. Issues of racism are further explored in Chapter 9, in which **Davidge, Lengthorne and Moore** reveal how a student's experience of racism acted as the impetus for a reconsideration of how teacher trainers engaged with curriculum planning. Educators became aware of the necessity to increase representation and diversity within pedagogical materials. The chapter illustrates how learner voice can lead educators on a reflexive learning journey with potential to positively impact on the wider student learning experience. Continuing a focus on marginalised learners, **Davis and Taylor** explore learner voice within prison and HE contexts in Chapter 10, examining the interactions and complexities of these settings. The chapter suggests a new framework for learning that utilises peer mentor-mentee relationships to scaffold learning.

The dynamic interface between local and global forces of educational change are explored in the following two chapters. Drawing on the lived experiences and perspectives of a Nigerian postgraduate student, in Chapter 11, authors **Findon and Malik** discuss the adaptation processes of international students and tease out the wider implications for universities. This piece emphasises the importance of learner voice in ensuring academic success and maintaining the reputation of universities as they seek to diversify their student cohorts. In Chapter 12, **Bracken et al**. provide a case study approach which illustrates how learner voice and agency were combined with the Universal Design for Learning (UDL) framework to enhance educational experiences for disabled learners. Highlighting the creative contributions of the learner co-authors, the chapter accentuates the importance of learner agency in the adoption of an anticipatory inclusive design approach to the formation of curriculum, assessment and learning resources. In Chapter 13, **Stephenson** challenges traditional school leadership notions, advocating for relational leadership that includes often unheard voices. Importantly, the chapter introduces the concept of the "listening leader" and outlines the requirements for creating inclusive school cultures.

Stephen Ward, Series Editor, Bath Spa University

References

Simon, C.A. and Ward, S. (Eds) (2019) *A student's guide to education studies*. Abingdon: Routledge.
Ward, S. (Ed.) (2004) *Education studies: A student's guide*. Abingdon: Routledge.

Foreword
Richard Woolley

The concept of voice is a powerful metaphor. How we express our views, whether these are "heard" or acknowledged and how they are acted upon or dismissed are all fundamental experiences of being human and making us feel valued or ignored. Our voice can be expressed in many ways, whether verbally, in writing, using gestures or signals, through art or music or, indeed, our actions and behaviours. We can use our voice to support, encourage, praise, nurture, protest, condemn or dismiss. In past generations, it was said that children should be "seen and not heard". Over past decades, this idea has changed and been challenged, not least through developments in international and national laws, conventions and policies which have focussed increasingly on learner voice and agency.

It is almost 50 years since the publication of the Warnock Report (1978), which transformed the educational experience of children and young people across the United Kingdon. It changed the way in which we talk about disability, introduced the notion of special educational needs and transformed the language used to talk about children and young people with needs in ways which set us on the journey towards a more inclusive education system.

Warnock still stands as the most wide-ranging report into special educational needs and disabilities to date. It claimed to be the most comprehensive review with the widest terms of reference in almost a century (since the *Royal Commission on the Blind, the Deaf and Dumb and Others*, which reported in 1889). The Warnock Report asserted the rights of those with special educational needs and disabilities, extending its exploration of their lived experience well beyond the classroom or indeed the education system. Significantly, it considered the medical aspects of children's needs and their ability to contribute within society through employment alongside their social needs. The latter was not a part of the terms of reference (Warnock 1978: 1) proposed by then Secretary of State for Education Margaret Thatcher, MP. The inclusion of social aspects pushed the boundaries of understanding and paved the way for educational developments that followed in subsequent decades. This once in a century review set out its ambition to inform transformation of special educational provision for the rest of the century and potentially beyond. In that, it succeeded.

When I worked at the University of Worcester, initially as the Head of Centre for Education and Inclusion, I was proud to see that a plaque remained in the Bredon Building (a single storey ex-military construction from the second world war) noting that Baroness Warnock had opened a Centre for Special Education there in the 1970s. It was one indication of the rich and sustained commitment of the University (and its predecessor institutions) to what we now call inclusion (Woolley, 2018).

Warnock talked of integration and paved the way for the diminution of negative labelling and segregation so that children and young people with diverse needs could access mainstream education and receive support and advice to enable them to explore their aspirations and ambitions for life. Her report flagged an ambition for universities to establish senior academic posts in special education, and for there to be at least one university department of special education in each region of the country (Warnock, 1978: paragraph 18.4), in addition to a national Special Education Staff College (paragraph 18.18). The University of Worcester has a strong track record in this regard, not least through the taught courses and academic research undertaken in its former Centre for Education and Inclusion and current Institute of Education.

Warnock set the tone for developments that followed, with the report's notion of integration subsequently being developed by others into an understanding of inclusion and associated concepts of empowerment, learner voice and agency. This book takes these concepts and builds on them through the creative co-construction of content by a range of stakeholders. Significantly this book explores how curricula are developed and enacted in order to promote and facilitate voice and agency, areas of education that have become more significant than ever in a post-pandemic world. This book champions the retention and enhancement of a democratic attribute within learning, rooting this in a rationale grounded in conceptual frameworks and core principles. Ideally, education is something that is done with others, and not to them. It is collaborative mutual, reciprocal and thus by its nature should be democratic. Importantly, the chapters in this book engage with concepts and issues in collaboration with learners, giving voice to their views through shared authorship with members of academic staff. This co-construction of scholarly activity gives this book genuine integrity, as it models the value of agency and voice within its pages.

The authors contributing to this volume bring a wealth of experience across a wide range of contexts, and with learners of diverse ages, backgrounds and lived experience. Collectively, they present an ambitious vision for developments in education to inform and empower students, researchers, academics and leaders of education to work for sustainable change. Readers will find some aspects of this book uncomfortable and challenging, as well as informative and inspiring. Concepts such as empowerment, agency and learner voice have huge potential to challenge the status quo and to question traditional hierarchies, power relationships and dominant discourses. For many of us, this is what learning is all about: it is about developing the skills to question and challenge, to critique and reconceptualise in order to transform the world in which we live and make it a better and more equitable place. One may argue that this is a hallmark of the dynamic and ever-evolving field of Education Studies (QAA, 2025).

The issues explored in each chapter of this book are fundamental to enacting key planks in conceptions of human rights. Firstly, education should be directed to the development of the human personality and fundamental freedoms (Article 26 of the United Nations Declaration of Human Rights). Secondly, the voices of children and young people should be sought and them given the right to express these freely (Article 12 of the United Nations Convention on the Rights of the Child, 1989). Thirdly, the dignity and rights of each individual person should be valued and should act towards others in a spirit of mutual appreciation and value (United Nations Declaration of Human Rights, Article 1). Further, it continues the aspirations of Warnock, siting them in the current educational landscape and reconceptualising them for a new generation of learners.

References

QAA (2025) *Subject benchmark statement: Education studies* (5th edition). Gloucester: Quality Assurance Agency for Higher Education.

United Nations (1948) *Universal declaration of human rights.* New York: United Nations.

United Nations (1989) *Convention on the rights of the child.* New York: United Nations.

Warnock, M. (1978) *The Warnock report: Special educational needs, report of the committee of enquiry into the education of handicapped children and young people.* London: HMSO.

Woolley, R. (Ed.) (2018) *Understanding Inclusion: Core concepts, policy and practice.* Abingdon: Routledge.

Contributing Authors

Seán Bracken is Principal Fellow of the Higher Education Association (HEA) and Doctoral Programme Lead for the College of Education Culture and Society at the University of Worcester. Seán is also an Adjunct Professor at Curtin University Australia. In 2019, he co-founded the International Collaboratory for Leadership in Universally Designed Education (INCLUDE) and coordinates the Inclusion by Design research group at the University of Worcester. Through research and practice, both networks advocate for learner voice and agency.

Rebecca Davidge was Senior Lecturer in Teacher Education at the University of Worcester, leading the PGCE for Religious Education, as well as being the course leader for the BA in Religion, Philosophy and Values in Education. Becky was a deeply valued member of our education community and is sorely missed. She was at the forefront of the University of Worcester's work on social justice, anti-racism and holocaust education.

Emily Davis earned a BA in Education Studies from the University of Worcester before returning as a postgraduate to achieve a PGCE. Her teacher training takes place in a prison, reflecting her commitment to emancipatory education for socially excluded adults. She is committed to enhancing the profile of prison education within the HE sector. Her research interests explore self-structured, non-institutional learning among imprisoned individuals and examines the impact of shame and trauma on learner voice.

Sara Dornan is an undergraduate student on the BA (Hons) Education Studies course at the University of Worcester. With current research interests in co-created curricula and acknowledging student voices in education, she is interested in refugee education and comparisons of education disparity within different countries of the United Kingdom.

Ruth Felstead has lectured within the Department of Education and Inclusion at Worcester University for ten years and was previously Lecturer and Senior Manager within the Further Education sector. Her research interests include the teaching and reception of societal values within curricula of schools past and present, which formed the basis of her recent doctoral thesis, *Teaching "Cheerful Obedience to Duty": Moral, Patriotic and Imperial Education in Birmingham and Worcestershire Elementary Schools c.1880–1902*.

Madeleine Findon is Senior Lecturer in Education and International Lead for the Department of Education and Inclusion at the University of Worcester. Madeleine's research interests concern educational leadership, inclusion, early years education, creativity and international student experiences. Her most recent publication is Findon, M., Johnston-Wilder, S. (2022) *Unit 1.3: developing your resilience: managing stress, workload and time.* Learning to Teach, 9th edition. Abingdon: Routledge.

Stuart Gallagher is Course Leader for Education Studies BA (Hons) at the University of Worcester. With a professional background in alternative education, educational welfare and multi-agency work, his research interests include social pedagogy, learning cultures in safeguarding and corporate parenting. Most recently, his article "Creating Hope in Dystopia: Utopia as Method as Social Pedagogy in Early Childhood Studies" (co-written with his colleague Niki Stobbs) was published in the *International Journal of Social Pedagogy*.

Mia Griffin is an undergraduate student on the BA (Hons) Education Studies course at the University of Worcester. Current research interests include the question, "Who is doing the work within schools and getting the acknowledgement for this?" She is particularly interested in the hierarchy of teaching staff, teaching assistants and site staff and the relationship to socio-economic status.

Lucy Gibson is an undergraduate on the BA (Hons) Education Studies course at the University of Worcester. As a mature student and mother, she found the motivation to return to education after deeming her initial school experience unsuccessful. She has navigated unique challenges faced by individuals in her position, which have driven her to explore and understand the experiences of others with similar journeys. She has developed a keen interest in the motivations and barriers of fellow returnees and hopes that through her studies, she can contribute valuable insights to promote accessibility in education.

Peter Gossman is recently retired from Worcester University. His most important article was written in conjunction with a PhD student and was the most cited, in the publication, in its publication year: Grant, T. Thomas, Y., Gossman, P., and Berragan, E. (2022). "I left feeling different about myself" – What students learn on their first practice placement. *BJOT 86*(2).

Niall Harris is an undergraduate student on the BA (Hons) Education Studies course at the University of Worcester. Current research interests include autism in education and exploring the experience of autistic students in mainstream settings, including HE.

Alice Hopkins is a student at the University of Worcester studying for a Master's in Research in Media and Culture. She is currently researching the representation and perceptions of characters with disabilities across media with a specialist focus on the depiction of blind characters within literature. Her studies explore the impact that representation can have on perception. Alice is also active in the Disabled Students' Network and is committed to empowering student voice to impact positive change.

Ellie Hill is Principal Lecturer at the University of Worcester and Course Leader for the PG Cert in Learning and Teaching in Higher Education. Her research interests include the use of narrative approaches for data collection and data analysis. Ellie is particularly interested in the stories of students in HE, and her PhD considered how the university journey impacted Gen Z students' personal values: Hill, E., Gossman, P., & Woolley, R. (2024). Using a bespoke, triad narrative analysis approach with Gen Z students: telling the story of their values. *Research in Post-Compulsory Education*, https://doi.org/10.1080/13596748.2023.2285628.

Jessica Jones is an undergraduate student on the BA (Hons) Education Studies course at the University of Worcester. Her current research interests include gender differences in SEN education and alternative education.

Anastasia Kennett is a PhD student and Associate Lecturer at the University of Worcester working in the field of equality, diversity and inclusion, with a particular interest in disability studies. Research interests include the UDL framework, student voice, student mental health and student–staff partnerships. More recently, Anastasia has sought to conceptualise Inclusive Student Voice in HE practice as part of their PhD research.

Harriet Lawrence is an MA in Education student at the University of Worcester. Whilst doing an undergraduate in a BA in History and Sociology, she was involved in Network and Committee roles, and this is how she became involved in UDL. Her research interests include a dedication to amplifying Special Educational Needs and Disabilities (SEND) voices, in which she aims to contribute to shaping an educational landscape that is accessible and equitable for all students.

Elena Lengthorn is University Lead Mentor on the Secondary PGCE Programme at the University of Worcester, working in the fields of Geography and Sustainability. Research interests include Climate and Ecological Emergency, Education for Sustainable Development, Flood Education and Nature Connectedness. Her project on Decolonising, Democratising and Diversifying the Secondary PGCE course received a UW Team Teaching Award. Elena seeks to nurture difficult conversations in education and recently published a chapter titled "Engaging Educators in Conversation on Our Climate and Ecological Emergency".

Rabiat Malik is currently studying for an MA Education (Early Childhood and SEND) at the University of Worcester. Her research interests are centred around, early years, educational administration and special education needs and disability.

Rachael Moore is the PGCE secondary subject lead for history at the University of Worcester. She spent over 17 years in secondary education teaching history in a comprehensive school in which she worked as a subject mentor for PGCE history trainees, professional mentor and helped run a successful "Schools Direct" partnership. Her research interests include working on a Masters module in Holocaust education with UCL.

Jeremiah Adebolajo Olusola is a Research Fellow at the University of Surrey. His research interests include British multiculturalism, post-racialism and Islamic epistemology. He has recently contributed to *The BERA Guides*: Davis, S., & Olusola, J. A. (2024). Decolonial praxis in Wales: Reflections on Research, Policy, and Anti-Racist Action. In M. L. Moncrieffe, O. Fakunle, M. Kustatscher, & A. Olsson Rost (Eds.), *The BERA Guide to Decolonising the Curriculum: Equity and Inclusion in Educational Research and Practice*. Emerald.

Emma Richardson is Senior Research Fellow of Inclusive Sport at the University of Worcester. Her work with disabled communities focuses on enhancing equity and opportunities for physical activity, and doing so through emancipatory, meaningful and impactful qualitative methods. She is a theme leader of the Inclusive Physical Activity, Wellbeing and Sport Research Unit at the University of Worcester.

Rebecca Russon studied BA (Hons) Education Studies at the University of Worcester and graduated in 2022. She completed her MSc Psychology of Education at University of Bristol in 2023. Her research interests include critical perspectives on special educational needs, and she is currently working within the Assessments Team of the SENAR (Special Educational Needs Assessment and Review) service at Birmingham City Council.

Alexandra Sewell is a HCPC registered Practitioner Psychologist and prior to embarking on a career in academia held positions as an educational psychologist and trainee educational psychologist across the West Midlands, United Kingdom. Her research interests range from social development in primary school to promoting student voice to enhance inclusive educational practice in HE. She has published her research in numerous peer-reviewed international education journals and has presented at educational psychology conferences in the United Kingdom.

Joanne Smith was a Primary School Teacher and Inclusion Manager for 15 years. She studied for her MA in Special and Inclusive Education at the University of Worcester and is now Head of Department for Education and Inclusion. She also owns a childcare business which was established in 2013. Her research interests lie within curriculum development, focusing on the incorporation of student voice across all phases of education, from early years to HE. Joanne has published articles in national educational journals and has presented at local specialist education conferences.

Sharon Smith is Senior Lecturer in Education and Inclusion at the University of Worcester. Sharon's research interests concern, inclusion, early years education and perspectives of inclusive education. Her most recent publication is Hill, E. & Smith. S. An exploration of the Peer Debriefer role: A walk in the park with Polly. *16th Annual International Conference of Education, Research and Innovation*, Seville, Spain. pages 127–131. ISBN: 978-84-09-55942-8, ISSN: 2340-1095, doi: 10.21125/iceri.2023.0068.

Marie Stephenson is Senior Lecturer in Education at the University of Worcester. She is pathway lead for the MA in Education (Leadership & Management) and has conducted qualitative research in the field of ethical leadership and ethical decision-making. She champions methods such as elite and specialised interviewing and is particularly interested in understanding how leaders develop through collaborative engagement within groups of their peers. Other recent work includes exploring the notion of *inclusive leadership* and its underpinning principles such as equality, fairness, dignity, respect and democracy.

Simon Taylor is Senior Lecturer and Course Leader at the University of Worcester. His professional background is working in the arts and cultural sector, and he has an MA in Museum and Gallery Education from UCL's Institute of Education. His research interests include the creative curriculum, arts-based interventions in SEND settings, critical pedagogy and possibility thinking. His most recent publication is entitled "Creativity in the Early Years: Engaging Children Aged 0–5".

Pai Usowicz studied BA (Hons) Education Studies at the University of Worcester, followed by PGCE Further Education (FE) with SEND subject specialism. Pai graduated in 2023. Her research interests included narrative inquiry and the experience of children who have experienced ACEs (Adverse Childhood Experiences). She works as Lecturer in FE and previously worked in advocacy roles with young people aged 10–17.

Kirsty Wedgbury qualified as a nurse from the Worcestershire and Hereford School of Nursing & Midwifery in 1991. She has enjoyed a long NHS career in a variety of roles, before moving into education as Senior Lecturer in Adult Nursing at Birmingham City University. Working at the University of Worcester since 2019 has given Kirsty further opportunities to develop her professional practice, focusing on innovative, inclusive and creative teaching approaches.

Christian T. Wilson is a Sports Coaching with Disability Sport graduate, and Wills-Edwards Spirit Disability Sport Academic Prize winner from the University of Worcester. Whilst at UW, Christian was Chair of the Disabled Students' Network. His particular interests include disability research within mainstream and SEND education, and representation and promotion of the learner voice.

Acknowledgements

We would like to thank series editor Stephen Ward for his support, encouragement and guidance during the preparation and writing of this book. His patience and attention to detail have been evident throughout the process.

Thanks also to Richard Woolley for his inspiring words and for placing this book in the wider historical context, both of Worcester and the concept of educational inclusion itself.

Lastly, but by no means least, thanks to all the many former and current colleagues, students, friends and associates who have made this collection possible by their inspiring work, research and ideas.

Simon Taylor and Seán Bracken

1 Education's purpose

Conceptions of teaching, conceptions of learning and learner voice

Peter Gossman, Anastasia Kennett and Sharon Smith

> **Vignette – Early career teacher experience**
>
> When I was a student, my knowledge was passively absorbed from lecturers and included following their instructions – for example, when structuring my undergraduate dissertation. However, participation in student voice projects has increased my confidence, and now, I use my voice frequently in developing my own work whilst listening to the guidance of others, for example, in my PhD work, which explores the development of my voice – spoken and written –using introspection. Through my self-exploration, I found the cause of my lost voice and the ways my voice could be improved further, which ultimately led to self-development and a greater understanding of self. I learnt that my educational experience was personal to me and that, in learning to use my voice, I could take ownership and have agency within my own educational journey.
>
> Now, as a new lecturer working in higher education, I can use my experience to benefit the students in my class, such as encouraging students to explore their own meta-cognition and to use their voices to negotiate (with me or their peers) how best to approach an activity and/or assessment. In this respect, I do not own students' educational experiences because students know their individual selves best. However, I can be empathic about students' past experiences and the processes involved in developing their voices. In doing so, students can become more autonomous, independent thinkers and navigators in their own lives.

Introduction

When considering student voice there are, amongst many things, contested aspects which include what is the voice to be about (curriculum content, assessment formats, etc.)? To whom it is addressed (teachers, institution, etc.)? What is the aim? Seale (2009) reviews the field and suggests that the roles ascribed to students provides a framing for the nature of their voices. Students are cast as stakeholder or representative, consumer or customer, teacher or facilitator, evaluator or informant and as storyteller. Each of these roles, Seale (2009) notes can be problematic and reveals something of the nature of the teacher/student relationship. Various authors report both positive and negative elements of student voice. For Brooman, Darwent and Pimor (2015), the student voice clarified, challenged and re-defined their approach to curriculum development. Conversely, for Seale (2009), there is evidence that students as evaluators or informants (which in

DOI: 10.4324/9781003406334-1

itself is a curious word with potentially negative overtones) can result in a rather one-way relationship between staff and students, reminiscent of what Briscoe et al. (2008, p. 10) describe as a "you said, we did" approach.

In the case of "you said, we did", Appleton (2013) notes the use of this format in professional services and goes on to state "such a consumer or customer relationship model of higher education can distort the relationship between the student and the university and suggests that 'the customer is always right' (p. 14). In turn, it can be argued that this has its own parallels with students, in a potentially customer frame of mind (and who in HE has not heard this), asking, 'What do I need to do to pass?'" It suggests a situation in which the student might be termed passive in their own education and has to simply follow a teacher's instructions without recognising or exercising their own agency – a concept of learning on the part of the student that might be termed "passive" or "surface".

This chapter will take a step back and review learners and their conceptions of learners and teachers and their conception of teaching in relation to student voice. It assumes then that student voice is a component part of students' learning, that it is a key aspect of a course of teaching (a programme or a module) and that having a "voice" is an important aspect of learning.

Conceptions of learning

The seminal work in students' conception of learning is Marton and Säljö's (1976) study of how students set about reading long pieces of writing. They identified that students differed in terms of what was learnt, as opposed to how much was learnt. They proposed that students could be considered as engaging in either surface or deep level processing. The authors later changed the term "level of processing" to approaches to learning (Marton and Säljö, 1984). Entwistle (1991) suggests that this was done to avoid any confusion with terms used in relation to memory and to illustrate that approach also involved an intention on the part of the student.

There are obvious links to motivation here, with intrinsic motivation associated with deep learning and vice versa (Alt and Boniel-Nissim, 2018).

Later work by Säljö (1979) refines conceptions of learning into five different forms:

1. Increase of knowledge (surface)
2. Memorising (surface)
3. Acquisition of facts/procedures retained and/or used in practice (surface)
4. The abstraction of meaning (deep)
5. An interpretative process aimed at understanding (deep)

Subsequently Marton et al. (1993) added a sixth:

6. Personal change

How might this relate to aspects of voice? If we equate, perhaps somewhat simplistically, the surface conception of learning as one where a customer or client is receiving a service, the delivery of knowledge, then a "you said, we did" approach might be suitable. Interestingly, the National Student Survey (NSS) question (2023, No. 32), "Overall, I am satisfied with the quality of the course", seems to encapsulate such an approach. The American parallel survey, the National Student Engagement

Survey (NSSE), within campus environment section asks "How satisfied are you with your educational experience?" NSSE (2021) describe the survey: "Each year the National Survey of Student Engagement asks students at hundreds of colleges and universities to reflect on the time they devote to various learning activities. The topics explored are linked to previous research on student success in college" (p. 1). Intriguingly, the American survey, within an arguably more market-driven/consumer-drive culture than the United Kingdom, focuses on student engagement, whilst the UK one examines satisfaction.

> Consumerist values appear to be a by-product of the increasingly transactional relationship that students have entered with their institutions, which has also heightened expectations about how beneficial their higher education experiences might be .
>
> (Tomlinson, 2017: 465)

> Education has always been a commodity to be bought and sold; the true danger lies in the move to a "rights-based" culture where students (and politicians) see education merely as something to be "consumed" rather than as an activity in which to participate.
>
> (Kaye, Bickel and Birtwistle, 2006: 85)

Within the notion of an "activity in which to participate" students need to exercise their agency, how students conceive the concept of teaching needs to be considered: Hämäläinen, Kiili and Smith (2017: 1106) note that "for universities to meet the twenty-first-century learning needs of today's students, it is important they allow students to take an active role in developing pedagogy and sharing their perspective. We may see different approaches in our students" understanding, and consideration should be given to the adult learner and how this might be different for undergraduates who are coming from formal secondary education into higher education. Knowles (1990) considers that an adult learner or mature student (defined as being over 21 years old) has a different approach to their learning. The term "andragogy" (Knowles, 1990) assumes that the adult learner has a desire to learn, is self-directed and the process of learning is often a certain need, such as employment. The voice of the adult learner is often more prominent in class, as there is a desire to learn and engage. The andragogical approach may certainly require some adaptation in the lecture's approach to allow for the students' voice to be heard. An understanding of how the lecturer might translate the activities into a learning process can be identified in Bloom's Taxonomy (1956), which suggests that learners acquire ownership of knowledge as they begin to analyse, synthesise and evaluate it (Smith, 2008). Adult learners are able to consider new knowledge and make comparisons or create subjective reasons relating to their own experience.

Conceptions of teaching

As with learning, there are conceptions of teaching. In their 1992 paper, Samuelowicz and Bain note that previous work in the field identifies a range of conceptions from information presenting to facilitation of student learning. It is easy to draw a parallel between surface learning, an increase in knowledge and teacher presentation of knowledge – i.e. its transmission from the teacher to the student(s) and deep learning, for understanding, and teaching as facilitation. Samuelowicz and Bain (1992) conducted 13 semi-structured interviews with academic staff from two Australian universities, seeking to explore their experiences of teaching. From their analysis of the interviews, they report (p. 98) five qualitatively different levels of conceptions of teaching as follows:

- (Level 5) imparting information
- (Level 4) transmitting knowledge
- (Level 3) facilitating learning
- (Level 2) changing students' conceptions
- (Level 1) supporting student learning

They note for level 5 that "this conception is seen as a teacher centred activity" (p. 101) and of level 1 that it was only reported in relation to postgraduate teaching. However, of level 2, they note that the "outcome of teaching is *different* knowledge rather than *increased* knowledge" (p. 98, emphasis in the original).

The work was revisited in 2001 (Samuelowicz and Bain, 2001) with 39 semi-structured interviews conducted across three universities in Brisbane, in which participants were asked about their beliefs and how they construed teaching and learning. A seven-level framework was created which they mapped onto teacher- or student-centred. The teacher-centred approach being that of transmitting information and the student-centred approach involving helping the learner to negotiate meaning, supporting the process of assimilation of knowledge.

In this framework the first three levels are quantitative, the others qualitative. In the quantitative conceptions, the teacher is seen as central to the learning process. They make decisions about what (content) and when learning (or at least teaching) takes place. In qualitative conceptions, teaching is seen as changing ways students perceive and use knowledge; teaching involves facilitating learning to develop students' understanding and ways of interpreting the world.

Samuelowicz and Bain (2001) also discuss the beliefs of teachers in relation to dimensions they asked about in the interviews. They include in their work a comparison of two teachers (one with a level 3 orientation, a chemist, and one with a level 4 one, an architect). Within the dimension of teacher-student interaction, the following two statements were recorded.

The Chemist:

He did interact with students, but primarily to ensure that they had understood what he had told them (and to clarify the ideas if they did not).

(p. 318)

The Architect:

She interacted closely with students to help them think and act as architects, in a process that involved two-way negotiation of what being an architect comprises.

(p. 318)

It is here at the teacher-centred/student-centred boundary that "voice", the "two-way negotiation", becomes a featured and key component of teaching (and learning).

A further model and conceptualisation of teaching comes from Carnell (2007). Her study involved eight participants from a range of disciplines and experiences, and each was appreciatively

Objective

1. Didactic	2. Co-operative
Individual = the process	Collective = knowledge is either given or constructed
3. Empowering	4. Community

Subjective

Figure 1.1 Adapted from two-way continuum of teaching (Carnell, 2007: 36)

Table 1.1 Adapted from "Community" approaches to teaching and learning (Carnell, 2007: 36)

	Community approach
Purpose of teaching	Collective knowledge construction
Teaching approach	Learning through co-constructive dialogue
Roles of teacher and learner	Teacher and learners have joint responsibility for learning

interviewed about their most effective experiences and what hindered them. Based on the interview analysis, a model was constructed by creating four quadrants derived from two scales related to approaches to teaching: one that opposes individual – collective views of teaching and one that opposes subjective – objective views about knowledge. The quadrants can be seen in Figure 1.1.

The horizontal "individual-collective continuum is to do with the process, or dynamics of teaching and learning" (p. 35–36), whilst the vertical "objective-subjective continuum is to do with how knowledge is seen, that is, knowledge is either given or constructed" (p. 36). Carnell (2007) states, "[T]he analysis of the data suggests *conceptions* (emphasis in the original) of effective teaching in HE sit squarely in the subjective-collective quadrant (community)" (p. 36). She then discusses the purpose of teaching, the teaching approach and the roles of the teacher and learner as they apply to each quadrant (see p. 36). For "community", these are reported in Table 1.1.

> **Pause for thought**
>
> Do you agree with Carnell's claim that effective teaching "fits" within the community quadrant? What does collective knowledge construction look and feel like in practice?

The confluence of conceptions

Teachers' conceptions of teaching and students' conceptions of learning have been neatly summarised by Trigwell et al. (1999). They note, just as Carnell did eight years later, that teachers' approach to teaching is related to their conception of it, just as students' approach to learning stems from their conception of it. In the middle of Figure 1.2, represented by the "?", is the point or confluence of these two streams of conception/approach. Clearly, one influences the other and vice versa.

There are many aspects of a teacher that influence the two boxes on the left-hand side of the diagram (just as there are for the two on the right) – for example, discipline, teaching experience,

6 Learner Voices, Perspectives, and Positionings

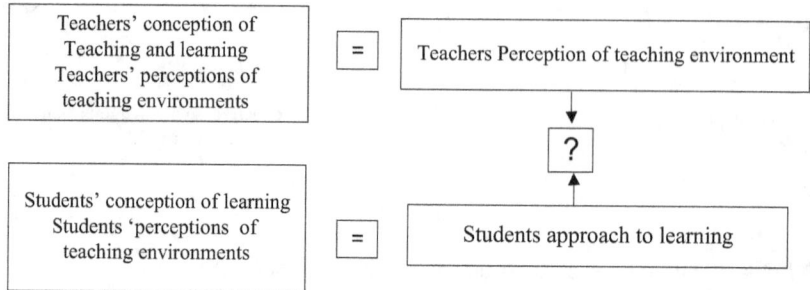

Figure 1.2 Adapted from 'Established Links Between Teachers' Conceptions of Teaching and Learning and Students' Learning Outcomes – slightly amended (Trigwell et al., 1999: 60)

level of teaching and so on. About the first, Palmer (1998) suggests that teachers are in some way drawn to their subjects because of who they are and what the subject is to them.

For teaching experience and its influence, a much earlier work can be drawn upon. Fuller (1970) proposes, for schoolteachers, a model which in his words "depicts the teacher concerns or growth motives which occur in a regular sequence" (p. 1) (Table 1.2).

Fuller (1975) describes phase I as pre-teaching concerns, phase II as survival concerns ("They are concerned about class control, their mastery of content to be taught and evaluations by their supervisors" (p. 38)) and phase III as teaching situation concerns ("[They are] concerned about [teaching] methods and materials" (p. 39)). He goes on from his 1970 model to add in 1975 a fourth phase of concern, one about pupils in which "teachers express deep concern about pupils, about their learning, their social and emotional needs, and about relating to pupils as individuals" (p. 40).

For higher education, Noben et al. (2021) provide a mapping of three teacher development models against each other (see Table 1.3).

Each clearly progresses from personal teacher/teaching concerns to student learning concerns. Noben et al. (2021) note,

> Fuller's (1969) theory of teacher concerns for studying teacher development is similar in terms of scope and conceptualisations to Kugel's (1993) and Åkerlind's (2003) theories described earlier, which acknowledge the progressive change from concerns about self to task to impact on student learning.

Table 1.2 Adapted from Fuller's (1970) model of teacher development – (Okas, van der Schaaf and Krull, 2014: 329)

Phase			Concerns about …
I	Early phase	0	… self (non-teaching concerns)
II	Middle	1	… professional expectations and acceptance
	phase(Competence)	2	… one's own (teacher's) adequacy: subject matter and class control
		3	… relationships with students
III	Late phase	4	… students learning what is taught
	(professionalism)	5	… students learning what they need
		6	… one's own (teacher's) contributions to student change

Table 1.3 Adapted from teacher development according to Fuller (1969), Kugel (1993) and Åkerlind (2003)

Fuller (1969)	Kugel (1993)	Åkerlind (2003)	
		Conception of teaching	Awareness of teaching development
Concern with self	Focus on self	Teacher transmission focused	Focus on self (teacher comfort)
Concern with task	Focus on subject	Student relations focused Student engagement focused	Focus on practice Focus on self (teacher comfort)
Concern with impact on student learning	Focus on student (i) Student as receptive		Focus on practice
	Focus on student (ii) Student as active	Student learning focused	
	Focus on student (iii) Student as independent		Focus on student learning

(*Source*: Noben et al., 2021: 91)

Their quantitative work using trained observers viewing 203 teachers focuses on teaching quality and skills; however, they conclude, "There is an indication that university teachers develop their teaching by gradually transitioning from focusing on transmitting the content to focusing on the learning of the student" (Noben et al., 2021, p. 102). Arguably, something can only come into focus for a teacher when students have a voice.

In addition, a study by Gibbs and Coffey (2004) that quantitatively researched using a case/control design teachers' approach to teaching, quantified into two categories, teacher focused and student focused. The case group received teaching development input in the form of at least 60 hours, whilst the control group did not. The authors report that, for the control group, teacher focus increased, and student focus decreased, whilst the case group "became less teacher focused and more student focused by the end of their training" (p. 93). Of learner (student-) centred learning, Bilimoria and Wheeler (1995) have written about teachers that they "are more likely to provide opportunities for [student] self-direction; reshape the authority relation in classrooms, implement experienced-based learning, [and] adopt a relational-learning approach" (p. 426).

Further considerations of academics' experience of teaching development

In a phenomenographic study in a research-intensive university in Australia 28 academics from a range of disciplines and with a range of teaching experience were interviewed. The intentions were to capture the academics' experience and understanding as they conceptualised their position allowing for their interpretation to be presented. The interviews, using a semi-structured format, explored the respondents' views around "what growing and developing as a teacher meant to them" (Åkerlind, 2007: 26). The analysis identified five different approaches to growing and developing as a teacher (see Table 1.4).

Table 1.4 Adapted from teacher development according to Fuller (1969), Kugel (1993) and Åkerlind (2003)

Fuller (1969)	Kugel (1993)	Åkerlind (2003)	
		Conception of teaching	Awareness of teaching development
Concern with self	Focus on self	Teacher transmission focused	Focus on self (teacher comfort)
Concern with task	Focus on subject	Student relations focused Student engagement focused	Focus on practice Focus on self (teacher comfort)
Concern with impact on student learning	Focus on student (i) Student as receptive		Focus on practice
	Focus on student (ii) Student as active	Student learning focused	
	Focus on student (iii) Student as independent		Focus on student learning

(*Source*: Noben et al., 2021: 91)

As with other models, there is a progression from self (what, to how) to students (facilitation of learning), with the latter seeking, via development, to "improve student learning" (p. 33). Åkerlind (2007) notes that this approach varies from the one that precedes it because it has a change of focus from student satisfaction to improved learning outcomes. She specifically notes that this approach is the "most complex" (p. 31). Table 1.5 summarises the developmental strategies, derived from the interviews, that can be employed to grow and develop as a teacher.

Note that Åkerlind states that the "intentional act of development" for the final step of development is to find out what works from the students' perspective – hearing and attending to their voices. In a formal way, this attending to voice might take the form of research (Gossman, 2008). The development from novice to expert (Dreyfus and Dreyfus, 1986), as a teacher, is hypothesised (Gossman, 2008) to follow a series of stages: Haigh's (2005) three Rs (rules, reflection and research) from where teachers follow a set of rules (the concern with the self and doing it "right", for example, sharing objectives with the students at the start of a session, or planning lecturers into 15–20 sections to aid attention) via experience and reflection to application of the rules has been refined and contextualised. This is then followed by a move towards greater expertise whilst still drawing upon experience and reflection and now involves research into and about their own practice (i.e. their work with their own students, for example, via action research). It is briefly worth mentioning the notion of the scholarship of teaching here (Boyer, 1990), which can be defined as systematic enquiry (research), and its publication, into student learning to advance higher education (Hutchings and Shulman, 1999).

> **Pause for thought**
>
> Can meaningful educational research take place with student voice forming a part of it?

Table 1.5 Adapted from developmental strategies associated with different developmental intentions (Åkerlind, 2007: 34)

Intentional act of development	Illustrative developmental strategies
Increasing content knowledge	Reading disciplinary literature, conducting research collecting up-to-date materials and examples
Acquiring practical experience	Engaging in teaching
Accumulating teaching strategies	As above, plus attending courses/workshops, reading educational literature, observing teaching colleagues
Finding out what works, from the teacher's own perspective	As above, plus experimenting with teaching methods, seeking feedback on student satisfaction, reflecting on the outcomes
Finding out what works form the students' perspective	As above , plus seeking feedback on student learning, including reflecting on student learning outcomes apparent from their assessment

Toshalis and Nakkula (2012) propose a spectrum of student voice that ranges from "expression" to "leadership" with students' involvement as stakeholders and collaborators increasing across it. Above we have discussed voice as it relates directly to the student experience of teaching (and their learning). The scholarship of teaching seems to fit most obviously in the spectrum at the level of consultation; however, this depends upon the nature and form of the work undertaken. As teachers refine, via reflection, being scholarly and scholarship, and as their conception of teaching becomes increasingly student-centred, it is arguable to that their research will move across the spectrum.

A final conceptualisation of teaching

Because of its unique terminology and perspective, one final conceptualisation of teaching is outlined: Ramsey and Fitzgibbons' (2005) "being in the classroom". Table 1.6 roughly equates how Ramsey and Fitzgibbons' modes of teaching and learning relate to the conceptions discussed earlier, Importantly, however, "being" is not simply being student-/learner-centred, it is where there is mutual responsibility for the learning outcomes, and where everything is a potential source of learning.

They describe, in the being mode, the role of the teacher as "servant-leader", creating learning opportunities and allowing community (see Carnell) to develop. They describe the classroom interactions as "fully present, intense, intimate and respectful, starting with the students and allowing them to move where they feel they need to be" (p. 336).

Table 1.6 Adapted from Ramsey and Fitzgibbons' conceptions of teaching (doing to, with and being) compared with traditional descriptions

Teacher-centred	←--------------------→	Student-centred
Doing something to the students	Doing something with the students	Being with the students

Of the being mode they note that students, too, have a changed role.

> Being classes recognize and honor interbeing: I am who I am because of who you are with me; our beings are in relation to one another. Interbeing is interconnectedness, interdependence and mutuality. All of these are emphasized in a being mode.
>
> (Ramsey and Fitzgibbons, 2005: 347–348)

> **Pause for thought**
>
> In an appendix to their article, the authors outline a set of minimum expectations for students on a course. It contains fairly standard things like attend, undertake the reading and checking email, but the assessment required a self-evaluation/reflection on how well the student had met the expectations. What effect do you think this approach might have on students?

The being mode is overtly about personal growth and development and requires some consideration of the contested function of higher education, which has a direct influence on students' conception of learning and teachers' conception of teaching. Space does not permit an extensive debate of this topic, but to provide an excellent starting point, Gert Biesta's functions of education are outlined next.

> **Pause for thought**
>
> What might "being with the students" mean, and feel like, in practice for a teacher and for students?

Biesta's functions of education

Biesta in various works (see, for example, 2010 and 2015 in the reference list) refers to domains of purpose within education and he puts forward three: qualification, socialisation and subjectification. Qualification is readily understood, students learning and demonstrating, in some way, their knowledge, skills and, according to Biesta (2015), their "attitudes and dispositions" (p. 263). Qualifications then are the proof that students are qualified (Biesta, 2015).

For socialisation, Biesta (2015) eloquently states that it as an education aim is "to provide our students with an orientation in the world, which comes with the invitation to find their own place within it" (p. 263), they become socialised. "Through its socializing function education inserts individuals into existing ways of doing and being" (Biesta, 2010: 19).

The final purpose, subjectification, is the aim of encouraging students to be "subjects of their own lives" (p. 265) as opposed to objectification which would seek to control student actions, thinking and judgements. There is an obvious parallel with notions of independent and self-directed learning. Biesta (2010) clearly encapsulates the idea in stating that through subjectification, "those educated become more autonomous and independent in their thinking and acting" (p. 20). Indeed, degree curricula tend to lead students towards autonomy with a capstone independent dissertation. Equally, doctoral degree holders, according to the QAA (2014) will have "the qualities and transferable skills necessary for employment requiring the exercise of personal responsibility and largely autonomous initiative in complex and unpredictable situations, in professional or equivalent environments" (p. 33).

Voice in all of this

Whereas most curricula and pedagogy seek to change the student in some way, either through the accumulation of new knowledge, the shifting of perspectives, or the alteration of behaviours, student voice activities and programmes position students as the agents of change. In this way, student voice is about agency. At its core, student voice is the antithesis of depersonalised, standardised and homogenised educational experiences because it begins and ends with the thoughts, feelings, visions and actions of the students themselves. This makes student voice profoundly student-centred (Toshalis and Nakkula, 2012: 23).

In the previous quote, aspects of Biesta's domains of purpose can be clearly identified: for example, accumulation of new knowledge – qualification, shifting of perspectives – socialisation, students as agents of change – subjectification. However, it is the final aspect actions, Biesta's (2015) ability of students "to make their own judgements, and to be able to act and act well" (p. 2640) and its association with student-centredness that is critical.

Conclusion

This chapter has reviewed students' approaches and conceptions of learning alongside teachers' approaches to and conceptions of teaching. It has considered how voice is a key aspect of a conception of teaching that is student-/learner-centred. We argue then that voice is an integral part of good facilitatory teaching (or to take it further a "being" mode) that has at its heart the personal growth and development of students.

Summary points

- The chapter explores how teachers' conceptions of teaching, both espoused and enacted, influence learners' conceptions of learning. This, in turn, impacts learner voice and agency on their educational journeys.
- Active participation and negotiation in learning processes can lead to greater autonomy and independent thinking among students.
- The chapter reviews seminal works on students' conceptions of learning, distinguishing between surface and deep learning approaches. It discusses how these conceptions relate to motivation and the role of student voice in fostering deeper learning.
- The progression of teacher development from focusing on self and teaching tasks to prioritising student learning and engagement is explored. Professional teacher development is pivotal to further enhance student voice and agency.

Recommended reading

The implications of the development of teachers' conceptions of teaching and its influence on students' approaches to learning suggest that teachers have a role in education that extends beyond their subject expertise.

Biesta, G. J. (2015) *Good education in an age of measurement: Ethics, politics, democracy*. Abingdon: Routledge.
Biesta, G. (2023) Outline of a theory of teaching: What teaching is, what it is for, how it works, and why it requires artistry. In *Theorizing teaching: Current status and open issues*. Cham: Springer International Publishing.

Second, as this chapter has considered teachers and their development further consideration of teacher identity and how it can be extended into notions of teacher authenticity in seeking to enhance student authenticity.

Kreber, C. (2010) Academics' teacher identities, authenticity and pedagogy. *Studies in Higher Education*, 35(2), pp. 171–194.
Kreber, C. (2013) *Authenticity in and through teaching in higher education: The transformative potential of the scholarship of teaching*. Abingdon: Routledge.
Kreber, C. (2014) Rationalising the nature of "graduateness" through philosophical accounts of authenticity. *Teaching in Higher Education*, 19(1), pp. 90–100.

Third, it is natural to move from the broad purpose of education, through teacher identity / authenticity to students, specifically the development of student agency and self-authorship.

Magolda, M.B.B. (2023) *Authoring your life: Developing your internal voice to navigate life's challenges*. London: Taylor & Francis.

References

Åkerlind, G. S. (2003). Growing and developing as a university teacher–variation in meaning. *Studies in Higher Education*, 28(4), 375–390.
Åkerlind, G. S. (2007). Constraints on academics' potential for developing as a teacher. *Studies in Higher Education*, 32(1), 21–37.
Alt, D., and Boniel-Nissim, M. (2018). Links between adolescents' deep and surface learning approaches, problematic Internet use, and fear of missing out (FOMO). *Internet Interventions*, 13, 30–39.
Appleton, L. (2013). A student partnership approach to developing library services. In *of the 10th Northumbria international conference on Performance Measurement in Libraries and information services* (p. 13).
Biesta, G. (2010). *Good Education in an Age of Measurement: Ethics. Politics, Democracy*. Oxford: Routledge.
Biesta, G. J. (2015). *Good education in an age of measurement: Ethics, politics, democracy*. Abingdon: Routledge.
Bilimoria, D., and Wheeler, J. V. (1995). Learning-centered education: A guide to resources and implementation. *Journal of Management Education*, 19(3), 409–428.
Bloom, B. (1956). A. and McGill, I. (1998). (pp.42) In Brockbank, A. and McGill, I. (1998) acilitating Reflective Learning in Higher Education Buckingham: Open University Press.
Boyer, E. L. (1990). *Scholarship reconsidered: Priorities of the professoriate*. Princeton University Press, Lawrenceville, NJ.
Briscoe, S., Patrick, S. and Read, A. (2008). Engaging students in quality assurance: the challenge of embedding unit feedback processes and enhancing the student learning experience. Paper presented at *Exploring the Hinterlands: Mapping an Agenda for Institutional Research in the UK*, Solent University, June 24–26, UK. Available online at: https://www.solent.ac.ukirconferenceresourcesBriscoe20et20al.doc (accessed 17 February 2009).
Brooman, S., Darwent, S., and Pimor, A. (2015). The student voice in higher education curriculum design: is there value in listening? *Innovations in Education and Teaching International*, 52(6), 663–674.

Carnell, E. (2007). Conceptions of effective teaching in higher education: extending the boundaries. *Teaching in Higher Education*, *12*(1) 25–40.

Dreyfus, H., and Dreyfus, S. (1986). *Mind over machine: The power of human intuition and expertise in the era of the computer*. New York: Free Press.

Entwistle, N. J. (1991). Approaches to learning and perceptions of the learning environment: Introduction to the special issue. *Higher Education*, 22(3), 201–204.

Fuller, F.F. (1969). Concerns of teachers: A developmental conceptualization. *American Educational Research Journal*, *6*(2), 207–226.

Fuller, F. F. (1970). *Personalized Education for Teachers*. An Introduction for Teacher Educators. Austin: University of Texas.

Fuller, F. F. and Bown, O. H. (1975). 'Becoming a teacher'. In *Teacher education: 74th yearbook of the national society for the study of education II*, 25–52. Kevin Ryan, ed. Chicago: University of Chicago Press.

Gibbs, G. and Coffey, M. (2004). The impact of training of university teachers on their teaching skills, their approach to teaching and the approach to learning of their students. *Active Learning in Higher Education*, 5(1), 87–100.

Gossman, P. (2008). Teaching development—experience and philosophy (Using the three Rs). *Teacher Education Quarterly*, *35*(2), 155–169.

Haigh, N. (2005). Tertiary teacher development: connecting policy, personal theory and practice. In P. M. Denicolo and M. Kompf (Eds.), *Connecting policy and practice: challenges for teaching and learning in schools and universities* (pp. 171–176). New York: RoutledgeFalmer.

Hämäläinen, R., Kiili, C., and Smith, B. E. (2017). Orchestrating 21st century learning in higher education: A perspective on student voice. *British Journal of Educational Technology*, *48*(5), 1106–1118.

Hutchings, P., and Shulman, L. S. (1999). The scholarship of teaching: New elaborations, new developments. *Change: The Magazine of Higher Learning*, *31*(5), 10–15.

Kaye, T., Bickel, R. R., and Birtwistle, T. (2006). Criticizing the image of the student as consumer: examining legal trends and administrative responses in the US and UK. *Education and the Law*, 18(2–3), 85–129.

Knowles, M. (1990). *The Adult Learner – A Neglected Species* (4th Edition) Houston: Gulf Publication.

Kugel, P. (1993). How professors develop as teachers. *Studies in Higher Education*, *18*(3), 315–328.

Marton, F. Dall'alba, G, and Beaty, E. (1993). Conceptions of learning, *International Journal of Educational Research*, *19*, 277–300.

Marton, F., and Säljö, R. (1976). On qualitative differences in learning: I—Outcome and process. *British Journal of Educational Psychology*, *46*(1), 4–11.

Marton, F., and Säljö, R. (1984). Approaches to learning, in Marton, F., Hounsell, D.J. and Entwistle, N. J. (eds.), *The experience of learning*. Edinburgh: Scottish Academic Press, pp. 36–55.

Noben, I., Maulana, R., Deinum, J. F., and Hofman, W. A. (2021). Measuring university teachers' teaching quality: a Rasch modelling approach. *Learning Environments Research*, 24, 87–107.

NSSE (2021). A Pocket Guide to Choosing a College: NSSE 2021 Answers from Students https://und.edu/analytics-and-planning/_files/docs/_files/nsse-2021-poc-guide.pdf

Office for Students (2023). NSS 2023 questionnaire Accessed 13.7.23 https://www.officeforstudents.org.uk/media/c2ddb4c1-34cf-4df4-8c26-b6469412768f/nss-2023-questionnaire.pdf

Okas, A., van der Schaaf, M., and Krull, E. (2014). Novice and experienced teachers' views on professionalism. *Trames*, *18*(4), 327–344.

Palmer, P. J. (1998). The Courage to Teach. *Exploring the inner landscape of a teacher's life*, San Francisco, CA: Jossey-Bass.

QAA. (2014). UK Quality Code for Higher Education. *Part A: Setting and Maintaining Academic Standards*. The Frameworks for Higher Education Qualifications of UK Degree-Awarding Bodies.

Ramsey, V. J., and Fitzgibbons, D. E. (2005). Being in the classroom. *Journal of Management Education*, *29*(2), 333–356.

Säljö, R., (1979). Learning about learning. *Higher Education*, 8(4), 443–451.

Samuelowicz, K., and Bain, J. D. (1992). Conceptions of teaching held by academic teachers. *Higher Education*, *24*(1), 93–111.

Samuelowicz, K., and Bain, J. D. (2001). Revisiting academics' beliefs about teaching and learning. *Higher Education*, *41*, 299–325.

Seale, J. (2009). Doing student voice work in higher education: An exploration of the value of participatory methods. *British Educational Research Journal*, *36*(6), 995–1015.

Smith, S. (2008). *Foundation Degrees: Further Education or Highering Aspirations? To what extent do Further Education Institutions support transition into Higher Education?* University of Worcester. Unpublished.

Tomlinson, M. (2017). Student perceptions of themselves as 'consumers' of higher education. *British Journal of Sociology of Education, 38*(4), 450–467.

Toshalis, E., and Nakkula, M. J. (2012). *Motivation, engagement, and student voice*. Boston, MA: Jobs for the Future.

Trigwell, K., Prosser, M., and Waterhouse, F. (1999). Relations between teachers' approaches to teaching and students' approaches to learning. *Higher Education, 37*(1) 57–70.

2 Why don't they teach education at school?

Listening to learners' voices and resisting polarisation to restore education as common ground throughout our lifetimes

Sara Dornan, Stuart Gallagher, Lucy Gibson, Mia Griffin, Niall Harris and Jessica Jones

> **Vignette**
>
> *Sara, Lucy, Mia, Jess and Niall are undergraduate Education Studies students. Stuart is the Course Leader. Together, they shared a research module in the first year of studies. Stuart chose lifelong learning as an example of education worth researching. Lifelong learning means different things to different people. For some, it means emancipation from schooling; for others, it means incarceration in insecure employment. Students must also be careful not to fall into the trap of polarisation, believing only one side of the story to be true.*
>
> *Sara, Lucy, Mia, Jess and Niall were invited to respond by choosing an area of education they wished to pursue as research. Each student's lived experience of education shaped their decision. By acknowledging that we are all subjects of education (however unconsciously), we might study how to shape it positively (hopefully consciously). As the module progressed, it became apparent that including all voices – that is, the voices of academic literature, the voices of librarians and university assessment, the voices of academic staff and, primarily, the voices of student learners – brought learning more fully to life.*
>
> *In this chapter, each learner's voice invites us to pause for thought. Each pause intends to broaden our knowledge and deepen our understanding of learners' diverse experiences of lifelong learning. And as we pause, we are invited to find our own learner voice.*

Introduction

What do the following have in common: life insurance, mortgages, communication skills and stress management? The answer: they should all be taught at school. Or so goes the occasional critical commentary on school curricula, at least. When what happens "in school" is seen to differ dramatically and disappointingly from what happens "in real life", critical voices might ask, "How does trigonometry pay my rent? How will Pythagoras's Theorem get me a job?" Disillusionment with curriculum and its relation to life suggests school and life are two distinct experiences. These voices argue that a more worthwhile and meaningful – *practical* – experience of education would blur the

DOI: 10.4324/9781003406334-2

distinction between the two. This would be done by overlaying school curricula (what gets taught in school) with the vicissitudes of life. In other words, the purpose of school is to prepare us for life.

What, then, are we to make of the claim that the national curriculum in England "prepares pupils at the school for the opportunities, responsibilities and experiences of later life" (DfE, 2014: para 2.1). The lesson we are expected to learn appears to be this: not now, but later, will life present you with opportunity, responsibility and experience. For now, bank knowledge and information; later, withdraw it when relevant. The greatest savers will benefit most from the opportunity and experience to come. The winners will be revealed in time and will be rewarded with the greatest opportunity and responsibility.

> *How cynical! Surely, since life is already so unpredictable and disorientating, we can enjoy school as one of the few constants we have. Its presence reassures us that continuity and constancy remain possible. Who dares to tinker with it, without knowing what chaos might ensue? Schools are schools and always will be, time immemorial.*

> *Oh, how naive! Secure the futures of the next generation! Financial precarity and social inequality disturb and sadden us. Are we not disturbed by the mere suggestion that our school system mimics the banking system and its inherent values? School curricula can remedy our malaise: teach sustainability, co-operation, intergenerational equity and conflict resolution. Time is running out!*

Already, a cacophony of voices demands our attention, hawking remedies to education's ills.

Who do we listen to? Who do we believe?

Some roots of Education Studies lie in the study of schools and the schooling system. Students must make that familiar world strange again. Core texts, seating plans, school hierarchies and quality standards might be familiar; none is neutral, natural, inevitable nor unavoidable. They are strange: they are cultural constructs that perpetuate social structures of power. Students of Education Studies may be interested to reveal such structures and to scrutinise the evidence base for them: what knowledge schools claim to be essential (curriculum), how schools communicate this knowledge to learners (pedagogy) and who stands to benefit from this practice of schooling (assessment) – in other words, the winners and losers.

Different perspectives can be taken. Certainly, different voices noisily clamour for our attention. Is it fair to evaluate them as either complicit, cynical or naive? The rhetoric might easily distract us from the reality of weighing the evidence. Students of Education Studies face this dilemma: who do we listen to and who do we believe? This is an example of the work of Education Studies. Its benchmarks indicate so:

> Graduates are able to participate in and contest changing discourses, exemplified by reference to debate about values, personal and social engagement, and how these relate to communities and societies. Students have opportunities to develop their critical capabilities through the selection, analysis and synthesis of relevant perspectives, and to be able to justify different positions on educational matters.
>
> (QAA, 2019: 4, para 2.4)

Pause for thought: Jessica

Does research mirror all educational experiences, values, and personal and social engagement with education?

From the very beginning, I was very eager to find the voices of those who have slipped through the cracks, such as young girls with learning difficulties. I started by focussing on ADHD/SEN in education, mainly focussing on the gender difference in attitudes, schools and diagnoses. I wanted to research this topic, as it is quite personal to me. I shifted my focus to gender differences in education. I took a step back and turned my attention to alternatives to early years education. While reading up on this, I stumbled across the geographies of alternative education. I found this topic really fascinating and came across advocacy groups online that spoke about girls' experiences of these alternative schools.

Academic articles mainly focused on young boys or parents and caregivers of children with special educational needs. Advocacy groups, though, discussed how girls are usually less likely to outwardly show ADHD symptoms like hyperactivity because they are better at masking symptoms. Some also mentioned the lack of research around what works for girls and how teachers are less confident at dealing with girls' behavioural problems. The goal should be making sure each child gets an education that is suited to them, whether that is in "mainstream" or alternative education.

As we can see, the work of students of Education Studies includes synthesising *relevant* perspectives. Dismissing perspectives as cynical or naive sidesteps our responsibility to analyse their respective relevance to the work of improving education. Where, instead, might we find places of robust connection rather than brittle incompatibility? The goal is to see education as common ground rather than a battle ground.

How do we decide which perspectives and voices are relevant or irrelevant?

We are the products of schools, at least in part. Most of us have enjoyed and endured a backstory of schooling. As students of Education Studies, we can reflect on our experiences from the perspective of our present circumstances. Our scrutiny of them will be shaped by those experiences, again, at least in part. One purpose of our scrutiny is to shape the school and schooling experiences of others more positively: to improve curriculum, to improve pedagogy, to improve assessment. Where preferable alternatives to existing practice exist, Education Studies would weigh sound evidence. Rather than being distracted by noisy debates, an opportunity of synthesis presents itself: to evaluate the respective merits of each perspective, to create innovative combinations of their strengths and to propose new possibilities for action based on the evidence.

The general direction of the Education Studies student's work would appear to be participation in decision-making around education's relationship to life. These include decisions about what counts as curriculum, pedagogy and assessment. How do we weigh up what each perspective has to say in relation to others' points of view, experiences and lives? Critically, we must ask: whose perspectives are relevant to the debate? We might find perspectives that are relevant to our enquiry but which do not noisily clamour for our attention.

Pause for thought: Mia

Who is best placed to contribute to education day after day? How well placed are we to listen to them?

Who does the work in the education system to make it work? Who does the graft and who gets the credit? Research often privileges some voices (for example, headteachers and senior leaders) over others' voices. Who contributes to a school's culture and organisation? For example, Teaching Assistants contribute remarkable amounts to a child's education and environment.

I was looking into education during COVID-19 and the impact it had on pupils and seeing if Teaching Assistants (TAs) gained any form of recognition for the work they had done. COVID-19 made the job lonely for TAs. The loss of face-to-face contact meant there was no collaboration or enjoyment between students and staff, and there was essentially no emotional support for them even though their school role is crucial when it comes to managing behaviour (Maitland and Glazzard, 2022). Why are their views and voices so absent in the educational research literature? The key phrases I used to search for literature changed drastically. "Voice" and "privilege" allowed me to acknowledge what was being written and what was not.

This approach does not relate to Education Studies' interest in schools and schooling only. It also relates to education more broadly, as we learn across the courses of our lives. It prompts us to consider other questions about who has a say in what we learn, who decides how we come to learn and who decides what value to place on what we have learned. Two examples might illustrate this point:

[The National Curriculum] provides pupils with an introduction to the essential knowledge they need to be educated citizens. It introduces pupils to the best that has been thought and said, and helps engender an appreciation of human creativity and achievement.

(DfE, 2014: para 3.1)

[It is] important for citizens to be able to make up their own mind […] also for everyone to have the *courage* to make up their own mind. [Education is an injunction] to be a self, that is, not to forget oneself and walk away from what the world is asking from you.

(Apple et al., 2022: 247–48, emphasis in original)

In the first example, the Department for Education and schools decide what's worth knowing; the mark of an educated citizen is their appreciation of pre-determined selections of human creativity and achievement. In the second example, learners decide what they think is worth believing; the mark of a citizen is courage and responsibility. Is a citizen, then, someone whose mind is made up for them or someone who makes up their own mind?

For students of Education Studies, the challenge remains: how do we establish criteria for relevance for each perspective? How might we synthesise the respective positive contributions (if any) of each position? There is work to be done to clear common ground. From such common ground, we might hope to propose education as inclusive and as a common good, and resist engaging in attritional tit-for-tat battles over the purpose and practice of education.

> ### Pause for thought: Niall
>
> How might our learner voice represent others?
>
> I am looking at autism in education and seeing how autistic students are doing with mental health and grades. This was partly because I was an autistic student and found it exceedingly difficult. Evidence points towards autistic students having a mental health crisis. Their stories spoke about how they felt like the system does not understand them, teachers do not understand them, students do not understand them and they do not understand themselves. Why is nothing being done about it? This really made a profound impact on my worldview, and I look forward though to how it might change more.
>
> I am at a stage where I understand the problem from not only looking at qualitative work and quantitative work but my own experience as well, and it is time to look at solutions: to find, critique, analyse and use solutions that academics produce, as well as putting forward my own ideas, to create a synthesis of the knowledge and pragmatic value that I can use.

Education's common ground

It is one thing to call for common ground, another to define its characteristics. In other words, what gets held in common there? This chapter explores three possible visions of educational common ground: lifelong learning, polarisation and listening to learners' voices.

Lifelong learning: Conflict avoidance as common ground?

First, perhaps every voice in our common ground is talking about the same thing: for example, lifelong learning. What gets held in common here is a singular subject. An attritional, adversarial approach to a "hot topic", such as the purpose of schooling, is sidestepped in favour of a relatively non-contentious, catch-all concept. Here, common ground is characterised by consensus and the preference for calm discussion over clamorous din.

Who could blame us for sidestepping controversial topics in the pursuit of synthesis? Why risk danger and damage? Why not dial down the din? We all have an educational backstory. This may be one of endurance, enjoyment or a blend of both. Through reflection, we might become aware that our respective experiences of schooling might determine the criteria we would each apply to decide which perspectives and which voices are relevant. Rather than reignite a noisy debate, we might pluck out lifelong learning instead.

Lifelong learning provides us with safe ground: compensation for those of us whose school experiences were negatives ones, and a challenge to complacency for those whose experiences were positive ones. Lifelong learning adeptly appeals to education's winners and losers. All can face the future as capable learners, curious about learning for the rest of their lives, whatever might lie ahead.

The span of the future can sometimes distort our understanding of lifelong learning. The turn of the millennium saw renewed interest in "skills for the future", and researchers busily drew up lists of skills that learners would need to acquire to the uncertainty of the future (see, for example, Coffield, 2002). Perhaps over-awed by the challenge of predicting a curriculum to last another thousand years, the focus of lifelong learning shifted from curriculum to assessment of learning dispositions, such as resilience, playfulness, and reciprocity, instead (for example, Carr and Claxton, 2002). On the one hand, learning how to learn is unsatisfactorily circular: learning how to learn how to learn how to learn how to learn, etc. On the other hand, this shift from curriculum to assessment means learning how to learn sidesteps decisions around what is worth learning. This matters because another meaning of lifelong learning undermines any value we might attach to learning across a lifetime. Lifelong learning, hitched to an economic agenda, has this to say: learners, to remain employable (and to remain employees) have no choice but to engage in lifelong learning (see Biesta, 2022). What's learned rapidly loses value, and knowledge and know-how become the latest casualties of throwaway culture. Here, lifelong learning offers neither compensation to learners nor a challenge to their complacency with qualifications but only insecurity, uncertainty and precarity. No wonder lifelong learning has shifted its focus to assessment rather than curriculum.

The student of Education Studies might reasonably have hoped to use lifelong learning as a quieter concept around which to synthesise relevant perspectives on education. Instead of a singular subject, they find lifelong learning is another contested concept, a battle ground rather than common ground.

> **Pause for thought: Lucy**
>
> How might lifelong learning reflect learners' expertise in lived experience? What might lifelong learning look like as a common good?
>
> *As a "mature" student who is female, has family commitments and a negative school experience, I can testify to the barriers faced on a journey back into education, in particular with a view to focussing on women who wish to return to education following a break to raise a family.*
>
> *The freedom of reading through opposing viewpoints, data, facts and research from a variety of experts is a new and liberating experience and has given me enjoyment in my own learning. Research has helped me to see viewpoints and areas of adult learning that I had not considered before. For example: Why do so few men in comparison with women return to education? Why do women seek to change careers after giving birth? What is being done to encourage workers to gain qualifications? And why does there appear to be resistance in the workplace to encourage employees into Further Education?*

Polarisation as common ground?

Second, perhaps common ground is characterised by only one voice: one view prevails. It enjoys a singular object. This is the polarisation option. One view only is admitted, and all are satisfied that it addresses all relevant issues comprehensively. No other is relevant; alternative views are irrelevant and can be dismissed. Here, common ground is characterised by a single story.

Polarisation offers one way out of the quandary: pick a side and enjoy the safety of the echo chamber. What you hear might lack harmony, but this space does not suffer from quite so much discord. That's because all voices there share a common goal, a singular object. This is a convenient criterion of relevance: that you are with us and not with them.

This chapter began with an example of what happens when school curricula do not mirror the lessons that the school of life has to offer. On the one hand, we saw, a national curriculum purports to prepare students for later life; on the other hand, those students' respective (and unequal) later life experiences provide them with grounds to be sceptical about that claim. It can be convenient to divide curriculum into us and them, where *they* are the curriculum designers and deciders, and *we* are those penalised for our compliance, or vice versa.

Polarisation asks, whose side are you on? It implies that an abyss lies between the two sides, making the space between them impossible to traverse. Students of Education Studies face a formidable challenge when weighing the relevance of each perspective, let alone synthesising them. Synthesis, in its shape as dialogic civility (Arnett, 2001), is impossible when we opt for a polarising approach to education. Common ground, here, is no more than the convenience of picking a side, listening to some voices and dismissing others.

Listening to learners' voices as common ground

Third, perhaps common ground is a space where all voices and views enjoy the common privilege of being heard equally. This space tolerates plural subjects and objects, and none dominates another.

There, we might hear diverse learners' voices. Here, common ground harbours the entanglement of our lives. Entanglement need not mean a contest to decide winners and losers. Instead, common ground might represent our entangled responsibility to learn together and to understand one another.

Listening to learners' voices pushes us towards common ground. If we view education as a public and common good (Locatelli, 2018), we might expect that work to involve making time to listen to the reasonableness of all views and move all towards greater inclusion.

This chapter listens to learners' voices in two ways. First, the chapter is co-authored – all authors are learners. Each voice invites us to pause for thought and to reconsider our positions. Authority – meaning the responsibility to author the chapter's argument – is shared, collaborative and inclusive. Listening to learners' voices offers a positive and progressive way to overcome the common problems posed by lifelong learning and polarisation. Learners' voices may not be the noisiest voices in debates about education's place in life; making the space and time to listen, though, means not being distracted by the clamouring din of dominant voices. Instead, we can better evaluate the merits of their respective arguments by listening to learners, whose lives are directly shaped by education and who seek to shape education more positively in turn.

Sharing our stories and listening to stories of others to understand the drama of learning characterises common ground. No one story seeks to dominate the space; all stories invite a deeper understanding of education. All of us involved in Education Studies, reflecting on our diverse experiences of being subjects of education and articulating our development as students of education, face the challenge of selecting, analysing and synthesising relevant perspectives. Do we choose domination or understanding to overcome that challenge?

> **Pause for thought: Sara**
>
> Co-creating educational curricula as shared understanding
>
> *After negative experiences throughout my education, I began to think about the fight for and against education. Educational journeys and resources should be democratised: reciprocal relationships built on mutual positive regard for the personal significance of learning and the professional skills of teachers leading to co-created curricula between students and staff. I believe these can be the foundation of a new structure, providing equal opportunities for both students and staff.*
>
> *I began my research looking at co-created curricula and education in the United Kingdom, which is where I discovered Catherine Bovill and her research for the first time. Bovill is a spokesperson for missing voices in education. I can only confess that this journey of discovering missing voices in education has not only developed my skills in reading academic papers and transforming it into literature but that I have also discovered new areas of the educational world that I wish to conquer.*

Conclusion

Why don't they teach education at school?

Educationalists might evade answering this question by making this observation. It depends, they might say, on whether education is a subject or an object or a discipline. Policymakers, similarly, might prefer to evade answering this question. It depends, they might say, at what Key Stage you're looking to introduce the children to education. Over-stretched teachers and TAs might reply, "I'm sorry. I am busy teaching my class".

It's one thing to imagine these answers and to put words in other people's mouths, quite another to listen to what they would really have to say. We are confident all are learning how to understand education and its place in people's lives more deeply. How might we invite them to share that story with us, for the common good?

This chapter has highlighted the tension between school curricula and their relationship to learners' lives and lived experiences. It asks, How are students of Education Studies to respond? Rather than being overwhelmed by a cacophony of competing voices clamouring for our attention and attempting to dominate the discussion, the chapter suggests we pause for thought and listen, foremost, to learners' voices. And as we pause, we might learn to understand the part our shared lives might yet play in shaping education positively. Common ground can be prepared so that we listen for work undertaken in schools that foster inclusive collaboration and not individual competition.

Summary points

- The study of education necessarily involves encounters with controversy. For example, what is the relationship between school and life? Education Studies introduces us to the different values and differences of viewpoints that provide diverse answers to such questions.
- In theory, students of Education Studies are expected to identify and synthesise all relevant perspectives so that they might be able to justify them. In practice, this currently involves encounters with a cacophony of dominant voices, all clamouring for relevance and justification.
- In search of synthesis, students wonder which voices, values and viewpoints to believe: which ones are relevant, which ones are justified. Polarisation and apparently non-contentious concepts, such as lifelong learning, might appeal as shortcuts to synthesis.
- But other voices can be heard too: their own and the voices of other learners. In this chapter, learners' voices invite us to pause for thought, and, more, they recommend further reading to us.
- Listening to learners' voices provides common ground. Listening provides space to weigh up the respective merits of different viewpoints and to build an inclusive experience of education that brings common good.

Recommended reading: Sara

Bovill, C. (2014) An investigation of co-created curricula within higher education in the UK, Ireland, and the USA. *Innovations in education and teaching international*, 51(1), pp. 15–25.

This paper focuses on a series of studies which ask whether having a say in what they are learning supports students further. Their purpose is to encourage students and staff to share ideas for co-created curricula and to recognise the importance of students' views.

Students prefer co-creation via self-directed learning, especially the individual responsibility, engagement, and autonomy that comes with it. Staff had a different viewpoint. They found co-created curricula to be time and skill-demanding – and nerve-wracking, though several staff enjoyed how student participation developed courses, which, in turn, became transformatory.

The paper found that there is a lack of approaches and designs for co-created curricula and that staff are continuously taking risks to support new curricula. However, the study draws attention to work that can give power to students while still having the structure and support of staff.

Recommended reading: Lucy

Mallman, M. and Lee, H. (2016) Stigmatised learners: mature-age students negotiating university culture., *British Journal of Sociology of Education*, 37(5), pp. 684–701.

This is a qualitative study discovering mature students' experiences during their first year of university. It tells a story of the differences between mature students and their younger peers in terms of the emotional impact of university life, both socially and academically. I found this refreshing and relevant.

However, mature students appear stigmatised. At a time when universities are being incentivised to increase enrolment of "non-traditional" learners, it appears the mature student must conform to university life. Commitments outside of university life are seen as "baggage". Mature students often held back on questions or opinions so as not to appear too keen in front of the rest of the class. The priorities of younger and older students are quite different. While I do not believe that this is necessarily a problem, we will have different priorities through various stages of life. Perhaps this contributes to the young/old divide seen in this study.

Recommended reading: Mia

Fraser, C. and Meadows, S. (2008) Children's views of Teaching Assistants in primary schools. *Education 3–13*, 36(4), pp. 351–363.

Can children tell the difference between teacher and TA? Children's first-hand experience and perspectives of a classroom and the teachers in a school are crucial to educational research. They are the ones spending the majority of their day in schools.

It was emotional reading how much the children all cared for the staff. The children reiterated how comfortable they felt with TAs and how TAs felt like friends. Children trusted them. In one part of the questionnaire, children were asked about qualities a TA would need. The children said it is important TAs like children and pay attention to them. Every characteristic was a warming positive one.

Recommended reading: Niall

Widnall, E., Epstein, S., Polling, C., Velupillai, S., Jewell, A., Dutta, R., Simonoff, E., Stewart, R., Gilbert, R., Ford, T., Hotopf, M., Hayes, R.D. and Down, J. (2022) Autism spectrum disorders as a risk factor for adolescent self-harm: a retrospective cohort study of 113,286 young people in the UK *BMC Med*, 20(137), p. 137.

This study looks at the association of mental health, suicide, suicide attempts and self-harm of autistic people when compared to non-autistic people. Evidence suggests a strong link between autistic young people and poor mental health and hospital visits related to suicide and self-harm. It made me sad how well researched the issue is.

Although solutions may not be the goal of the study, highlighting an issue and not going into pragmatic ideas is scary, especially for an autistic reader. Young people probably have a lot to say on this; adding some qualitative information would greatly enhance the emotional impact. It is important to remember the numbers and figures represent real people, young people who have a developmental disability.

Recommended reading: Jessica

Salehi, H. et al. (2024) ADHD learners as victims or survivors in L2 learning contexts: a case of application of dynamic assessment to selective attention and reading comprehension ability. *Asian-Pacific Journal of Second and Foreign Language Education*, 9(10), pp. 10–21.

This study of a 13-year-old girl diagnosed with ADHD focuses on whether dynamic assessments could be helpful in teaching students with ADHD regarding L2 learning (learning a second language). Dynamic assessment improved the student's reading comprehension and selective attention when it came to learning a second language.

Although the authors note that no generalisations based on the findings can be made, it is interesting to see how ADHD learners might potentially succeed and flourish in education. As a fellow student with ADHD, I certainly feel I could have benefitted from an interactive form of assessment.

Acknowledgements

Sincere thanks to Sarah Purcell (Library Services) and Penny Golightly (Centre for Academic English and Skills), both colleagues at the University of Worcester, for their support and assistance in producing the work that has informed this chapter's collaboration. Thanks also to Simon Taylor and Dr Seán Bracken, editors of this book, for their patience as this chapter was prepared.

References

Apple, M.W., Biesta, G., Bright, D., Giroux, H.A., McKay, A., McLaren, P., Riddle, S. and Yeatman, A. (2022) Reflections on contemporary challenges and possibilities for democracy and education. *Journal of Educational Administration and History*, 54(3), pp. 245–62.

Arnett, R.C. (2001) Dialogic civility as pragmatic ethical praxis: an interpersonal metaphor for the public domain. *Communication Theory*, 11(3), pp. 315–38.

Biesta, G. (2022) Reclaiming a future that has not yet been: The Faure report, UNESCO's humanism and the need for the emancipation of education. *International Review of Education*, 68(5) pp. 655–72.

Carr, M. and Claxton, G. (2002) Tracking the development of learning dispositions, *Assessment in Education: Principles, Policy and Practice*, 9(1), pp. 9–37.

Coffield, F. (2002) +Skills for the Future: I've got a little list. *Assessment in Education: Principles, Policy and Practice*, 9(1), pp 39–43.

DfE (Department for Education) (2014) National Curriculum in England: Framework for Key Stages 1 to 4, Statutory Guidance, available online: https://www.gov.uk/government/publications/national-curriculum-in-england-framework-for-key-stages-1-to-4/the-national-curriculum-in-england-framework-for-key-stages-1-to-4, (Accessed 30 September 2024).

Locatelli, R. (2018) Education as a public and common good: Reframing the governance of education in a changing context. *Education, Research, and Foresight: Working Papers 22* (UNESCO), available online: https://unesdoc.unesco.org/ark:/48223/pf0000261614?posInSet=3&queryId=ef6c7815-3ddf-4302-bd6a-f37baa66d9d2, (Accessed 30 September 2024).

Maitland, J. and Glazzard, J. (2022) Finding a way through the fog: School staff experiences of the Covid-19 pandemic. *Cambridge Journal of Education*, 52(5), pp. 555–77.

QAA, (2019) *Education Studies Subject Benchmark Statement*. The Quality Assurance Agency for UK Higher Education. Available at: https://www.qaa.ac.uk/docs/qaa/subject-benchmark-statements/subject-benchmark-statement-education-studies.pdf?sfvrsn=3ae2cb81_5 (Accessed 30 September 2024).

3 Finding the voice of children past
How do we do it, and what does it tell us?

Ruth Felstead

Case studies from late nineteenth-century schools

The following are quoted directly from school "Logbooks" and were written by the headteachers in 1896.

1. "A…was very rude to his teacher and on being punished by the Mistress he attempted to hit her with a slate, also with a brush. The Mistress communicated with the Managers. (His mother) asked for him to be forgiven and re-admitted. He was forgiven on condition that he apologise and take a caning before the children, which was administered by the Mistress in the presence of the Rector and his mother" (Belbroughton-Fairfield School *Logbook*, October 1896, in Hogarth, 1975).
2. "An act of insubordination (took place) by 12 boys across standards 3–7 who had previously arranged to run away; after playtime instead of falling in for drill they ran off over the fields. Parents were visited and told that their offspring would be punished on Monday. Boys were reprimanded in front of whole school then taken to classroom but refused to hold out their hands for punishment. They were then placed on one of the desks and received three cuts with the cane on the lower part of their backs" (Crabbs Cross School *Logbook*, 27/11/1896).

Introduction and context

This chapter is about attempting to locate the voices of schoolchildren from the past, so ensuring that they do not go unheard. Unlike today, in the late nineteenth and early twentieth centuries in publicly funded "elementary" schools, there was no specific way in which children had the opportunity to express themselves and their viewpoints. In other words, they apparently had no 'voice'. Attendance at school for children aged 5–10 was compulsory from 1880 but not free until 1891. In 1893, the school leaving age rose to 11, and in 1899, it rose to 12. From 1862, headteachers in government-funded schools had been required to write daily in a "Logbook". This was where they recorded the events of the day, including, amongst other things, attendance and issues with behaviour.

The previous extracts are Logbook entries from two schools in Worcestershire. Schools in the late nineteenth century had many differences from those of the early to mid-twenty-first century; for instance, they could legally physically punish children with the cane (corporal punishment). The right of a school to physically punish a child (where there was "just cause") had been, for many years, generally viewed as acceptable; the punishment, however, should be "proportionate" to the offence. This was legally upheld in 1889 following the *Gardner vs. Byfield* test case in which a parent attempted but failed to prosecute a teacher for caning the hand of their child (Middleton, 2008: 254). Whilst corporal punishment was not always desirable, it was very much part of the classroom experience, as shown by the following comments of two influential educationists.

Joseph Landon, the Principal of Saltley Teacher Training College in Birmingham, wrote in his 1894 teaching guide that the point of discipline was to create a frame of mind in children to curb "evil tendencies and bad habits" and to "cultivate a sense of honour and duty" (Landon, 1884: 205). This showed a visibly moralistic approach to schooling, which will be explained further in this chapter. David Salmon, the Principal of Swansea Teacher Training College, identified in his guide *The Art of Teaching*, published in 1898, that "bodily chastisement" was one of the "punishments available" to "prevent the offender repeating the offence, (or) to prevent others from copying it" (Salmon, 1898: 35–37). These comments show the ways in which the "official" views of children were then presented to teachers. There is nothing here to suggest that the child had a way to make their voice heard.

Seeking the child's voice

Today, the child's voice is frequently sought by care and education professionals, reflecting the current assumption that, as stakeholders in the institutions that govern their lives, children's opinions and feelings are valuable. This voice is much harder to locate when it comes from the late Victorian period. Harry Hendrick (1997) stated that it is missing largely due to a lack of documentation emanating from children themselves. Whilst there is a considerable amount of material relating *to* children, it was generated mainly by adults: for example, parents, teachers, doctors, civil servants and other officials who were talking *for* or *about* them. The voice of the child itself, therefore, is under-represented, and this can sometimes lead to it being ignored:

> Not only is the voice of the child more or less absent, there is always the related likelihood that the historian will be tempted to omit any representation of the child's viewpoint, or even fail to recognise that such a perspective exists.
>
> (Hendrick, 1997: 3)

Unable to directly "hear" the child's voice, a historian of education therefore needs to seek it in different ways. There are several methods of doing this. As you read through the chapter, you will find the opportunity to "pause for thought", which will enable you to try to locate the children's voices yourself.

Pause for thought

Look at the case studies on the first page of this chapter.

What are the teachers' views of the child(ren) in each extract?
What are the parents' views of the children and of the school?
From these extracts, what can you learn about the children themselves? Can you see anything that would give you a clue about their views and feelings?

It is sometimes possible to find out the view of children by reading very carefully what others (adults) have written about them. This involves searching for hidden meanings in their use of words, which may give some indication about what the child is thinking or feeling, including, for example, what prompted them to take the actions that they did. This has become known as "reading against the grain". This term was initially used by the historian Ranjit Guha (1983), who was researching the voice of indigenous groups in India during the colonial period, finding that, despite their ostensible lack of both power and voice, these people were still able to act to make their feelings known.

When looking at the extracts, it is easy to see that punishments were often harsh within many schools and that many parents were generally accepting of corporal punishment being meted out to their children if it was regarded as justified. Furthermore, it was regarded by successive nineteenth and early twentieth-century governments as essential to instil in children the morals required for future citizens, which would, it was hoped, result in lower criminality and raise the moral tone of communities (Wright, 2017: 220). Schools, therefore, were urged to institute a strong punishment regime to encourage these desired behaviours. It would appear that children had very little control over these circumstances. However, the previous extracts also show us that children were often oppositional and challenging, although they made their feelings known in a variety of ways. They were, therefore, showing their voices through their actions. The child in the first case resorted to physical violence towards the teacher. We have no knowledge of why, but there was clearly anger in the child's action, perhaps also frustration at the lack of any other means of enabling their feelings to be known. In the second case, the children were acting together in a premeditated attempt to run away from the school. This suggests that, although schools had a repressive punishment regime, children were still able to organise themselves to take this sort of collective action, even if unsuccessfully. It also shows something important about the process of punishment in general, which was that children were expected to accept it without question; that these boys did not do so and chose to refuse to hold out their hands for punishment was also a form of expressing their voice, even though eventually they capitulated and apparently accepted it.

Children and agency

The point of having a voice is not just to be heard but also to be able to bring about changes. This is known as having "agency". Human agency, states Houston (2010), is the ability of individuals, alone or with others, to purposefully make a difference to their circumstances as Bandura elucidates: "People are partly the products of their environments, but by selecting, creating, and transforming their environmental circumstances they are producers of environments as well" (Bandura, 2000: 75). The action of the children from Crabbs Cross School who ran away shows a form of what is termed "collective agency" – that is, working together for a common purpose (Bandura, 2000: 75–78). Children today are, as Oswell (2013: 3–4) indicates, regarded as having a stake in decision-making processes, including at school, indicating that they have agency. Therefore, there has clearly been a change in the degree of agency afforded to children over the past hundred years or so, raising the question of how this came about.

This change in children's agency is partly due to the evolving nature of how children were viewed by society in general. Children in early twentieth-century Britain were, Allison James identifies, seen only as in the process of "becoming" adults, rather than as individuals with the capacity for independent thought (James, 2009: 34–35). As such, they would appear to have little agency. For example, structuralist/functionalist sociologists such as Talcott Parsons (1954) saw children as not independently motivated: instead, automatically and without question, they became socialised into the societal structures (such as school and family) which made up their lives and which they were unable to change until they reached adulthood. In a similar vein, developmental psychologists like Jean Piaget (1936) conceptualised children as being strictly bound by age-related fixed developmental stages which prevented them developing independent thought until they reached a certain age. Both Piaget and Parsons, therefore, saw children as having relatively little opportunity for making a difference to either their own or other people's circumstances. This perception of children as unable to act independently was challenged by Phillipe Ariès (1962), who put forward the view that "childhood" was a social construct – that is, not fixed by biology or psychology, but instead based upon social norms and values about what a child should be. Moreover, from the mid-1970s, the rise of Lev Vygotsky's social constructivist and Albert Bandura's social learning theories led to greater understanding that children could learn and think independently of adults, along with a growing perception of children being capable of agency in their own right (Vygotsky 1978; Bandura, 2000).

At the same time, there was a change in how the 'child's voice' was characterised. Previously of interest mainly through what it revealed about the development of young people on the road to adulthood, it now became understood that children had an ability to construct their own meanings of situations as they developed. Children, therefore, could be seen as social actors in their own right, with the capacity to accept, resist or change the social structures that made up their lives – in other words, to show their voice through their actions.

Pause for thought

Reflect on what you have read about the changing understanding of the nature of childhood and children in history.

Think about the different conceptualisations of childhood expressed by structuralist, social constructivist and social learning theorists. How do you think these different views about the nature of childhood might affect how the authors viewed the ability of children to make their voices heard?

The child's voice and agency in nineteenth-century schools

In the late nineteenth century, there was general concern that urbanisation had a negative effect on the morals of the working classes, who became viewed as "degenerate" and lacking in morals. For example, drunkenness, "immorality" and "Godlessness" were seen to be destabilising communities (Duncan, 2013:). Children were frequently regarded as in need of being "civilised" into good citizens, with schools being identified as the main institution through which the moral values appropriate for future citizens could be instilled (Wright, 2017). It also needs to be remembered that Great Britain at this time was a country with a large and growing empire, the defence of which was frequently a matter of governmental concern. Instilling behaviours such as obedience to authority at an early age was, therefore, seen as important for children who might, in the future, be required to militarily defend the empire, as happened in the South African Boer War of 1899–1902, and also in the First World War of 1914–1918 (Horn, 1988). Children were expected to exhibit, among other things "cheerful obedience to duty" (Committee of Council on Education, 1875: 6). Effectively, this meant that children should obey teachers, parents and others in authority willingly, and without question. It included the expectation, seen at the beginning of the chapter, of submitting "cheerfully" to punishment if it was deemed to be deserved.

The doctoral research of the author (Felstead, 2024), which compared a sample of elementary schools in the neighbouring areas of Birmingham and Worcestershire, found, through an investigation of school Logbooks, that although the two areas were very different in terms of types of school and educational philosophies, each, in different ways, sought to foster a school environment which effectively promoted these required values. This could be through the taught curriculum, for example, reading books and stories, songs and poetry and the teaching of military "drill" but also through punishment for undesired behaviour, such as disobedience and truancy, and rewards, such as prizes or 'treats' for compliance with the rules.

Children, it therefore seems, appeared to be in a very weak position, with little chance of having the ability to make a difference to the school, let alone the world they lived in. For children, expressing their voices and showing agency was difficult, especially in schools. James and James (2004: 21) characterised schools of the time as institutions of adult hegemony: the rules and values set entirely by adults, who sought to impose their vision and purpose upon pupils to encourage them to fit the accepted ideal. However, although schools *were* clearly hegemonic institutions, evidence suggests that in certain circumstances, despite the constraints and rules which surrounded them, children were able to find opportunities within the structures of the school to show their own potential for agency. In other words, children were able to find ways of tactically disrupting schools' expectations and requirements.

Agency in schools is more readily seen if the focus is placed, not on the children themselves, but instead on the degree of 'agentic action' that is visible (Wyness, 2015: 10, 11). These are actions that children took to change their school environment or structure. Anthony Giddens' (1986) theory of 'structuration' suggests that schools, because of their opportunities for conflict, often have the capacity for children to show agentic action. Similarly, Michel de Certeau's (1984: 37–40) theory of the "power of the weak over the strong", states that even powerful institutions like schools had areas of weakness which could be exploited by pupils, so bringing about change. The weak (in this case, the pupils) would then be able to tactically alter and reverse the power of the strong (the teacher or the school as a whole) through their knowledge of the environment, as seen in the following case study.

Case study: Evesham Church of England School, 1883–1886

A number of episodes of serious behavioural issues took place in Evesham National School Girls Department between 1883 and 1887, leading to the resignation of four headmistresses during this period. Initially, this appeared to have occurred during a period of staff shortage following the extended sick leave of the assistant mistress, leaving the headmistress to cope alone with teaching the whole school.

The death of the vicar in 1883 meant that his wife, who had previously been of considerable support to the headmistress, no longer visited the school, and this lack of effective supervision seems to have provided the initial opportunity for girls to exert their power to behave in a disruptive

Finding the voice of children past 31

manner. This resulted in punishment, which led in turn to an escalating cycle of disobedience and to further "punitive measures". These are identified in the Logbook entries written by the headmistresses in the first table that follows:

1883	26/1	"Punished two girls for behaving very rudely – detained them until 2.45".
	9/2	"Punished xxx for being rude".
	16/2	"Punished three girls for bad conduct".
	23/2	"Detained xxx all the dinner hour for disobedience".
	2/3	"Had to keep xxx without her dinner as she refused to do her dictation before she went to dinner – made her do it in the afternoon".
	9/3	"Punished three children for rudeness".
	22/3	"Resigned my duties as Mistress".

This cycle continued until September 1886 and successive Logbook entries described the girls as "disobedient, disorderly, and rebellious". This is illuminating as it suggests that much of the power within the school at this time was in the hands of the pupils and not the teachers, despite the continuation of retributive punishments. Order was restored finally when the fifth incumbent headmistress completely changed the disciplinary method, shown in the second table.

1886	10/9	"Found the whole of the classes in a most disorderly and rebellious condition and the work of the year in a backward state".
	27/9	"It was only with the utmost vigilance that any sort of order could be maintained yesterday and today".
	28/9	"As soon as there was any undue noise manifest the bell was rung, lessons stopped, and the children obliged to sit still. This took place several times".
	1/10	"Order improving but still very poor. No corporal punishment used this week. Tried to impress on the children's minds the necessity of good behaviour".

(Felstead, 2024: 189–190)

> **Pause for thought**
> 1. Read the explanation and the Logbook entries in the case study.
> 2. Can you suggest reasons why the pupils became, and remained, so disorderly?
> 3. What were the results of the disorderly behaviour for teachers and pupils?
> 4. Can you find anything from these extracts that relates to the agency of the pupils?
> 5. What does this tell us about the children's voices?

Using Gidden's theory of structuration and de Certeau's conception of power of the weak over the strong, the events at Evesham tell of a breakdown in order which appears to have been caused by an increase in harsh punishment. Although the pupils were relatively weak, their reaction to continuing severe punishment was not to "give in" but to become even more disorderly. That the head teacher used the word "rebellious" to describe them tells us that this was more than just "bad behaviour" and that the rebellious action may have included an element of organisation. Also interesting is that although the pupils continued to be punished, it no longer had the desired effect, so it did not stop the rebellious actions. Therefore, although the pupils were constrained within the structure of the school, and subject to its punishment on account of their oppositional behaviour, they effectively prevented the school from operating, leading to resignations of several headteachers. After the fourth change of headmistress, the severe punishment regime was abandoned, and behaviour slowly returned to normal, which suggests that the punishment in itself had prolonged the disturbance. We can, therefore, see that this was an example of pupil agency, as the pupils, although "weak" in terms of apparent power, were in a position to exploit through indiscipline the continued weakness of the school systems, and therefore able to exert their own power to make clear their dissatisfaction. This was very long-term, but it does show that changes were made in the structure of the school environment in that, not only did a number of headteachers resign but also there was a change (for the better) in the punishment regime.

Logbooks from Birmingham and Worcestershire indicate that children's power was mainly expressed in three ways: truancy, disruptive or hostile behaviour and lack of effort (Felstead, 2024). The previous case study was an example of disruptive behaviour. Truancy was also an effective way of making the school take notice; at this time schools were partly financed through the number of attendances over the course of the year, and truancy could therefore make a difference. Persistent or organised truancy was, therefore, punished severely (as shown in extract 2 at the beginning of the chapter). However, schools were also affected by "occasional" truancy. This might mean not attending on a specific day, for example, on days when a local event such as a show, or a circus was in town. This kind of truancy was commonplace. Examples of this were the Birmingham Onion Fair, Sayers Circus, and Bromsgrove Fair. Some schools accepted poor attendance on such days, simply recording it in their Logbooks. On the day of the annual Horse Fair in Birmingham in 1882, Bristol Street Board School noted in its Logbook: "Kept school open (Horse Fair Day) – only about a dozen boys present." At Dodford-with-Grafton school near Bromsgrove, the school simply gave in and closed on the day of the Bromsgrove Fair in 1883 (Dodford-with-Grafton Logbook, 1883). It was, of course, technically an offence for children not to attend, but schools rarely punished this sort of absence, suggesting that there was a kind of unofficial agreement in operation. This indicates that schools *were* (in this case) hearing the child's voice and allowing them to have an "unofficial holiday".

The role of parents

At this time, not only was the voice of the child hard to find but also that of the parent. Parents sometimes deliberately kept children at home. This could be for economic reasons– for example, in rural communities, children were needed to work in the fields at harvest time, or to look after younger siblings whilst the parents worked. Preventing a child's attendance at school was often the only way that a parent could express disapproval about either something specific that had happened at school, or just with schooling in general. Parents might, after being told by their child about a disciplinary incident, decide to move their child from one school and to re-register them in another one nearby. Relevant Logbook entries record:

> "Kept a boy named … in school for bad conduct but he was fetched away by his mother who declared her intention to send him to some other school".
>
> Crabbs Cross School Logbook (16/4/1880)

"Girl punished for idleness and carelessness in exam work. Mother came to school and abused me very much declaring intention to move child to another school".

Evesham National School Logbook (18/10/1889)

This removal of children to another school was more commonly observed in Worcestershire than in Birmingham, probably because schools in Birmingham tended to be over-subscribed, making it harder to find another place if a parent were to withdraw a child. Bandura (2000: 75) terms this sort of behaviour "proxy agency", i.e. when relatively powerless individuals "try to get other people who have expertise, or wield influence and power, to act on their behalf to obtain the outcomes they desire".

If the parent and child worked together to bring about change, this would be a form of collective agency, as discussed previously. In the second extract, the parent felt strongly enough about her daughter's punishment to come into school to argue with the teacher. Both proxy and collective agency are therefore visible in these extracts. When acting together, parents and children could enhance the effectiveness of each other's actions. Both parents and children, therefore, were making their voices heard when acting together for their common goal.

The importance of children doing 'good work' was another weak point within schools through which children could find the opportunity to voice displeasure. Schools were financed not just through attendance but also through examination success. All pupils were tested for their learning by Her Majesty's Inspectors of Schools (HMIs) once a year, and if a child failed, the school would lose part of their government grant. Children who attended school could, therefore, show their alienation from lessons through their work or lack of it. Punishments for idleness, carelessness and lack of effort or care, were mentioned in three Logbooks from Worcestershire: one at Belbroughton-Fairfield; one – eventually leading to an expulsion – at Evesham; and another at Crabbs Cross. Birmingham schools were required to keep punishment books. Barford Road School cites "careless work", "continually careless" and "idle" on numerous occasions, with caning as punishment, and Icknield Street School recorded several instances of children being punished for "inattention" (Barford Road Board School Punishment Book, 1895–1910; Icknield Street Board School Punishment Book, 1883–1946). Whilst not all "careless work" or apparent idleness was a deliberate attempt to make a point, failure to make an effort could give a message of, for example, lack of interest, dislike of teaching methods or a lack of relevance of school to the pupil. This was not something that a headteacher would want an HMI to see, as it could lead to reduction of the "merit grant", paid at three levels, and which could easily be reduced if concerns with teaching arose.

Independent thinking

Agency was not just about a child making their views known but also about their ability to accept or reject some of the material they were taught and the rules they were expected to follow. The assumption was that children would become "civilised" (well behaved, polite, and morally responsible people) through attending schools, and growing into exemplary citizens, which would eventually improve the morals of local communities. The intention for this to happen is shown in the following extract:

> Children as they return from the happy hours of school bring with them, to the worst homes as well as the best, memories, impressions and influences which must ultimately raise the whole tone of working-class life to a higher pitch, and so benefit the community throughout.
>
> (Committee of Council on Education, Report, 1881–1882: 177)

Children, however, could show their independent thought, and so their agency, through rejecting or adapting some of these messages, as can be seen by the following extract from an HMI:

> Teachers have often told me in sorrow that children who are irreproachable in school often appear to leave their good manners behind them when they go into the streets … one of my sub-inspectors heard a child in a tramcar addressing the guard in the most vile and violent language. His head teacher happened to be there also, unbeknown to the child, and he informed my sub inspector that the child in question was his very best scholar and that if he had not heard what had passed, he could not have believed it possible.
>
> (Board of Education *Report*, 1899, p. 179)

This shows an awareness of a more sophisticated kind of agency where children were consciously discerning about what they learned, able to identify which behaviours were required for school and which were acceptable outside and to change their behaviour accordingly. It shows very clearly their capacity for thinking independently and rejecting what they did not believe was relevant to their lives. The ability for independent thought amongst schoolchildren has led to much discussion about how much the moral messages of "behaviour" and "duty", as well as values of patriotism and imperialism, were received and internalised by children. This has formed the basis for investigations into voting behaviour in General Elections and the likelihood of young men volunteering for service in both the 1899–1902 South African War and the 1914–1918 First World War.

Conclusion

This chapter has examined ways in which the "learner voice" can be found in schools of the late nineteenth century, during which period it apparently seems to be completely absent due to there being no formal ways in which children were able to make known their views or to influence decision-making processes. It shows that, even though there is very little written by working-class children themselves, through a searching and careful reading of material written by others, the previously hidden voice of the child emerges. Issues around punishment were often a particular opportunity for conflict, and for this voice to become apparent. Sometimes this happened when children (or their parents) were able to exploit weaknesses within the school system, such as the need for attendance, appropriate behaviour and careful work. Children could, through oppositional behaviour in these areas, cause schools, in response, to make changes in their actions or regimes. These oppositional actions showed also that children were capable of agency, in that they could think independently and behave accordingly. These agentic actions can still be observed in schools today, although of course, it is much easier in the twenty-first century to find examples of the learner voice through official channels such as school councils and formal requests for evaluations. Yet, there are, even now, pupils, either as individuals or groups, whose voices are harder to locate than others, some of which are examined elsewhere in this book.

Summary points

- The "voice" of working-class pupils in nineteenth-century state-funded schools has been historically hard to hear, mainly because there were no mechanisms in schools for it to be garnered.

- The conceptualisation of childhood as a "social construct" allowed children to be seen as individuals in their own right.
- Using techniques such as "reading against the grain", it is possible to hear pupils' voices through materials written about them by others.
- Theories such as Gidden's theory of "structuration" and De Certeau's "power of the weak over the strong" enables investigation of situations within schools where pupils were able to exploit weak points and so succeed in initiating change.
- Evidence of independent thought on the part of children further suggests their degree of agency, even in a situation where there appears to be little opportunity to express it.

Recommended reading

As with all historical investigation, it is good to be able to find materials from the period being studied. Joseph Landon's (1884) *Principles and Practices* is free to view online; larger libraries usually have an archive department where you can find school Logbooks. However, this can be time-consuming, so books and articles from the reference list also contain such extracts. Especially useful are the following:

Oswell, D. (2013) *The agency of children: From family to global rights*. Cambridge: Cambridge University Press.

Provides an overview of some of the concepts raised in this chapter, i.e., the nature of agency from historical, current and international human rights perspectives.

James, A. and James, A.L. (2004) *Constructing childhood: Theory, policy and social practice*. London: Palgrave.

Focuses on the social construction of children, widening from education to include citizenship, family and health. For a more historical perspective looking at punishment, see

Middleton, J. (2008) The experience of corporal punishment in schools, 1890–1940. *History of Education*, 37 (2) pp. 253–275.

References

Ariès, P. (1962) *Centuries of Childhood: A social history of family life*, (New York: Random House).
Bandura, A. (2000) Exercise of Human Agency Through Collective Efficacy. *Current Directions in Psychological Science*, 9 (3).
Barford Road Board School, Birmingham, (1895–1910) *Punishment Book: Senior Boy's Department*, Birmingham Archives and Heritage Service (BAHS).
Belbroughton-Fairfield School, *Logbook* (October 1896) Worcestershire Archive and Archaeology Service (WAAS).
Board of Education, (1899) General Report for the year 1899 by T.S. Aldis, one of Her Majesty's Chief Inspectors, on the Schools in the West Central Division of England, *Report, Vol III, Appendix to Report* (1899–1900).
Committee of Council on Education, England and Wales (1875) *New Code of Education 1875*, (London, HMSO).
Committee of Council on Education, England and Wales (1882) *Report with Appendices 1881-2*, (London: HMSO).
Crabbs Cross School *Logbook* (27/11/1896) WAAS.
De Certeau, M. (1984) *The Practice of Everyday Life*, (Berkely: University of California Press).
Dodford with Grafton *Logbook*, (1883) WAAS.
Duncan, R.G. (2013) *Pubs and Patriots: The Drink Crisis During World War One*, (Liverpool: Liverpool University Press).
Felstead, R. (2024) Teaching 'Cheerful Obedience to Duty': Moral, Patriotic and Imperial Education in Birmingham and Worcestershire Elementary Schools, c.1880–1902, PhD Thesis, Liverpool Hope University.
Giddens, A. (1986) *The Constitution of Society: Outline of the Theory of Structuration*, (Cambridge: Polity Press).

Guha, R. (1983) *Elementary Aspects of Peasant Insurgency in Colonial India*, (New Delhi and Oxford: Oxford University Press).

Hendrick, H. Children (1997) *Childhood and English Society 1880 – 1990*, (Cambridge: Cambridge University Press).

Hogarth, W. (1975) *Fairfield School, Bromsgrove: one hundred years of history 1875–1975*, (Unpublished, Bromsgrove Library Local Collection).

Horn, P. (1988) English Elementary Education and the Growth of the Imperialist Ideal, 1880–1914 in Mangan, J.A. *Benefits Bestowed? Education and British Imperialism*, (Manchester and New York: Routledge).

Houston, S. (2010) Further reflections on Habermas s contribution to discourse in child protection: An examination of power in social life , *British Journal of Social Work*, 406, 1736–1753.

Icknield Street Board School Birmingham *Punishment Book* (1883–1946) BAHS.

James, A. Agency, Qvortrup, I. N. J., Corsaro, W., & Honig, M. (Eds), (2009) *The Palgrave Handbook of Childhood Studies*, (London: Palgrave).

James, A. and James, A., (2004) *Constructing Childhood: Theory, Policy and Social Practice*, (Basingstoke: Palgrave).

Landon, J. (1884) *The Principles and Practice of Teaching and Class Management*, (New York: Macmillan and Co.)

Middleton, J. (2008) The Experience of Corporal Punishment in Schools, 1890–1940, *History of Education*, 37,2, 253–275.

Oswell, D. (2013) *The Agency of Children: from Family to Global Human Rights*, (Cambridge: Cambridge University Press).

Parsons, T. (1954) *Essays in Social Structure*, (Glencoe, USA: The Free Press).

Piaget, J. (1936) *The Origins of Intelligence in the Child*, (London: Routledge and Kegan Paul).

Salmon, D. (1898) *The Art of Teaching*, (London: Longmans).

Vygotsky, L.S. (1978) *Mind in Society: The Development of Higher Psychological Processes*, (London: Harvard University Press).

Wright, S. (2017) *Morality and Citizenship in English Schools: secular approaches 1897–1944*, (London: Palgrave Macmillan).

Wyness, M. (2015) *Childhood*, (Cambridge: Polity).

4 Beyond the survey metrics

A narrative approach to higher education student voice

Pai Usowicz and Ellie Hill

> **Vignette**
>
> *As I sit here, my mind is filled with doubt and despair. The words that echo in my home are suffocating – "You are not good enough". "You're a disease". "Dumb dumb". I'm too afraid to show any emotion because if I do, I'm seen as weak. But deep down, I know that my teachers share the same opinion as my so-called parents. I can never seem to avoid getting caught for talking or not doing my work. It's not that I don't want to, it's just that I have too much on my mind. What's the point of doing all this schoolwork if I'm going to end up with a dead-end job or living on the street? At least, that's what my stepdad tells me. All I wish for is that my teachers would ask me if I'm okay. But I'm too scared to tell them what's happening at home. My stepdad threatens me, saying that I'll be taken away from my friends, my grandparents, and forced to attend a school where I won't be allowed to leave. I want to reach out and speak up, but I'm convinced that my teachers don't care. They see me as a lazy, burdensome student who just doesn't care about anything. But that's a lie – I care deeply.*

Introduction

This chapter will incorporate genuine learner voice with academic discussion and research. To indicate learner voice, italics are used.

Higher Education often presents the student voice as important for quality, seeing the student as a customer, paying for their education, with the National Student Survey (NSS) exemplifying this transaction (Canning, 2017). This chapter will explore how a narrative approach to data collection can enable the authentic and honest student voice to be heard in all its richness and uniqueness. The chapter uses narrative research to shine a spotlight on the experiences of the individual (Kim, 2015; Cresswell and Poth, 2018). In order to understand stories of challenges in education and to respectfully appreciate the journey into higher education for some non-traditional students, the narrative of one's schooling is an opportunity to hear the interpretation of that time. The importance of this is explained by Clandinin and Murphy (2009: 601): "We, too, see the possibility through narrative research to change the dominant narratives, to shift the taken-for-granted social, cultural, and institutional narratives".

Pai – introduced in the case study – struggled with social, emotional, and mental health (SEMH) due to adverse childhood experiences (ACEs), which had a profound impact on her academic performance during high school and the General Certificate of Secondary Education (GCSE). Despite facing challenges in her home life and being a looked-after child (LAC), as well as having poor relationships with her teachers, she did not allow these experiences to shape her future negatively. Instead, she used them as a catalyst for change and growth.

The following part of this chapter moves on to explore how the narrative data were gathered. Then, the themes from the data are defined and illustrated with a range of narrative techniques. These themes are ACEs, learner voice, relationships in education and survivor advocacy.

Gathering narrative data

Listening to people's voices takes time. The narrative data drawn upon for this chapter includes photo elicitation (Harper, 2010), diary entries (Kim, 2015), poetry (Furman, 2007) and field notes (Clandinin and Connelly, 2000). The reflection process undertaken allowed Pai the opportunity to choose what was important to share about her school experiences. It was important to research ethically, understanding the personal investment, but also having control of how her voice was being represented to the reader (Squire et al., 2014).

Data was analysed using photographs of transitional objects that represented Pai's experiences, such as, "Albert the safety bear", which was taken during her fieldwork of narrative data (Kara et al., 2021). The use of transitional objects as a method of exploring contemporary issues was considered a novel approach. The use of transitional objects is a well-known therapeutic tool in the fields of psychology and education (Ecclestone and Hayes, 2009; Kiely, 2016). Research has shown that it can help to reduce anxiety and stress when discussing personal experiences and sensitive issues (Kara et al., 2021).

Poetry is a way to deliver critical judgement through data analysis and promote personal discovery of oneself (Hanauer, 2010). In poetry, emotions, personality and a creative manner of conveying sensitive experiences can be represented in a poetic form. Using poetry as a research approach allows for the retention of ambiguity, the investigation of transitional places and the reflection on silence, which may be difficult to achieve with more traditional research methods, such as quantitative analysis (Johnson et al., 2017).

The selection of personal diary entries was edited to protect the identities of teachers, students and locations where the experiences took place. The diaries preserve historical facts and provide exact times and dates (Clandinin and Connelly, 2000). Researchers value the use of diaries in narrative research because each experience is unique, and two individuals entering the same lesson may have different experiences and opinions during the reflective process (Clandinin and Connelly, 2000). The rich data produced from personal diaries capture critical moments of Pai's experiences, offering the freedom to reflect and express herself authentically (Noyes, 2008).

ACEs and disaffection

ACEs refer to traumatic and adverse events that individuals have faced within their family units, including physical, emotional and sexual abuse (Smith, 2018). Such experiences are prevalent in children who have undergone parental separation, which significantly increases their vulnerability to abuse (Radford et al., 2011). The consequences of ACEs can be severe, leading to various mental health disorders like depression, anxiety, personality disorders, and post-traumatic stress disorder (PTSD) in the affected children and young people (Smith, 2018).

Research has established a clear connection between SEMH and ACEs, showing how these experiences can deeply impact an individual's behaviour (Treat et al., 2020). ACEs can significantly influence the daily lives of children and young people, affecting their academic performance and, in turn, influencing their future opportunities in adulthood (Radford et al., 2011). Educators play a crucial role in breaking this cycle by providing a safety net for their pupils, improving their life chances and preventing disaffection in education (Williams and Pritchard, 2006; Swann, 2013).

Disaffection is an overarching term used to identify pupils who are considered statistically at risk, often associated with aberrant behaviours (Swann, 2013). Research indicates that those who have experienced trauma or adversity are more likely to become disengaged with academic study and withdraw from the world around them (Vizard, 2009). Consequently, such experiences can significantly impact their behaviour in an educational setting, ultimately hindering their academic success and limiting their future prospects for successful careers and positive relationships in adulthood (Williams and Pritchard, 2006).

The concept of ACEs, their impact on academic performance and the reasons behind students' behaviour remain ambiguous in the educational context. Behaviours that deviate from the norm are often misunderstood, and negative societal labels are used to define individuals without recognising their cry for help (Swann, 2013). The literature has consistently demonstrated the link between ACEs and disaffection in education, revealing the challenges that pupils face, which act as barriers to their learning:

Reflecting on my own experiences, I can see how ACEs affected my behaviour and engagement during my school years. I used to intentionally provoke teachers to receive detentions, as staying in school felt safer than going home. Growing up in a household where my mother's drinking led to abusive and controlling behaviours from both biological and stepparents, I felt trapped in a vicious cycle with seemingly no escape. Emotions were suppressed, as showing vulnerability would lead to punishment, and the reasons for punishment were often trivial.

As I reflect on my life experiences and academic journey, I have come to understand and appreciate them in a more positive light. Drawing from my personal experiences and my work as an educator with young people who have become disaffected and struggle academically, I can empathise with their feelings and struggles. I see aspects of myself in them and recognise the importance of investing time and effort in nurturing their growth and helping them strive for greatness because I believe everyone is capable of achieving their potential. My experiences have taught me that by providing understanding and support, we can use our own journey to positively impact the lives of others and guide them towards a better future.

"When I grew up, I couldn't show emotion. If I cried, I would be beaten".

(Conversation between Pai and Ellie)

June 2005

Dear Diary,

I had a rough time at school today. I was in science, and I don't like science, I didn't want to go home, and I wanted to make some trouble to get a detention. Yet again I don't think it was right but I needed to, Mr J was talking and talking and talking as normal. I said can we just get on with work or what. Mr J said get out of my classroom right now P you rude little girl I will deal with you in a minute. RUDE I THINK NOT! I stood outside I really didn't care about his stupid talk about how oxygen does this it does that blah blah blah.

I hate catch up lessons, they are stupid I am not going to do well the teachers at my school only care about the boffins the goody 2 shoes have the perfect life perfect parents at least they are safe wish I was. Anyway, back to the stupid science lesson, Mr J came out and started shouting at me. I just started smiling I just did not care. I wanted a detention after school, so I didn't come home another hour away is better than nothing. Anyway, Mr J said that I was trying to control the class I wasn't, he said that I am rude, disrespectful, and telling him how to do his job. I told him I was not trying to tell him how to do his job and I am sorry. But it was too late for apologies he sent me to Mr B office, all I got was writing lines at lunch. This is stupid I don't like writing lines nothing ever goes the way I want it to.

It another day in the hell hole, I hate my life, my house, my so called parents, I hate school, the teachers everything. I like my friends they get me but they don't see what I have to go through do they. Goodnight Diary write again soon xx

The historical diary entries I produced provided a valuable insight into the traumas I was enduring and the underlying reasons behind my behaviours. They became a window into the distressing experiences I faced at home, and why I resorted to acting out at school as a cry for help. My reluctance to go home was a clear indication of the turmoil I was enduring within my family unit. Those diary entries served as my attempt to shed light on the painful happenings at home, which were severely disrupting my education and well-being. The connection between these experiences and the impact on my academic disaffection became apparent through the emotions and struggles expressed in those diary pages. They revealed how ACEs had a profound effect on my behaviour, making it vital for educators to understand and address these underlying traumas to help students like me break free from the cycle and thrive in their educational journey.

> **Pause for thought**
>
> How can educators effectively address ACEs to prevent disaffection and foster academic success for students facing trauma?

Expressing your learner voice

Through research and reflecting on my educational experiences, it became increasingly evident that my voice was not heard. One significant moment that stands out in my memory is during the exam period for my GSEs. I was put into isolation, with teachers convinced it was for my own good. Despite my pleas not to be secluded in a room alone, my wishes were not respected, and I felt abandoned and ignored. It seemed unfair that I was treated this way simply because I was experiencing ACEs, which my adolescent mind struggled to process effectively. The whole time was overwhelming, and, unsurprisingly, I did not perform well in those exams.

During those trying times, I found solace in Albert, my safety bear. Writing poems and diary entries became my way to escape and process my feelings when I felt most abandoned. However, on the day of receiving my exam results, a turning point occurred. The teacher handed me the results and uttered words that stung deeply: "This is the most important mail you will ever receive; you will amount to nothing". But these hurtful words also ignited a fire within me. I vowed to prove him wrong, to show him and others that I am capable of achieving greatness.

From that moment onward, I refused to let negative experiences hinder my progress. I persisted through adversity, demonstrating that individuals like me could indeed attend university, even if it took a little longer. My achievements now serve as a model for others who find themselves in similar situations, showing them that hard work and determination can lead to success and realising their true potential.

Albert, my safety bear, played a crucial role in helping me feel secure. Engaging in dialogues with Albert offered me an outlet to communicate my thoughts and emotions more easily than with other people. Much like my maternal grandmother, who provided a sense of security during my formative years, Albert became a comforting presence in my life. In my diary entries, it is evident that adversity at home was impacting my performance at school. However, I was afraid to speak the truth about what was happening at home, opting to confide in my diary or talk to Albert instead. My fear of separation and abandonment played a significant role in my reluctance to share the truth. Trusting those responsible for my well-being was vital, and I feared the consequences of speaking up. The use of transitional objects, like Albert, proved to be effective in the home environment, even when ACEs were present.

Figure 4.1 Albert the Safety Bear

Albert the Safety Bear has been around for 22 years. Albert was given to me by my maternal grandmother when I was 10 years old since she was my safe person. This is the origin of the name Albert the Safety Bear. Albert has become and continues to be a significant part of my life. If Albert had the ability to communicate, I am confident that he would be able to share some of his secrets with you. My experience with Albert was excellent in that I was able to express my emotions and not be afraid to confront the reality of what was happening around me. Albert provided me with the courage to talk about my flaws, relationships, feelings and concerns with my peers and teachers.

> **Pause for thought**
>
> Think about your experiences as a learner or teacher, and any use of transitional objects such as Albert. How could you incorporate these into your teaching (for example, during Circle Time or puppets used with children for communication)?

Relationships in education

During my high school years, the relationships I experienced with teachers and peers were far from positive. I consistently found myself labelled by others, influenced by my background, mental health struggles and resulting low-level disruption in class. Amongst the teachers, there was only one who showed genuine concern and asked if everything was alright at home. However, I froze and couldn't find the courage to reveal the real reasons behind my behaviour.

Unfortunately, these negative labels hindered the relationship between me and my teachers, affecting my learning, attention, and overall quality of work. I knew I was intelligent, but my circumstances prevented me from fully applying myself in school. The impact of ACEs and my disaffection with education were undeniable factors behind my actions (Corcoran and McNulty, 2018).

In the midst of this challenging environment, one teacher stood out, showing a willingness to invest time in getting to know me. This simple act of reaching out began to chip away at the cycle of negative connections that often plague the teacher-student relationship. It became evident that when a teacher took the time to establish positive relationships and effective communication with their student, it transformed the entire educational experience (Vizard, 2009; DfE, 2014). On reflection, the impact of these unfavourable relationships, labelling, ACEs and my psychological wellbeing was profound. My behaviour and disengagement with learning were all products of this complex web of challenges. However, I recognised that I could not continue living up to the negative labels as a solution to my problems. There had to be a better way forward. As I progressed through my educational journey, I began to understand the limitations of professional teaching practice when it comes to establishing positive relationships with students. The most common concerns revolved around interactions with both peers and teachers. Regrettably, the labels that were frequently used to describe me, such as "rude", "dumb" and "disrespectful", painted a bleak picture of the relationships in my school life (Peterson, 2020).

Nonetheless, the impact of that one teacher who took the time to connect with me was profound. This experience demonstrated the transformative power of building positive relationships in education (Vizard, 2009; DfE, 2014). Their efforts taught me that not all teachers perceived students through the lens of negative labels, and it planted a seed of hope within me.

> **Pause for thought**
>
> Consider this scenario: a young person comes into the educational setting, and before they enter the classroom, you notice they have a black eye and a split lip. What do you do?

Survivor advocacy

Throughout my education journey, I have undergone tremendous growth as an individual, celebrating my successes, and gaining a fresh perspective on life. I no longer see myself as a victim, burdened by self-blame. Instead, I proudly embrace the title of a survivor, someone who can advocate not only for myself but also for others facing difficult times. Education has served as a transformative escape for me, renewing the purpose of my life. My newfound calling is to teach young individuals who find themselves in situations like mine, showing them that success is attainable, and challenging the notion that "people like us" are destined to fail, unable to pursue higher education or promising careers (Delker, Salton, and McLean, 2020).

Survivor advocacy - as I have come to learn - is not merely an inherent trait but rather a skill that develops through a series of transitional processes (Ross, 2006). The poetry I have written has been deeply influenced by my personal experiences with ACEs and my feelings of disconnection from education. These poems have served as both a testament to my ongoing transformative learning process and a means to strengthen my survivor advocacy skills (Ross, 2006). Moreover, they have shed light on the opposition I have faced due to my experiences (Delker, Salton and McLean, 2020).

> Who am I? (February 2022)
>
> My resilience can be traced back to the early trauma I endured and overcame. I chose to make use of those sad days in order to assist others who are experiencing similar difficulties,
> Making the best of a bad situation, taking responsibility for one's actions and remaining strong,
> I'm determined to move on at long last, and I'm looking for a method to make use of my past,
> My Beautiful Scars have now been shown, despite the fact that my wounds have been healed for a long time,
> Despite difficulty, my educational journey is merely a sampling of who I am,
> As time progressed, I discovered that I was not a victim, but a survivor advocate,
> Put my strength into action in order to assist others in giving their adversity the power of voice.

In the pursuit of understanding myself better, I have delved into autobiographical memory and skilfully weaved these recollections into my poetic expressions (Kara et al., 2021). This experience has been instrumental in challenging and reshaping my inner belief systems, allowing me to grow as a survivor advocate. In line with Ross's (2006) assertions, my use of autobiographical memories in a therapeutic approach mirrors the positive transformation undergone throughout the process of becoming a survivor advocate.

I am driven by the desire to dismantle the prevailing belief that disaffected individuals are destined for failure and have limited prospects. Through my own success story, I aim to prove that with determination, resilience and access to education, we can carve out a fulfilling future, defying expectations. By becoming an advocate for young people in similar circumstances, I hope to impart the transformative power of education and instil in them the confidence to embrace their own survivor identity.

The journey of becoming a survivor advocate has been one of self-discovery and empowerment. My experiences with ACEs and educational disaffection have shaped my perspective, but they do not define me. Instead, they have become a source of strength and inspiration to advocate for myself and others. Education, as a form of escape and renewal, has been the key to unlocking my potential, allowing me to rise above adversities and rewrite my narrative.

My mission as a survivor advocate and educator is to inspire and empower young individuals, showing them that they too can rise above their circumstances and create a brighter future for themselves. Education is the key to unlocking their potential, just as it has been for me. By sharing my journey, I hope to be an advocate for those who need it most, proving that we are not defined by our past but by the strength and resilience we exhibit in shaping our own destinies.

"You're nothing like school said. You are really intelligent. You are going to do good in the world".
Health and Social Care lecturers to Pai – Christmas party in the classroom (2006)

> **Pause for thought**
>
> How could you advocate for survivors, showing their strengths to other students to give them confidence and develop a community?

Conclusion

Pai's stories enable us to see higher education as more than just a set of metrics and survey data. Sharing her lived experience through a narrative approach highlights what really matters and the impact that truly listening to student voice can have, both on the student and the reader.

Now, Pai has completed her Post Graduate Certificate in Education (PGCE) in Further Education with a subject specialism of Special Educational Needs and Disability (SEND) and has become a qualified teacher. She reflects that as she moves forward, she knows that her past does not define her future. Learning from her experiences, she believes that education has the potential to be a catalyst for change and empowerment. Her goal as a teacher is to contribute to a positive learning environment for others who may have faced similar challenges in their lives. Pai vows to be a teacher who actively seeks to understand and support her students, regardless of their circumstances. She wants to make a difference in their lives, just as that one caring teacher made in hers.

Whilst her high school years were characterised by challenging relationships, negative labels, and a lack of engagement in learning, she knows that ACEs and disaffection with education heavily influenced her behaviour during that time. She is filled with gratitude for the opportunities that have come her way, seeing education as a lifeline, offering a pathway to personal growth and empowerment.

"Looking back to me as a child, I'm unrecognisable. It's just wanting better in life".
(Conversation between Pai and Ellie)

Summary points

- The voice of the higher education student is nuanced and individual. Narrative research can create a space for these authentic voices to be heard.
- Childhood experiences can influence our adult life and, specifically, our belief in ourselves to be a student in higher education. This is even more so for those that experienced ACEs. Educators have the opportunity to listen and support and make a difference.
- A survivor advocate is someone who takes back the power from those who did not listen and seeks to transform themselves and others through re-writing their narrative and advocating for others.
- Higher education is more than metrics and survey data. Knowing the whole person, the higher education student and being aware of their past and present through listening to their voice is our mission.

Further reading

Caine, V., Chung, S., Steeves, P., and Clandinin, D. J. (2020) The necessity of a relational ethics alongside Noddings' ethics of care in narrative inquiry. *Qualitative Research*, 20(3), 265–276. https://doi.org/10.1177/1468794119851336

If you are interested in using a narrative approach to research this article shows a narrative account. Written by experienced narrative researchers in the field of education the article intertwines their research with the theoretical roots of their work.

Wearmouth, J. (2004) 'Talking Stones': An Interview Technique for Disaffected Students. *Pastoral Care in Education*, 22(2), pp. 7–13.

In this article, Wearmouth (2004) introduces the 'Talking Stones' interview technique, a novel approach for connecting with disaffected students. The study delves into the practical application of this method in the context of pastoral care and education. By utilising 'Talking Stones,' educators can gain deeper insights into the experiences and emotions of disaffected students, fostering better understanding and support to address their needs effectively. The article presents valuable findings and recommendations that can greatly benefit educators and professionals seeking to create a more inclusive and supportive environment for students facing disaffection.

Coomber, S. (2019) *Trauma-informed education. Education* (Sydney. 1919), pp. 1–3.

Coomber's article, "Trauma-Informed Education" (2019), promises to be a compelling read as it delves into the crucial topic of trauma-informed approaches in education. The article likely explores how trauma affects students' learning experiences and provides insights into implementing effective strategies to support them better. With growing recognition of the impact of ACEs and traumatic events on students' academic and emotional well-being, Coomber's work is likely to offer valuable research and practical applications for educators and professionals. By understanding trauma-informed education, readers can gain essential tools to create safe, empathetic learning environments that promote resilience and growth in students affected by trauma.

References

Canning, J. (2017) Conceptualising student voice in UK higher education: four theoretical lenses. *Teaching in Higher Education*, 22(5), 519–531. https://doi.org/10.1080/13562517.2016.1273207

Clandinin, D. J., and Connelly, F. M. (2000) *Narrative Inquiry: Experience and Story in Qualitative Research*. Jossey-Bass Publishers.

Clandinin, D.J. and Murphy, M.S. (2009) 'Relational ontological commitments in narrative research', *Educational Researcher*, 38(8), pp. 598–602.

Corcoran, M., and McNulty, M. (2018) Examining the role of attachment in the relationship between childhood adversity, psychological distress and subjective well-being. *Child Abuse and Neglect*, 76, pp. 297–309. https://doi.org/10.1016/j.chiabu.2017.11.012

Cresswell, J. W., and Poth, C. N. (2018) *Qualitative Inquiry and Research Design: Choosing Among Five Approaches* (4th Edition). London: Sage.

Delker, B.C., Salton, R., and McLean, K.C. (2020) Giving Voice to Silence: Empowerment and Disempowerment in the Developmental Shift from Trauma 'Victim' to 'Survivor-Advocate'. *Journal of Trauma and Dissociation*, 21(2), pp. 242–263. https://doi.org/10.1080/15299732.2019.1678212

Department for Education (2014) Promoting the education of looked-after and previously looked-after children. Available at: https://www.gov.uk/government/publications/promoting-the-education-of-looked-after-children (Accessed 11 February 2022).

Ecclestone, K., and Hayes, D. (2009) *The Dangerous Rise of Therapeutic Education*. Abingdon: Routledge.

Furman, R. (2007) Poetry and Narrative as Qualitative Data: Explorations into Existential Theory. *Indo-Pacific Journal of Phenomenology*, 7(1), 1–9. https://doi.org/10.1080/20797222.2007.11433939

Hanauer, D.I. (2010) *Poetry as Research: Exploring second language poetry writing*. Pennsylvania: John Benjamins Publishing Company.

Harper, D. (2010) Talking about pictures: A case for photo elicitation. *Visual Studies*, 17(1), pp. 13–26.

Johnson, H., Carson-Apstein, E., Banderob, S., and Macaulay-Rettino, X., (2017) "You Kind of Have to Listen to Me": Researching Discrimination Through Poetry. *Forum: Qualitative Social Research*, 18(3), pp 1–28. https://doi.org/10.17169/fqs-18.3.2864

Kara, H., Lemon, N., Mannay, D., and McPherson. (2021) *Creative Research Methods in Educations Principles and Practices*. Bristol: Policy Press.

Kiely, H.M. (2016) Transitional objects in therapy: not just for kids. Available at: https://tribecatherapy.com/4308/4308/ (Accessed 7 March 2022).

Kim, J.-H. (2015) *Understanding Narrative Inquiry: The Crafting and Analysis of Stories as Research*. London: Sage.

Noyes, A. (2008) Using video diaries investigate learner trajectories Researching the to 'unknown unknowns', in Thomson, P (ed.), *Doing Visual Research with Children and Young People*. London: Routledge Taylor and Francis. pp. 132–145.

Peterson, T.A. (2020) Igniting Hope in Youth from High-Risk Settings. *Journal of Organizational Psychology*, 20(3), pp. 30–38.

Radford, L., Corral, S., Bradley, C., Fisher, H., Bassett, C., Howat, N., and Collishaw, S. (2011) Child abuse and neglect in the UK today. Available at: https://learning.nspcc.org.uk/media/1042/child-abuse-neglect-uk-today-research-report.pdf (Accessed 1 February 2022).

Ross, C.A. (2006) Brain self-repair in psychotherapy: Implications for education. *New Directions for Adult and Continuing Education*, 2006(110), pp. 29–33. https://doi.org/10.1002/ace.216

Smith, L. (2018) Adverse Childhood Experiences (ACEs): educational interventions. Available at: https://www.iriss.org.uk/resources/esss-outlines/aces (Accessed 1 February 2022).

Squire, C., Davis, M., Cigdem, E., Molly, A., Harrison, B., Hyden, L.-C., and Hyden, M. (2014) *What is Narrative Research?* London: Bloomsbury Academic. https://doi.org/10.5040/9781472545220

Swann, S. (2013) *Pupil disaffection in schools: Bad boys and hard girls*. Farnham: Ashgate.

Treat, A.E., Sheffield-Morris, A., Williamson, A.C. and Hays-Grudo, J. (2020) Adverse childhood experiences and young children's social and emotional development: the role of maternal depression, self-efficacy, and social support. *Early Child Development and Care*, 190(15), pp. 2422–2436. https://doi.org/10.1080/03004430.2019.1578220

Vizard, D. (2009) *Meeting the needs of disaffected students: Engaging students with social, emotional and behavioural difficulties*. London: Network Continuum.

Williams, R., and Pritchard, C. (2006) *Breaking the cycle of Educational Alienation A Multiprofessional Approach*. Berkshire: Open University Press.

5 Transitions in education
The importance of learner voice and identity

Joanne Smith and Anastasia Kennett

This chapter draws upon personal experiences, both as a practitioner and as a learner. Throughout the text, we will be referring to Anastasia's perspective as "the learner" and Joanne's perspective as "the practitioner". This concurs with the argument that diverse learner voices need to be heard (McLeod, 2011).

Case study of education – Learner voice and belonging (AK)

The learner's heuristic inquiry (Moustakas, 1990) PhD research is used for this case study; that which explores the evolution of students' silence within educational institutions from home to higher education (HE). In the following, the learner discusses their experiences:

> I was often ridiculed for incorrectly answering questions in primary school, to being bullied and failing my GCSE exams in High School. I retook my exams in college to gain the entry requirements to support my transition to university but, although I was diagnosed with dyslexia and received support from tutors, I still struggled with exams. Consequently, I felt excluded from entering university. The world told me that the repetition of failure would improve my resilience, but it had the opposite effect by creating an identity of self-blame, anxiety and silence. What was the point in improving my resilience when I had no voice to express how this cycle impacted me?
>
> I re-joined college a decade later, taking an Access Course involving assignments rather than exams. My academic achievement improved and ultimately contributed to gaining the entry requirements to HE. In university, I was further diagnosed with dyspraxia which also explains my previous difficulties with exams. But in university, students are encouraged to have a voice, so I became a student representative speaking up on behalf of my peers. However, voice was only considered within the confines of the university rather than considering the wider dilemma of entry requirements and assessment methods that had previously excluded me. Therefore, although the role increased my sense of belonging, this was juxtaposed with the historical exclusion of transitions.

Context

This chapter will explore the shifts in identity as the learner progresses through education, how being listened to and the sense of belonging is valued throughout the learner's educational journey. A particular focus on the transition to HE and the concept of *university readiness* based on the

DOI: 10.4324/9781003406334-5

practitioner's early PhD research literature findings will be included. Following this a discussion on the exclusive nature of HE entry requirements that hinder successful wider participation and the impact on learner identity.

When considering education beyond high school, the changing sector has seen an increase in fees, marketisation and commodification of education, sustained by mechanisms such as the National Student Survey and Teaching Evaluation Framework (Thompson, 2017), which is discussed further in this chapter.

The learner's reflection of legislation pertaining to transitions from high school to HE (AK)

This section will reflect on legislation pertaining to the learners PhD research to discover whether the concept of readiness during educational transitions is adequately supported by governmental policy. Later, the learner will discuss the importance of listening to students during transitions.

Prior to the learner attending HE, significant policies had already attempted to change the structure of HE, from providing an institution solely for the rich towards an institution open to all students with the capacity to succeed (Committee on Higher Education, 1963), encouraging HE to include more diverse students. However, resistance was received that blamed the government for becoming too involved in university autonomy, leading many HE institutions to reject the principles (Scott, 2014). As a result, the government opted for a "binary system" in which universities and local-authority-run polytechnics created the HE system that included a gender and class divide between the high university earners and the middle polytechnic earners (Department for Education and Skills, 1966; Scott, 2014; Carpentier, 2021).

This brings us to the Education Reform Act, 1988, which is largely responsible for the current structure of education that the learner would be familiar with, such as bringing to pass a National Curriculum throughout tertiary education and instructing educational institutions to assess students' capabilities using examinations, such as the Statutory Assessment Tests (SATs) in primary school and the General Certificate of Secondary Education (GCSE's) in high school. The Education Reform Act, 1988 aimed to improve the standard of education by comparing students' assessment results across all national institutions, highlighting those institutions that were successful whilst holding others accountable for less desirable outcomes by using government funding as an incentive. This also meant that students capabilities were assessed against each other using examinations. However, the case study demonstrates that some students were excluded from this type of assessment method, not because they are incapable but because of their diverse needs.

The Further and Higher Education Act, 1992 granted university status to many polytechnics removing the HE divide (Scott, 2014; Carpentier, 2021). Although initial discomfort was felt in implementing the Robbins report, the principles discussed in the 1963 report were beginning to be used (Scott, 2014) to instruct the Further and Higher Education Act and HE institutions to widen participation to more diverse students (see National Committee of Inquiry, 1997; Kennedy Report, 1997). Diverse students were now able to take advantage of widening participation strategies which saw a boost in student enrolment in post-1992 polytechnics (now universities), including high enrolment of part-time students, women and those who are ethnically diverse (Scott, 2014; Carpentier, 2021).

The Brown report (2010) placed emphasis on, not just accepting more diverse students but encouraging institutions to compete for the highest performing students. This shifted the educational system away from widening participation to introducing further competitive entry requirements, excluding many diverse students from attending HE, which Scott (2014) suggests will increase their positions on national league tables. The impact of this on students' transitions can be seen in the case study, whereby the resilience needed to obtain the entry requirements through examinations impacted on the student's mental health. It is at this point that the learner abandons their educational journey due to feeling excluded from participating in HE.

Referring now to the learner's later experience in Further Education, Smith et al. (2013) stated that the choice of assessment methods in HE was pivotal in whether Access students performed well in HE, stating that examinations were the least effective way to present students' strengths, whereas students performed equally as well as others in written assignments and practical work. The learner demonstrates this through their improved academic performance during their course, which ultimately led to their enrolment in HE. Expecting students with diverse needs to perform highly using exams and entry requirements could result in these students losing their identity, voice, and purpose within education, all of which are necessary ingredients to providing a meaningful educational journey (Mann, 2001).

In conclusion, legislation has fragmented the positive impact that widening participation could have had on individual students with diverse needs entering HE. This fragmentation arose from the influence of university competition, exclusive entry requirements and assessment methods on students' individual identities (Lygo-Baker et al., 2019; Mann, 2001; Scott, 2014). Inclusive practice is unlikely to occur whilst educational institutions persistently utilise examination-style assessment methods and entry requirements because exams rely heavily on memory and knowledge acquisition rather than incorporating practice-based skills (Lygo-Baker et al., 2019). "Universities are not passive victims of Government policy" (Canning, 2017: 524), and they could or at least they should listen to the voices of students by challenging the rhetoric of entry requirements and assessment methods in favour of the individual student.

Key concepts

The learner's reflection on the importance of being listened to in education (AK)

In a hierarchical system, such as education, many greater influences and voices are prioritised over students, and this is evident from the earlier discussion regarding national legislation and policies that are often created by government officials. This section will further reflect on government policy and provide the reasons for the importance of listening to diverse students in education. The learner's case study and heuristic inquiry (Moustakas, 1990) PhD research will be used to further explore exams, entry requirements and university readiness.

The learners PhD research and associated introspection highlighted the impact that learning needs can have on the feelings of shame through repeatedly making mistakes in home and at school and the ways in which shame leads to silence (Gilbert, 2014). Examples of these include, answering incorrectly to questions in class, repeatedly taking exams and failing them or applying for university and not being accepted as mentioned in the learner's case study. All of which can exacerbate the student's feelings of shame leading to poor mental health. Therefore, it is important for HE to understand the development of shame within their prospective students and the ways in which students learning needs prevents the students from feeling a sense of belonging and inclusion in HE institutions (Marriott et al., 2020).

Governmental departments have now begun to understand the challenges that some students face in self-advocacy and are now beginning to push towards enabling student choice throughout education (see for example, Children and Families Act, 2014; Department for Education and Department of Health, 2015). However, not all students are able to make independent choices based on their own individual wants and needs. Therefore, it is imperative that support is provided to enable students to develop their own self-advocacy skills, as these skills may still be under-developed or still developing for students, particularly so for those students with diverse needs (Department for Education and Department of Health, 2015).

In respect of transitions, students voice is still disregarded above others. Firstly, it has always been the right of universities to choose the required assessment and entry requirements that students need to achieve to transition into HE (Department of Education, 2023), and there have been moments of relaxation around these. For instance, it has been suggested that universities could partially relax entry requirements to enable more diverse students to enter HE in previous policy (Department of Education and Science, 1987), but this seems to have been introduced more as a sign of pity rather than a distinction of university readiness. Therefore, relaxed as they may seem, there continues to be no student choice regarding university readiness other than using exam-based assessment methods and entry requirements that dictate (through grades achieved) when the student is ready for university.

Recent parliamentary discussions demonstrates that this hierarchical transitional decision making from people in positions of power could continue. As recently as February 2022, the government requested a consultation to discuss (amongst other items) achieving a grade 4 in English and Maths at GCSE level as a minimum level of entry for university and to obtain a student loan (Department for Education, 2022). But where this is not achieved, students will be encouraged to retake exams or choose an alternative pathway (Department for Education, 2022). Although it is worth recognising that there are notable exceptions to this rule, such as part-time students, students who already hold a high qualification in their A-levels, level 4 and/or level 5 qualifications and mature students (Department for Education, 2022). The Institute for Fiscal Studies (2022) believes that many students will be impacted by this change should it be enacted, such as students from different socio-cultural backgrounds and those from low-income families who would be deprived the benefits of achieving a degree and the improved income that the degree would bring. The institute also expresses that enacting the suggestions from government would juxtapose many widening participation strategies currently being enacted (Institute for Fiscal Studies, 2022).

This policy warning comes after discussions pertaining to an increase in higher degree classifications awarded to students (HESA, 2020), otherwise known as *grade inflation* with pre-1992 universities awarding more higher-grade classifications than post-1992 universities, but this is often attributed to quality education, whereas a higher student population (such as those seen in post-1992 universities) often leads to lower degree classifications, possibly due to the universities inability to accommodate such diverse populations (Bachan, 2017). However, there is no evidence that university quality has changed, therefore, where there is *grade inflation*, this could be due to universities reducing student expectations to increase student numbers (Bachan, 2017) as had been advised by previous policies. Therefore, it is reasonable to suggest that policies can contradict each other, adding to the confusion and messiness when enacted into practice (Ball, 2017), leveraging the blame with diverse learners and/or educators for the outcomes of old policies.

This chapter also identifies two further impacts on students' identity. As previously discussed, the learners PhD research demonstrates that being rejected from such courses can lead to increased levels of shame. Furthermore, students must attempt to become the person they want to be whilst also being forced to make transitional decisions based on what entry requirements they must avoid (Markus and Nurius, 1986) resulting in some students being unable to take the courses that best aligns with their identity. The learners PhD research explores this dilemma, and it was established that the learner's own sense of belonging decreased when they were unable to make transitional decisions based on who they would like to be because of the barriers placed upon them in policy and by those in positions of power (Markus and Nurius, 1986; Harrison, 2018; Harrison and Waller, 2018).

The government responded to the consultation, stating that opposition was received that showed evidence diverse students would experience unequal treatment in the transition process, whilst the desirable outcomes would not be achieved showing the strategy to be highly inappropriate (Department for Education, 2023). For instance, the institute of Fiscal Studies (2022) states that a very high number (around 80 per cent) of students without English and Maths GCSE qualifications do go on to pass their degree courses. However, irrespective of this research, the government continued to place a warning for universities that more would be done by the government should universities continue to fail to improve standards (Department for Education, 2023). Other alternative suggestions included reducing the required entry requirements for diverse students (Augar, 2019; Institute for Fiscal Studies, 2022) which, with careful precision, could present a more equitable system.

The learner in this chapter, however, feels that a transition system is required that reduces students' feelings of shame by removing the need to build on students' resilience through exam repetition. Instead, students need to feel a sense of belonging during their transition to university. However, this would require a new widening participation agenda that focuses on students' voice, choice and individual identities. HE should not only be considering exam results, but to accept students as holistic individuals, such as students in-class capabilities, personal attributes and/or their ability to independently learn information.

The practitioner's literature findings on the importance of belonging when transitioning to higher education (JS)

During initial explorations of the literature for my PhD research, the theme of *belonging* appears to be of significance, especially within sources that explore the experiences of non-traditional students (first generation, mature, international, low socio-economic status). Also discussed is the contrast between the experience of home versus commuter students.

Van Harpen et al. (2020) describes *belonging* as students being able to *feel at home* and *fitting in*. Further concepts of belonging include students being members of communities. Meehan and Howells (2018) explain that learning communities can be home, work-based and university. They can be accessed physically and virtually, and institutions should recognise and adjust to these different communities. Mkonto's (2018) evaluation of peer-facilitated learning (PFL) activities utilises Tinto's (2003) learning communities model in which students are responsible for their own and the group members learning. There is shared knowledge from each other formally and informally; shared knowing, with the tutor sharing subject knowledge; and shared responsibility, creating a culture of interdependence.

Another facet of the notion of *belonging* is that of being supported by friends, family, employers, as well as academic staff (Xavier and Meneses, 2022). Gazeley and Hinton-Smith (2018) suggest that college staff in advice roles should provide education around issues likely to be experienced by those not familiar with such settings (as discussed previously). They found that admission processes were insufficiently adapted to take care of diverse needs. The community of support gives meaning to student experiences, without which students may not accept new learning experiences or build up relationships necessary for success.

Returning to Mkonto's (2018) evaluation of PFL, tutors provide the guidance and support necessary for students to solve problems. This relies on interdependence and connections between people and the socio-cultural context in which they interact. Institutions should allow students to check on misconceptions with peers and staff (Van Harpen et al., 2020). Seary and Willans (2020) found that students appreciated being made to feel comfortable, where lecturers catered for *lack of knowledge*, whilst also having opportunities to build on prior skills and enhance future opportunities.

Personal history influences this sense of belonging (explored further in the next chapter) and could help students to assume the role of HE student (Van Harpen et al., 2020; Seary and Willans, 2020). Meehan and Howells (2018) claim that student's complex lives with multiple responsibilities may limit student engagement with physical learning communities. Virtual and online platforms provide a forum for positive participation and engagement, especially for those choosing to live at home. Meehan and Howells (2018) explain that living at home is more than a financial choice: it may be due to family commitments/responsibilities, local community support structures and work commitments. Kahu and Nelson (2018) agree that the transition metaphor is not useful, as it does not capture the lived experiences and constant reworking of self; institutions should reconceptualise these *lived realities* (Gale and Parker, 2012).

Through embracing these *lived realities*, further exploration of the importance of the relational aspect of this enabling education is needed (Seary and Willans, 2020). In HE the student: staff interactions differ to the relationships students may have experienced in a school or FE context, where a *teach-to-test* culture is established (Christie et al., 2016; Jones, 2018; McCallum and Milner, 2021). In higher education institutions (HEIs), particularly those that are widening participation universities, the pedagogy is a lot more relational and collaborative, focussing on learners having autonomy and independence (Meehan and Howells, 2018). "Teachers become facilitators and motivators, constructing a collaborative learning environment which encourages student engagement" (Schütze, Bartyn and Tapsell, 2021: 852). Collaborative and individual activities allow students to learn as they construct knowledge and stimulate critical thinking, which could lead to better outcomes (Smart and Csapo, 2007: Gibbs, 1988).

As well as facilitating learning, university tutors may also be involved with the pastoral care of their students. Pastoral care is concerned with physical, social, intellectual, emotional and even spiritual development (Seary and Willans, 2020) and cannot be separated from educator's daily work (Hamblin, 1978). Best (1988) poses that pastoral care starts with students' needs, and HEIs develop structures and processes to support. Noddings (1998) suggests that caring teachers have a significant impact on their students: "[S]tudents care if we care about them" (Meyers, 2009: 206). This can be a positive experience for both students and teachers. Caring teachers know their students, authentically and consistently responding to them in a timely manner (Seary and Willans, 2020; Noddings, 1998; Tarlow and Haaga, 1996).

Continuing with the concept of *belonging*, Mkonto (2018) highlights the need for affirming cultural diversity: for instance, international students may find it a *culture shock* coping with life in a different country. Equally, those *non-traditional* students may also experience social class and ethnicity difference (Ball, Maguire and Macrae, 2000). Mkonto (2018) stresses the importance of feeling accepted by other students and treated equally by tutors. Historically, HEIs were seen as white, middle class and male in terms of domination culture (Savage, 2015). Therefore, intercultural interaction is an essential opportunity to share diverse cultural, racial and religious backgrounds in learning sessions to support the transitions of students identified as *non-traditional*. Further exploration on the topic of diversity will be explored in the next chapter on identity.

Returning to the discussion on group interactions, Van Harpen et al. (2020) suggests these interactions can be informal and/or formal and take place both in and outside the classroom. Meehan and Howells (2018) found that those who connected online prior to starting university, remained in close-knit friendships throughout university. These interactions contributed to their sense of belonging, as well as informal interactions with staff, discussing personal matters and well-being. However, commuter students could have more difficulty adjusting to teaching styles, as they do not always participate in social activities/events (Meehan and Howells 2018). Astin (1991) identifies that those who live on campus are more likely to attend and have increased interaction with peers and faculty, concurred by Hartman and Schmidt (1995) who claim the importance of social integration. This is further explored in the next chapter when discussing identity. Students may also feel anxious due to time poverty and conflicts, as well as discussion around teaching, learning and producing academic work (Farrell, Brunton and Trevaskis, 2020, Xavier and Menese, 2022). Workshops that support fitting in and making friends, although initially challenging and uncomfortable, can alleviate anxiety and enable students to engage socially (Farrell, Brunton and Trevaskis, 2020, Mkonto, 2018).

Drawing our two key concepts together, we realise that without being listened to, you don't feel like you belong. This feeling of alienation can result in leaving education. The authors feel that with "no choice there is no voice".

> **Pause for thought (JS)**
>
> Is understanding and supporting transition beyond the notion of access?
> Should the barriers people face when progressing to HE be considered?
> Can the need for students to be autonomous and more individually responsible create anxiety?
> Is it "critical to ensure there is not a mismatch of students' expectations and experiences"?
> Do students on vocational courses have different skills, experiences and expectations than those on traditional A-level routes?

Research in Focus

Part 1: Gale and Parker's (2012) "Typology of transition" (JS)

This typology focusses on three types of transition: Induction (T1), Development (T2) and Becoming (T3); this concurs with my experiences as a course-leader on an undergraduate programme. T1 and T2 are time bound and linear, taking the student from FE to HE, both through reforming their student identity and through the different physical environment and institutional structures. T3 is more "rhizomatic" and focuses on the student's whole life experiences, identifying those external contextual factors – accommodation, finance, work, assessment as likely contributors to students' perceptions of satisfaction with the transition process (Gruber et al., 2010). Taylor and Harris-Evans (2018) agree that transition is entangled, non-linear, iterative and recursive. In contrast, Van Herpen et al. (2020) propose four phases of transition: preparation, encounter, adjustment and stabilisation. This suggests that transition is still a linear, temporary process, whereas I agree with the position of Gale and Parker (2012) and Taylor and Harris-Evans (2018) that transition should be considered a continuation of experience.

Part 2: Aim higher evaluation report (OfS, 2020) (JS)

This report evaluated phase 1 of a longitudinal study. The OfS cited Bourdieu's (1977) cultural, social, and intellectual capital and Bandura's (1977) self-efficacy theory, saying that widespread research demonstrates a strong association between socio-economic/ demographic factors and attainment/progression to HE (citing Davis and Kurzban 2012). Non-cognitive psychological factors such as: aspirations/expectations, attitudes and behaviours, knowledge and understanding of HE and self-efficacy play an important role in attainment and HE participation. The study found that greater cultural knowledge and parental help with information about HE increased the likelihood that learners would apply to college (citing Dumais and Ward, 2010). Heckman and Rubinstein (2001) said that developing non-cognitive functions may help close the gap between advantaged and disadvantaged young people. Choudry (2014) agrees that non-cognitive skills could be the key determinant of a student's likelihood of going to university. The report discusses a *Theory of Change model*, using the following five key barriers: Awareness, Aspiration, Application, Access and Attainment.

Part 3: Harrison (2018) "Using the lens of 'possible selves' to explore access to higher education: A new conceptual model for practice, policy, and research" (AK)

This article explores the wider social context disadvantages faced by diverse students before entering HE by using the theory of *possible selves*. The article discusses the many ways in which students envisage their future selves through what they need/must avoid. They conclude that diverse students need more opportunities that align with their "possible selves", as these students are more likely to avoid desired transitional pathways, resulting in these students being unable to reach their *possible selves*. To achieve this, they suggest encouraging diverse students to visualise whom they would like to be leading to improved motivation to succeed: providing activities on campus to ease the transitional process, increasing the limited course choices available for diverse students and supporting students voices and control over their educational journeys.

Part 4: Harrison and Waller (2018) "Challenging discourses of aspiration: The role of expectations and attainment in access to higher education" (AK)

This article explains that the differences experienced in diverse students' participation in HE has little to do with students' aspirations to transition but more to do with lower academic achievement.

They argue that diverse students are more likely to be influenced by their wider social context, such as the family or the socio-economic status of the neighbourhood. Due to this, diverse students are more likely to question the expectations of HE and their own perceived capabilities. They conclude that diverse students need to be encouraged to create multiple *possible selves* to increase the likelihood of more diverse students progressing into HE. Furthermore, HE should be encouraged to work with parents and teachers so that the student is surrounded by adults who share the same philosophy.

The practitioner concludes (JS)

This summary is based on evaluations made by Thompson (2017). The current heterogenous students' body presents problems both in generalisation to research and for HEIs in terms of recruitment, retention, progression and achievement. Many students do not define or label themselves in ways of "under representation". The postmodern condition is that there is no *typical* student anymore. However, a normative construction still exists, and assumptions are made without acknowledging complexities. HEIs need to know more about the challenges students face, both academically and pastorally (Thompson, 2017).

Delivery and content need to be rebalanced with activities such as flipped lectures and problem-based learning. Students paying to commute want to extend knowledge and understanding and be challenged. This calls for new pedagogic models such as developing supportive relationships with staff and peers by adapting Learning and Teaching in HE (Thompson, 2017).

Marketisation has seen a reduction in access initiatives, overlooking cultural and social barriers. Thompson (2017) considers HE landscape and the student's own "micro-climate". He argues that it is not just about the student negotiating the landscape but also how HEIs respond to the changing climate and complexities of society. HEIs must display empathy, consider authentic and real experiences, without falling into assumptions. They must be innovative and experimental, contest the "norm" by reworking and reimagining the curriculum.

HEIs must understand the priorities of students within the context of shifting HE policy (Thompson, 2017). This concurs with Scott's argument (2015) that HE for most will be abandoned leaving HEIs to scramble for business in the marketplace. We must consider the responsibility HEIs have in terms of local/community needs. Is it time for a new widening participation agenda?

The learner concludes (AK)

A conclusion can be drawn that shows that listening to the learner's voice during transitions is imperative to the learner's own identity formation and sense of belonging. Traditionally utilising students' examination results and entry requirements has done little for students' resilience and has instead only perpetuated a decline in students' own feelings of shame. It is concluded by the learner of this chapter that building students' resilience is a fallacy that can be detrimental to students' mental health. It is, therefore, time to consider a new agenda to widening participation that focuses on nurturing students' voices and *possible selves* (Markus and Nurius, 1986) when discussing the many elements of transitions to ensure a seamless journey. If learners are not listened to in this regard, learners may feel as though they do not belong in HE, thus hindering their HE journeys.

Summary points

- The *widening participation* agenda has resulted in an increase in diverse learners attending HEIs.
- Effective transition to HE relies on the students being listened to, which can be demonstrated through various methods and by a number of stakeholders.
- Across a learner's trajectory, educational establishments must respond to the voices of diverse learners.
- Therefore, by understanding and accommodating diverse voices, this improves the learner's sense of *belonging*, which research shows positively affects attrition rates.

Further reading

Markus, H. and P. Nurius. (1986) 'Possible selves', *American Psychologist*, 41(9), pp. 954–969. doi: 10.1037/0003-066x.41.9.954

Reay, D. (2018) 'Working class educational transitions to university: The limits of success', *European Journal of Education*, 53(4), pp. 528–540. doi: 10.1111/ejed.12298

In this article, the author questions whether individualism is valued, arguing that academic identity holds more value (within HEIs) over social identity.

In this article, the authors discuss the concept of self in relation to the internal conflict between who we want to be juxtaposed against and what we need to avoid.

References

Astin, A. W. (1991) The changing American college student: implications for educational policy and practice 1, *Higher Education*, 22(9), pp. 129–143.

Augar, P. (2019) Independent panel report to the review of post-18 education and funding. Available at: Independent panel report to the Review of Post-18 Education and Funding (publishing.service.gov.uk) (Accessed: 21/09/2023).

Bachan, R. (2017) Grade inflation in UK higher education. *Studies in Higher Education*, 42(8), pp. 1580–1600. doi: 10.1080/03075079.2015.1019450

Ball, S. (2017) *The education debate*. Bristol: Policy Press.

Ball, S.J., Maguire, M., and Macrae, S. (2000) *Choice, Pathways and Transitions Post-16: New Youth, New Economics in the Global City*. London: Routledge Falmer.

Bandura, A. (1977) Self-efficacy: Toward a Unifying Theory of Behavioural Change. *Psychological Review*, 84(2), pp. 191–215.

Best, R. (1988) Care and Control—Are We Getting It Right? *Pastoral Care in Education*, 6(2), pp. 2–9. doi: 10.1080/02643948809470611

Bourdieu, P. (1977) Outline of a Theory of Practice. (J. Goody, Ed.), *Cambridge studies in social anthropology*. 16. doi: 10.1590/S0103-20702013000100001

Brown, J. (2010) *The Brown Report: Securing a sustainable future for higher education: An independent review of higher education funding and student finance*. GOV.UK. Available at: https://www.gov.uk/government/publications/the-browne-report-higher-education-funding-and-student-finance (Accessed 21/09/2023).

Canning, J. (2017) Conceptualising student voice in UK higher education: Four theoretical lenses. *Teaching in Higher Education*, 22(5), pp. 519–531. doi: 10.1080/13562517.2016.1273207

Carpentier, V. (2021) Three stories of institutional differentiation: resource, mission and social inequalities in higher education. *Policy Reviews in Higher Education*, 5(2), doi: 10.1080/23322969.2021.1896376

Children and Families Act, 2014, c. 6. Available at: Children and Families Act 2014 (legislation.gov.uk) (Accessed: 21/09/2023).

Choudry, A. (2014) From struggle knowledge and movement learning to the university classroom. *Postcolonial Directions in Education*, 3(2), pp.252–291.

Christie, H., McCune, V., Tett, L. and Cree, V. (2016) "It all just clicked": a longitudinal perspective on transitions within university. *Studies in Higher Education*, 41(3). doi: 10.1080/03075079.2014.942271

Committee on Higher Education (1963) *Higher education: report of the committee appointed by the prime minister under the chairmanship of Lord Robbins 191—62 (CMND 2154)*. London: HMSO.

Davis, L., & Kurzban, S. (2012) Mindfulness-based treatment for people with severe mental illness: A literature review. *American Journal of Psychiatric Rehabilitation*, 15(2), 202–232. https://doi.org/10.1080/15487768.2012.679578

Department for Education (2022) Higher education policy statement and reform consultation: government consultation. Available at: *DfE command paper template (publishing.service.gov.uk) (Accessed: 21/09/2023).

Department for Education (2023) Higher education policy reform: government consultation response. Available at: *CP876: Higher Education policy statement and reform - government consultation response (publishing.service.gov.uk) (Accessed: 21/09/2023).

Department for Education and Department of Health (2015) Special educational needs and disability code of practice: 0 – 25 years. Available at: assets.publishing.service.gov.uk/government/uploads/system/uploads/attachment_data/file/398815/SEND_Code_of_Practice_January_2015.pdf (Accessed: 21/09/2023).

Department for Education and Science (1966) *A plan for polytechnics and other colleges*. London: HMSO.

Department for Education and science. (1987) *Higher education: Meeting the challenge (Cmnd 1541)*. HMSO.

Dumais, S. and Ward, A. (2010) Cultural capital and first-generation college success. *Poetics*, 8(3), pp. 245–265.

Education Reform Act. 1988, C. 40. Available at: Education Reform Act 1988 (legislation.gov.uk) (Accessed: 21/09/2023).

Farrell, O., Brunton, J. and Trevaskis, S. (2020) "If I had missed it I would have been the lost little sheep": Exploring student narratives on orientation to first year. *Journal of Further and Higher Education*, 44(7), pp. 865–876. doi: 10.1080/0309877X.2019.1614543

Further and Higher Education Act. 1992. Available at: Further and Higher Education Act 1992 (legislation.gov.uk) (Accessed: 14/08/2024).

Gale, T. and Parker, S. (2012) Studies in Higher Education Navigating change: a typology of student transition in higher education. *Studies in Higher Education*, 39(5), pp. 734–753. doi: 10.1080/03075079.2012.721351

Gazeley, L. and Hinton-Smith, T. (2018) The "success" of Looked After Children in Higher Education in England: near peer coaching, "small steps" and future thinking. *Higher Education Research & Development*, 37(5), pp. 952–975. doi: 10.1080/07294360.2018.1467384

Gibbs, G. (1988) *Learning by Doing. A Guide to Teaching and Learning Methods*. Oxford: Further Education Unit at Oxford Polytechnic.

Gilbert, P. (2014) The origins and nature of compassion focused therapy. *British Journal of Clinical Psychology*, 53, pp. 6–41. doi: 10.1111/bjc.12043

Gruber, T., Fuß, S., Voss, R. and Gläser-Zikuda, M. (2010) Examining student satisfaction with higher education services: Using a new measurement tool, *International Journal of Public Sector Management*, 23(2), pp. 105–123. doi: 10.1108/09513551011022474

Hamblin, D. (1978) *The teacher and pastoral care*. Oxford: Basil Blackwell.

Harrison, N. (2018) Using the lens of 'possible selves' to explore access to higher education: A new conceptual model for practice, policy, and research. *Social Sciences*, 7(10), pp. 209. doi: 10.3390/socsci7100209

Harrison, N., and Waller, R. (2018) Challenging discourses of aspiration: the role of expectations and attainment in access to higher education. *British Educational Research Journal*, 44(5), pp. 914–938. doi: 10.1002/berj.3475

Hartman, D. and Schmidt, S. (1995) 'Understanding student/alumni satisfaction from a consumer's perspective: the effects of institutional performance and program outcomes.' *Research in Higher Education*, 36(2), pp. 197–217.

Heckman J.J., and Rubinstein, Y. (2001). The importance of non-cognitive skills: Lessons from the GED testing program. *American Economic Review*, 91(2), pp.145–149.

HESA (2020) How does the return to a degree vary by class of award. Available at: https://www.hesa.ac.uk/files/Return-to-degree-by-class-Summary-20200310.pdf (Accessed: 21/09/2023).

Jones, R. (2018) 'The student experience of undergraduate students: towards a conceptual framework', *Journal of Further and Higher Education*, 42(8), pp. 1040–1054. doi: 10.1080/0309877X.2017.1349882

Kahu, E. R. and Nelson, K. (2018) 'Higher Education Research & Development Student engagement in the educational interface: understanding the mechanisms of student success', *Higher Education Research and Development*, 37(1), pp. 58–71. doi: 10.1080/07294360.2017.1344197

Kennedy, H. (1997) *Learning works: widening participation in further education*. The Further Education Funding Council.

Lygo-Baker, S., Kinchin, I., and Winstone, N. (2019) The single voice fallacy. In S. Lygo-Baker, I. Kinchin, and N. Winstone (Eds) *Engaging students voices in higher education* (pp. 1–15). Palgrave Macmillian.

Mann, S. (2001) Alternative Perspectives on the Student Experience: Alienation and engagement. *Studies in Higher Education*, 26(1), pp. 7–19. doi: 10.1080/03075070020030689

Markus, H. and P. Nurius. (1986) Possible selves. *American Psychologist*, 41(9), pp. 954–969. doi: 10.1037/0003-066x.41.9.954

Marriott, C., Parish, C., Griffiths, C. and Fish, R. (2020) Experiences of shame and intellectual disabilities: two case studies. *Journal of Intellectual Disabilities*, 24(4), pp. 489 – 502. doi: 10.1177/1744629519844091

McCallum, S. and Milner, M. M. (2021) The effectiveness of formative assessment: student views and staff reflections. *Assessment & Evaluation in Higher Education*, 46(1), pp. 1–16. doi: 10.1080/02602938.2020.1754761

McLeod, J. (2011) Student voice and the politics of listening in higher education. *Critical Studies in Education*, 52(2), 179–189. doi: 10.1080/17508487.2011.572830

Meehan, C. and Howells, K. (2018) "What really matters to freshers?": evaluation of first year student experience of transition into university. *Journal of Further and Higher Education*, 42(7), pp. 893–907. doi: 10.1080/0309877X.2017.1323194

Meyers, S. A. (2009) Do your students care whether you care about them? *College Teaching*, 57(4), pp. 205–210.

Mkonto, N. (2018) Peer-Facilitated Learning: Students' Experiences. *Africa Education Review*, 15(2), pp. 16–31. doi: 10.1080/18146627.2016.1224599

Moustakas, C. (1990) *Heuristic research: design, methodology, and applications*. London: Sage.

National Committee of Inquiry into Higher Education (1997) *Higher education in the learning society*. London: HMSO.

Noddings, N. (1998) *Philosophy of Education*. New York: Routledge.

OfS (2020) *Does Engagement in Aimhigher Interventions Increase the Likelihood of Disadvantaged Learners Progressing to HE?* West Midlands: AimHigher.

Savage, M. (2015) *Social Class in the 21st Century*. London: Penguin Random House.

Schütze, H., Bartyn, J. and Tapsell, A. (2021) Increasing self-efficacy to improve the transition to university: an Australian case study. *Journal of Further and Higher Education*, 45(6), pp. 845–856. doi: 10.1080/0309877X.2020.1826034

Scott, P. (2014) Robbins, the binary policy and mass higher education: binary policy and mass higher education. *Higher Education Quarterly*, 68(2), pp. 147–163. doi: 10.1111/hequ.12040

Seary, K. and Willans, J. (2020) Pastoral Care and the Caring Teacher – Value Adding to Enabling Education. *Student Success*, 11(1), pp. 12–21. doi: 10.5204/ssj.v11i1.1456

Smart, K. L. and Csapo, N. (2007) Learning by doing: Engaging students through learner-centered activities. *Business Communication Quarterly*, 70(4), pp. 451–457. doi: 10.1177/10805699070700040302

Smith, C., Mahon, M. and Newton, C. (2013) Speech and language therapy students: How do those with 'non-traditional' university entry qualifications perform? *International Journal of Language and Communication Disorders*, 48(4), pp. 394–401. doi: 10.1111/1460-6984.12016

Tarlow, E. M. and Haaga, D.A.F. (1996) Negative Self-Concept: Specificity to Depressive Symptoms and Relation to Positive and Negative Affectivity. *Journal of Research in Personality*, 30(1), pp. 120–127. doi: 10.1006/JRPE.1996.0008

Taylor, C. A. and Harris-Evans, J. (2018) Reconceptualising Transition to Higher Education with Deleuze and Guattari. *Studies in Higher Education*, 43(7), pp. 1254–1267.

The Institute for Fiscal Studies. (2022) The impact of student loan minimum eligibility requirements. Available at: *The Impact of student loan minimum eligibility requirements (ifs.org.uk) (Accessed: 21/09/2023).

Thompson, D. W. (2017) 'Widening participation research and practice in the United Kingdom on the twentieth anniversary of the Dearing report, reflections on a changing landscape', *Educational Researcher*, 71(2), pp. 182–197. doi: 10.1080/00131911.2017.1380606

Tinto, V. (2003) Student success and the building of involving educational communities. *Higher Education Monograph Series*, pp. 1–11. Available at: https://www.researchgate.net/publication/228541701 (Accessed: 8 October 2022).

Van Herpen, S.G. A., Meeuwisse, M., Hofman, W. H. A. and Severiens, S.E. (2020) A head start in higher education: The effect of a transition intervention on interaction, sense of belonging, and academic performance. *Studies in Higher Education*, 45(4), pp. 862–877. doi: 10.1080/03075079.2019.1572088

Xavier, M. and Meneses, J. (2022) Persistence and time challenges in an open online university: a case study of the experiences of first-year learners. *International Journal of Educational Technology in Higher Education*, 19(31). doi: 10.1186/s41239-022-00338-6

6 Advocating for the learner and their diverse needs

Sharon Smith

> **Vignette – Reflection on practice**
>
> I have worked with many learners with needs during my professional practice and have witnessed the growth of advocacy during this time. One particular learner's journey highlights this for me. The agency and motivation they showed echoed through many other learners I have worked with. For the purpose of this reflection, I will call the learner Jim. On starting to study for his degree, he felt challenged by academic writing, particularly spelling. During his studies, I suggested some screening for dyslexia, which showed aspects of difficulties with visual discrimination relating to Meares-Irlen syndrome. This required some adjustments, and glasses with tinted lenses were required. This diagnosis enabled Jim to recognise that he had struggled with reading and spelling. It had made him feel "unintelligent" but with the new knowledge of his needs, Jim's confidence and skills grew. This extended into everyday life, as Jim highlighted that looking at road signs and reading shopping signs was much easier.

What is advocacy?

The starting point for this chapter is to highlight the importance of advocacy and consider how we can support our learners to become independent and have agency for their own learning, as highlighted in the vignette. During my career teaching several adults with learning and complex needs, I have gained a healthy perspective on the notion of supporting and enabling, through encouraging the students/learners to problem solve to enable and facilitate their empowerment. Sutcliffe (1990: 20) identifies this as "advocacy" and highlights that it requires us to provided "choices for students with learning difficulties about their lives'". This approach was pivotal in recognising the individual and allowed for a meaningful educational experience. From my own practice, I have witnessed a development in the approach to learners with individual needs at different levels. I have witnessed the emergence of changes which have resulted in the development of legislation and cultures – for example, the changes in terminology used for individual needs. Tomlinson's report (1997: 3) highlighted that education should "support each student to develop his or her potential and to aim for the highest personal achievement".

My own experience of supporting individuals with learning needs was the limited amount of concern for supporting self-advocacy, when often the lecturer involved with the learner took on the role

DOI: 10.4324/9781003406334-6

of "surrogate parents" and the learners relied on them to make decisions for them. Advocacy requires learners to be decision makers – Sutcliffe (1990: 14) recognised this and stated, "We should not see adults with learning difficulties as 'boys and girls' – eternal children". In addition to the lecturer, the role of the teaching assistant (TA) can impact on the learning journey, and learners may rely too heavily on the TA support. Webster et al. (2021) highlight the historical development of the TA and concur that appropriate support by TAs should include suitable training and planning for them to access. Lehane (2017) examines the role of the TA and identifies the concerns of TAs supporting learners with SEND, recognising that appropriate pedological approaches need to be addressed through training. This role is also seen with support workers in HE, where their role is defined by the students' disability assessment. The level of support provided within formal education can often be over compensated and indeed can remove the learner's responsibility for "self". The role of the adult is to scaffold the learning and support independence, as too often, what is known as the "Velcro" model of support is not productive, as it does not promote such independence (Kamen, 2003).

Historical changes

The impact of legislation ensured that the changes for learners promote inclusive approaches. Tomlinson (1997: 2) reflected on the changes in social attitudes and highlights that "nearly 40 years ago, some of our citizens were deemed uneducable and never offered any formal educational opportunity". Considering the developments that have occurred there is still a question as to exactly how far inclusive practice has developed. This was highlighted by Low (1997), who states that it was a desirable outcome but recognised the issues underlying it with regard to attitudes to learners with any "difficulties" (Smith, 2021).The relationship between recognising learners needs and widening participation has enabled those with individual needs to access education beyond the traditional formal provision. The recognition of Lifelong Learning defined by the Institute for Adult Continuing Education (NIACE) has endorsed that learning should be "*cradle to grave*". For the non-traditional with individual needs, learning this may continue on beyond formal education. Changes in policy and legislation have enabled more diverse communities to explore and engage with learning. I have witnessed these changes through my career and have been able to develop my pedagogical approaches accordingly. This chapter certainly does not represent a full account of how educational institutions have engaged with learners with individual and diverse needs. Elliot (1999: 19) highlights that the tutor's role is to support the student's learning and that this "is best carried out by directing the student's attention to how they learn in different contexts".

The debate about inclusive approaches to education and students' entitlement is a significant aspect of this chapter. In approaching the discussion, it will provide a viewpoint based on the experiences of higher education and not mainstream education. The systems in mainstream firmly sit with within a legal framework and policy and procedures to address the needs of individual pupils, and it could be argued that this process is based on "labelling" the learners. Recognising our "learners" needs can be quite challenging and often present as a difficulty during assessment time. The case study highlights a learner whose needs may not be obvious within class. As lecturers we need to consider how we meet the needs of the learners whose needs are hidden or not identified and may not have been declared. The voice of the learners is often silent in declaring their needs, or they may not even know they have needs. I have noted over the years of teaching that learners often comment that they thought they were unintelligent because they found spelling difficult; however, often, this has been diagnosed as dyslexia.

Knowing our students' needs is pivotal to allowing us to support their learning. In considering the diversity of the student cohort within HE and the requirements to recognise and support these needs, the approach to teaching and learning needs to consider accessibility to learning, the learning environment and assessment approaches. This chapter will continue to focus on supporting learners with defined needs of learning such as dyslexia, ADHD, autism, physical and sensory needs and mental well-being needs, but it also offers a broader discussion about the identification of needs and identity.

> **Pause for thought**
>
> **Case study from SCALE**
>
> Carol was diagnosed with *dyspraxia* at an early age and has had varying levels of help with this during childhood, which have increased her confidence with motor skills and co-ordination. However, her more hidden difficulties remain. Carol describes herself as clumsy and forgetful, and she has difficulties with reading, writing, spelling, time management and organisation, as well as co-ordination. These in turn have impacted on self-confidence and self-esteem, which is a long-standing impact stemming from her childhood experience of living with *dyspraxia*.
>
> Carol has difficulties with information processing and memory, which impact on her ability to understand, retain and recall information that she has heard or read. Carol's experience is that study tasks generally take her longer than others to complete, and she feels that she isn't always able to do justice to her true knowledge and ability, particularly in written work, presentations, and timed assessments, such as exams.
>
> **Reflect**
>
> 1. What might be the difficulties faced by Carol when she is asked to join a group task?
> 2. How might Carol be helped to manage any set task?
> 3. What could the lecturer do to support Carol's needs?

How do we know our learners' needs?

The provision within HE for supporting learners with individual needs is very much driven by students declaring their individual needs at the point of application. This then enables them to access HE systems and procedures, resources and support available to them through disability funding (Hubble and Bolton, 2021). The Equality Act (2010) sets out clearly the requirements for those with individual needs. However, there are challenges to meeting individual needs; often, resources and funding can impact on access to suitable resources (Smith, 2018). Lord Holmes (Weale, 2022) reports that in 2019–2020 only 29 per cent of students who declared their disability received the funding which was attributed to the bureaucracy of the application process. There were 20 recommendations from this report; one of these was to ensure students had "passports" to highlight their needs which could be carried through school to HE. The rise in the number of students declaring needs has steadily increased by 7 per cent from 2010/2011 to 2018/2019, and within these statistics the greatest need is reported is cognitive or learning difficulties, the next highest being mental health needs with the data showing an increase from 0.5 per cent to 4.5 per cent (Hubble and Bolton, 2021).

Reflecting on my own approach to teaching in higher education, I advocate that my teaching should incorporate the principles of Universal Design for Learning (UDL; Bracken and Novak, 2019). This approach champions a more inclusive perspective of the learners within the classroom and relies on the lecturer to consider a variety of individual needs that they can support through their teaching. This can be challenging for the lecturer, as it requires a thoughtful and considered approach to teaching to support the learners. Moore (2019: 231) conveys this requires highlighting "the design of learning experiences that centre on clear and rigorous leaning outcome, identification of anticipated barriers". Advocating for our learners requires a consideration of any barriers to learning and not just individuals' needs to be addressed. Moore considers that we might view these barriers as "students' problems" and not the instructor's responsibility. In exploring how we can advocate for the learners Moore offers a structure that offers alternatives (Moore 2019: 2.36; see Table 6.1).

Roy (2016) argues that we should consider a rethinking of our approach to supporting those with individual needs, through the process of "Design Thinking", and highlights five steps to doing this – namely, by defining the problem, observing the problem, thinking of ways to solve the problem, then "fourth, prototyping: gathering whatever you can, whatever you can find, to mimic your solution, to test it and to refine it" and finally, implementation. She confirms that we should consider designing for disabilities first, and she highlights that the invention of text messaging was to support those with hearing loss, but now, this has become a universal tool.

Table 6.1 Reframing barriers from students' problems to environmental limitation

Situation	Students' problem perspective	Environmental limitation perspective
Students in a morning class are falling asleep when instructor dims a light and begins a power point.	Students are lazy (I'm focussed) and stay out too late the night before a morning class.	Dimming the lights is an ineffective way to engage learning in morning classes.
Students frequently use their laptops to engage in off task behaviour. (e.g. social media, shopping) during class.	Students don't know how to manage themselves with technology; they are irresponsible and unfocussed.	Students may need routines and strategies for when and how to use technology as a tool for learning.
Essays related to understanding of topics studied in class are of poor quality.	Students lack knowledge from learning or lack skills in essay composition.	Essay writing is irrelevant to content and objectives. Students may be provided options to maximise their ability to communicate their understanding.

Whilst the main focus of this chapter is on advocating for learning needs and disabilities within the conceptual framework of diversity, there is a need to focus beyond it and consider the range of diversity covered within the Equality Act (2010). The extent of developing inclusive resources and approaches recognises the importance of equity of experiences. The language we use within our teaching, and, indeed, the resources we use should reflect a diverse range of needs. I recognise and champion that we use language in describing our learners that provides an opportunity for equity and not one which just considers policy but which takes an approach that values individuals (Smith, 2018). We can see how language is now recognising the individuality of those within the LGBTQ communities and how the use of pronouns can promote diversity by the use of he/her, him/he or the use of "them". Rosen (2018) argued that language has developed and that we should consider what is appropriate at any given time, and indeed what the individual prefers to be identified as. Within my own teaching I have explored the terms used to describe dis/ ability and have found that many students have preferred to be called "disabled" or "deaf" rather than "hearing impaired". In recognising the use of language as a tool to advocate for learners, it remains important to consider the individuals and support the diversity of the student cohorts (Smith, 2018). Girma (2021) argues that individuals' needs can be defined within our language and that we can state our needs, as not doing so can only promote a negative implication.

If you say I have special needs, I'll assume you're referring to my need for fresh-picked figs. I'm a Californian and this is non-negotiable. But if you're not referring to figs, then just say the word "disabled".

Euphemisms only fuel ableism. Disability is not a dirty word.

(Girma, 2021: np)

What is equity?

Doscher (2018) argues that approaching learners' needs is more than just recognising the demographics of the students within the universities. Indeed, she maintains that if we just consider the demographics, then we begin to measure inclusivity in terms of the data generated through admissions and graduate rates. She confirms my own belief in stating that inclusion means not all students feel they belong on all parts of the campus or in all aspects of life. She also highlights intersectionality and the importance of individual identity. In understanding identity, we need to advocate for the learners. Ward (2022) confirms this, as we can often position our teaching from a white privilege standpoint. It is argued that from this position, race and ethnicity become actions in which, for example, whiteness and brownness are defined in ongoing relation to each other. The term "Critical Race Theory" (CRT) argues we do not identify white people in the same way as we determine blackness. Rico (2016) states many people have multiple identities and that we need to teach from a point of intersectionality. For example, in our teaching, we must use a diverse range of teaching materials, and indeed our analogies needs to be from a broader experience, not just based on our own. We can adapt our teaching by using a variety of appropriate resources, as Woolley (2018) advocates. He highlights the need for reading materials to represent society as a whole. In adapting our teaching to support our learners' diverse needs, we can then develop learning relationships. Budge and Parrett (2017) consider that in advocating for learners, it is important to develop a relationship with the student which may be through a mentoring approach which models learning behaviours. Their work highlights engaging learners who are experiencing poverty and recognises the barriers this creates for learning. This echoes with the words of Rita Pierson (2013) who defines relationships as being pivotal to supporting learning, and she confirms the importance of relationships and highlights that you "cannot learn without building strong relationships". Garriy (2016) highlights the importance of language in defining individual needs but also addresses and confirms the importance of professional relationships with lecturers. Whilst she explores her own learning needs, she confirms that students need to have agency and advocate for themselves. She explains how the use of mnemonics is a supportive tool to her learning and how through collaboration the needs of individual learners can be addressed, with the emphasis on the relationship between lecturer and student.

Within recent years, we have become more aware of diverse needs, such as individual characterises such as transgender communities and the need to enable those individuals to be recognised within our communities. The language that we use in defining individuals' needs can have an impact on society's acceptance and cultural developments (Smith, 2018). In identifying the difficulties of transgender dysphoria and in enabling understanding of this within the community we can advocate for these individuals (Meyer et al., 2021). As educators we need to advocate for diverse needs to ensure social justice in order to reduce discrimination. In enabling self-advocacy learners can ensure they understand their self-identity. Vincent (2003, p. 2) recognises the important of education and educators in stating,

> "Education, because of its crucial role in the production and reproduction of particular identities and social positionings, is a particularly fruitful site in which to consider the playing out, or the performance, of social justice and identity issues".

Understanding how we advocate for all learners requires us to develop skills and knowledge which can be time-consuming and, in some cases, quite overwhelming. However, it enables us to take an approach which allows learners to be present in the classroom without necessarily giving them a "label". Having been involved in the development of online resources to support secondary school teachers with pupils with individual needs, the GUIDE Project (2013) was developed to inform policy within the European Union and support good practice for individuals with needs. The outcome of the project highlighted some of the concerns of teachers but particularly recognised the importance of developing self-advocacy and self-direction (Smith, 2018). The GUIDE Project provided an opportunity to reflect on working with our European partners and share and develop good practice.

A subsequent project, SCALE (Student-Centred Adult Learning Engagement in Higher Education) a three-year Erasmus+ funded project, ending in July 2021, was led by Worcester University. This project concentrated on the development and use of more effective resources and was designed to support lectures in higher education. The university worked with three European partners in Italy, Poland and Spain (https://scale.wp.worc.ac.uk/). The SCALE Project advocates a university-wide establishment of research focussing on inclusive approaches and further highlighted the international work on UDL.

The SCALE Project enabled the opportunity to explore the notion of inclusion with our European partners. This was achieved through a clear methodological approach. We were able to meet prior to COVID within our individual countries and institutions. During COVID, we made effective use of synchronised online meetings, which enabled us to share ideas and agree on some mutual conceptual ideas of inclusion. The GUIDE Project had previously identified that there were a number of different understandings of inclusion. For example, the notion of inclusion and the terminology and language used, as well as working practice, had been developed using definitions derived from World Health Organization (2001, DSM IV in Smith, 2018).

Project methodology

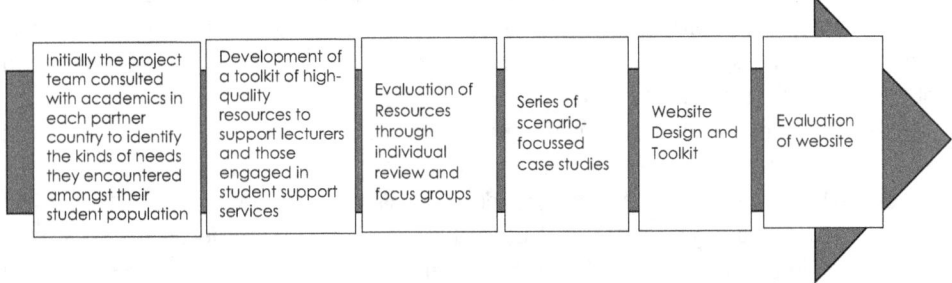

The project set out to

- identify the key learning needs and disabilities with which lecturers working on degree-level courses felt they needed support with,
- identify examples of best practice and evaluate their effectiveness/usefulness develop a toolkit of resources to support lecturers in their work with students, and
- create an online learning course as professional development for those teaching on degree-level courses and others working in student support services.

The project methodology was set out firstly to identify the specific needs lecturers required support with; this was achieved through online questionnaires across the project partnership. The five areas of needs were identified as follows:

1. Specific Learning Difficulties (SpLD): dyslexia, dyscalculia and dyspraxia
2. Autism
3. ADHD
4. Physical needs, language, speech, language needs, deafness, epilepsy, Tourette's, maturational delay, visual impairment
5. Mental health, anxiety, borderline personal disorder, highly sensitive person, addiction, maturational delay

In addition to identifying the individual needs, the project then considered a number of effective pedagogical strategies. These were group work, presentations, tutorials, reading and student skills, lecturers and classroom teaching and online learning.

The project aim was also to create a resources bank which would provide a toolkit for the website. In using literature and online searches, an appropriate resource would be created for the website. An initial literature search of meta-analysis of systematic literature reviews was conducted, and the priority was given to meta-analyses or systematic reviews to provide an overview of current research findings. The initial literature search included terminology such as "dyslexia", and the articles were limited to open access from the year 2011 to 2019 to ensure accessibility and current relevance. A total of six to seven resources for each identified area were included (dyslexia dyspraxia dyscalculia, ADHD/ADD, mental well-being, physical disability and autism). For each identified subject area, relevant webpages and downloads were recorded on an excel sheet for further evaluation. The resources were audited and finally moderated by the university of Worcester using a focus-group approach; this was to ensure the resources would be accessible to all the partners. In terms of challenges in collecting resources for the project, there is a sense that each partner took a slightly different approach to the collection of resources: e.g. focussing on international resources or resources from their own context. It was not always easy to decide what constituted best practice, as the term is relative and perhaps context-specific.

The SCALE Project team then created a number of modules. Five of these focus on student needs, namely, autism, ADHD, mental health, physical needs and SpLD which provided an interactive resource and the modular approach to this provides a structure to enable a lecturer to research and find solutions for supporting the students. Subsequently, a series of scenario-focussed case studies was developed to explore the areas of need most commonly encountered by the lecturers. Before the launch of the website, an evaluation was completed with a number of stakeholders and participants commenting on the website. The accessibility of the website enables lecturers to understand the students' needs and access information to support and enable the students to have agency.

Conclusion

Hearing our learners' voice and coming to some point of understanding allows for a negotiated response. We don't need to ensure we do it all for our learners: we need to understand what they would like for the process. Learning indeed from my own experience is a two-way process. When educators advocate for their learners, then learning relationships develop, this allows for a journey of discovery. I have found I have learnt from the learners I have taught and discovered how best to navigate the journeys they are on in their studies. Whilst I want to be correct in the terminology I use to describe my learners, how they want to be identified is pivotal in the pursuit of success on the journey to advocacy.

Summary points

- The chapter explores how lecturers can advocate for learners with diverse needs, emphasising the importance of supporting students to become independent and have agency in their learning.
- It discusses the SCALE Project, which developed resources and an e-learning course to support lecturers in higher education, focussing on bespoke provision for students along with a UDL approach.
- The chapter highlights the historical changes in legislation and social attitudes towards learners with individual needs, noting the progress and ongoing challenges in promoting inclusive practices.
- Drawing on insights gleaned over time, the author emphasises the importance of understanding and addressing the diverse needs of students, including those with hidden or undeclared needs.

- The chapter draws attention to the importance of language and terminology in supporting diversity and equity in education.

Recommended reading

In exploring explicitly debates about inclusion, the broader "complexities" are presented by Banks.

Banks, J. (2022) *The inclusion dialogue: debating issues, challenges and tension with global experts.* London: Routledge.

In understanding individuals, Brown presents the voices of academic staff presenting the same struggles that students may face.

Brown, N. & Leigh, J. (2020) *Ableism in Academia: Theorising Experiences of Disabilities and Chronic Illnesses in Higher Education.* London: UCL Press.

References

Bracken, S. and Novak, K. (2019) *Transforming Higher Education through Universal Design for Learning: An international perspective.* Abingdon: Routledge.

Budge, K. and Parrett, W. (2017) *Disrupting Poverty: Five Powerful Classroom Practices, Association for Supervision and Curriculum Development, 2017.* ProQuest Ebook Central, https://ebookcentral.proquest.com/lib/worcester/detail.action?docID=5231645

Doscher, S. (2018) Universal Global Learning, Inclusive Excellence, and Higher Education's Greater Purposes. *Peer Review.* Association of American Colleges & Universities. Available at (fiu.edu) (Accessed 27 November 2024).

Elliot, G. (1999) *Lifelong Learning: The Politics of the New Learning Environment.* Philadelphia: Jessica Kingsley.

Equality Act (2010) Available at https://www.legislation.gov.uk/ukpga/2010/15/contents (Accessed 15/06/23).

Garriy, L. (2016) Learning Disability in Higher Education and the Professor Student Relationship. Learning Disability in Higher Education… | Lexie Garrity | TEDxVanderbiltUniversity.

Girma, H. (2021) [Twitter] 3rd September. Available at: https://twitter.com/HabenGirma/status/1433899224203096067 URL (Accessed: 25 April 2023).

GUIDE (2013) Guidelines for Teachers Working with Students with Medium-light Cognitive Impairment. Available at https://www.project-guide.eu/ (Accessed: 27 November 2024).

Hubble, S. and Bolton, P. (2021) Briefing paper Number 8716, 22 February 2021 Support for disabled students in higher education in England. Available at https://commonslibrary.parliament.uk/research-briefings/cbp-8716/ (Accessed: 27 November 2024).

Kamen, T. (2003) *Teaching Assistant's Handbook.* London: Hodder and Stoughton.

Lehane, T. (2017) Teaching Assistants and Inclusion In R. Woolley (Ed.) *Understanding Inclusion Core Concepts, Policy and Practice.* London: Taylor and Francis.

Low, C. (1997) Point of View - Is Inclusivism Possible? *European Journal Of Special Educational Needs* 12(1), 71–79. Available at: https://doi.org/10.1080/0885625970120107

Meyer, D., Sledge, R. and Cameron, E. (2021) Gender Dysphoria and Transgender Concerns in School Counseling: Advocating for Students. *Journal of LGBTQ Issues in Counseling*, 15(4) https://doi.org/10.1080/15538605.2021.1938334

Moore, E. (2019) From Teaching content to teaching strategies. In S. Bracken and K. Novak(Ed.) *Transforming Higher Education through Universal Design for Learning: An International Perspective.* Abingdon: Routledge.

Pierson, R. (2013) Every Kid Needs a Champion. Available at https://www.ted.com/talks/rita_pierson_every_kid_needs_a_champion (Accessed: 27 November 2024).

Rico, N. (2016) Overcoming ableism: what you know as an able bodies person. Available at https://www.youtube.com/watch?v=X1xnyVCBYNQ

Rosen, M. (2018) Michael Rosen talks language and gender identity with CN Lester. *Word of Mouth.* Retrieved from: https://www.bbc.co.uk/programmes/b09r4k4l (Accessed: 27 November 2024).

Roy, E. (2016) When we design for disability, we all benefit. Available at https://www.ted.com/talks/elise_roy_when_we_design_for_disability_we_all_benefit (Accessed: 25 April 2023).

Vincent, C. (Ed) (2003) *Social Justice, Education and Identity*, Taylor & Francis Group, Available at ProQuest Ebook Central, https://ebookcntral.proquest.com/lib/worcester/detail.action?docID=181897 (Accessed 09.04.2024).

Smith, S. (2018) Dis/ ability. In: R. Woolley (Ed.) *Understanding Inclusion Core Concepts, Policy and Practice*. London: Taylor and Francis.

Smith, S. (2021) What's in a word? Rephrasing and reframing disability. Brown (Ed.). *Lived experiences of ableism in academia Strategies for Inclusion in Higher Education*. Bristol: Policy Press.

Sutcliffe. J. (1990) *Adults with learning difficulties: Education for choice and empowerment*. Leicester: National Institute of Adults Continuing Education.

Tomlinson, J. (1997) Inclusive Learning: the Report of the Committee of Enquiry into the postschool education of those with learning difficulties and/or disabilities, in England, 1996. *European Journal of Special Needs Education, 12*(3), 184–196. https://doi.org/10.1080/0885625970120302

Ward, G., Richards, R. and Best, M. (2022) Negotiating whiteness through brownness: Using intersectionality and transactional theory to capture racialised experiences of university campus life. *Studies in Higher Education*, 47(8), pp. 1736–1749. https://doi.org/10.1080/03075079.2021.1957814

Weale, S. (2022) Just 29% of students in England with disabilities receiving DSA allowance – analysis. *The Guardian*. https://www.theguardian.com/society/2022/mar/10/just-29-of-students-in-england-with-disabilities-receiving-dsa-allowance-analysis

Webster, Rob., Bosanquet, P. and Franklin, S. (2021) *Maximising the impact of teaching assistants in primary schools: a practical guide for school leaders*. Abingdon; Routledge.

World Health Organization (2001) *International Classification of Functioning, Disability and Health (ICIDH- 2)*. Geneva: World Health Organization.

Woolley, R. (2018) *Understanding inclusion: Core concepts, policy and practice*. Abingdon: Routledge.

7 Examining how academic self-concept and agency shaped a SEND learner's identity across the educational lifespan

Rebecca Russon and Alexandra Sewell

> **Vignette ("voiced" by Rebecca Russon)**
>
> It is almost cruel how mental health difficulties and Specific Learning Differences (SpLDs) often coexist. One factor alone can be overwhelming for students to face while studying, yet for neurodiverse students with a mental health condition, this can feel incapacitating. Terms often used to describe the experiences of such students are "debilitating" and "incapacitating". "Debilitating" suggests a weakness in the individual, and "incapacitating" suggests an individual cannot function in a "normal" way.
>
> Based on my lived experiences, portrayed narratively in this chapter, I hold a strong belief that this mindset, and even the use of such language, must change. I am in no way denying the daily and frequent difficulties I, and other neurodiverse individuals, have and continue to face. But society recognising the strengths of neurodiversity and in doing so for ourselves can have a positive impact on mental health.
>
> My own academic self-concept and agency have significantly changed and improved throughout my educational experience. However, I recognise this was not always the case, and it has not been a continuous progression. Therefore, I would like to encourage those who face difficulties with mental health, including current students, to seek support as soon as possible to grow your own self-concept and agency, as I tell with my story here.

Introduction

Learners with additional needs have predominantly been the subject of nomothetic, positivist research (Sewell, 2020; Sewell and Park, 2021; Sewell, 2022). This means that research has largely focused on identifying general laws and patterns that apply across groups of individuals with additional needs rather than exploring the unique experiences of each learner. The nomothetic approach aims to establish universal principles by comparing groups, often through quantitative methods, while the positivist paradigm emphasises objective measurement and the use of scientific methods to study observable phenomena, with the goal of producing replicable and empirically validated findings.

However, there is also complementary ideographic literature concerned with "the personal experiences of schooling" of individuals with additional needs (Glazzard and Dale, 2013: 26); due concern

DOI: 10.4324/9781003406334-7

is given to the layered, complex nature of individual's lived experiences (for example, see McAdams, 2001: 100–122). The idiographic approach focuses on understanding the unique, subjective experiences of individuals, using qualitative methods to explore the complexities and nuances of personal narratives and contexts.

Considering this literature, this chapter presents a qualitative research study that sought to explore the lived experiences of a learner with multiple additional needs throughout their educational experiences. The study aimed to explore how the experience of co-occurring SpLDs and mental health needs shaped the academic self-concept and agency of an undergraduate higher education student through the course of their education lifespan.

It is hoped that the personal biography, presented as an educational life history, will provide further commentary on the importance of considering "personal experiences of schooling" for individuals with additional learning needs (Glazzard and Dale, 2013: 26), and the implications for inclusive educational practice. By engaging with the educational life history that arose from the biographical narrative study, readers will have the opportunity to appreciate how personal experiences of education offer profound avenues for enhancing inclusive educational practices at all educational levels.

Chapter overview

In this chapter, we outline and explore the research methodology and methods used in the study. The educational life history is presented as a series of chronological life "scenes", with an emphasis on the protagonist's direct speech to highlight their personal experiences. The chapter concludes by situating the life history within existing research on academic self-concept and agency for neurodiverse learners, drawing connections between the individual narrative and broader theoretical frameworks.

The choice has been deliberately made to avoid language use such as "participant" or "subject"; terms traditionally associated with empirical-analytical research. Throughout the study, Rebecca is referred to as "the speaker". Purposive sampling was used to recruit the speaker, Rebecca Jones, in line with life history research methodology recommendations (Goodson and Sikes, 2001; Glazzard and Dale, 2013). The co-researcher, Dr Alexandra Sewell, had a professional relationship with Rebecca. Alexandra had been a tutor to Rebecca during her first-year modules at undergraduate level. They had taken part in research projects together. Alexandra had provided ad hoc tutorials to Rebecca to support her with her academic additional needs and provide career guidance. This prior professional relationship meant that Rebecca, the speaker, was open to sharing sensitive and personal information, which Glazzard and Dale (2013) argue is a strength of purposive sampling methods in life history research.

At the time the study was conducted, Rebecca was a mature student (aged 23) when she began studying for an undergraduate degree in a humanities subject at a post-1992 university in the United Kingdom. She arrived at the university with prior experience and diagnosis of depression and anxiety, and she received an assessment and diagnosis of dyspraxia and dyslexia during her first year at the institution. Rebecca considered herself an engaged student and wanted to do well at university. She came from a working-class background and was the first generation in her family to study at a higher education level. She aspired to postgraduate study after graduation, dreaming of doing a doctorate and having a career as a professional in the education sector. She achieved average grades at the beginning of her studies. Her grade point average improved progressively throughout her time at the university, and she graduated with an above average grade. She had a happy and secure friendship group throughout this time.

Methodology and methods

The research adopted a life-history approach to developing the narrative case study. A life-history approach prioritises individuals' stories as a means of providing data that is rich in nuance that other social science research methods cannot achieve (Goodson and Sikes, 2001). Stake (1978) presented the privileging of story in case studies as more appropriate than a traditional technical reporting style, as verbatim quotation allows for greater illustration of experience. This is furthered by Zeller's (1995) narrative case report approach, which argues for "narrative as a mode of communication more resonant with human experience...inherently more understandable" (Zeller, 1995: 75). There is, therefore, a phenomenological aspect to a narrative case study. A desire to understand the focus experience as storied by the experiencer. Yet, the final case narrative does not fully represent a life (Goodson and Sikes, 2001). It is lived experience rendered textual, and the methodology, whilst allowing for depth, can never fully elucidate the complexity of the human condition (Goodson and Sikes, 2001; Zeller, 1995).

Data collection

The researcher first interviewed the speaker during the first term of the first year of their undergraduate study. The interview lasted approximately two hours, and was audio recorded and transcribed. The speaker was then interviewed again during the first semester of their third year. The interview lasted approximately two and a half hours (with breaks), and was audio recorded and transcribed. No firm interview schedule was developed before either interview, as the researcher wished for the speaker to feel free to lead the topics being discussed. Field data, in the form of brief notes, was also kept by the researcher over the course of the speaker and researcher working together on the narrative life history.

Data analysis

Qualitative narrative accounts have been critiqued for lack of transparency, and associated validity, of data analysis processes (Dhunpath, 2000). Time is taken here to establish the approach to analysis and how its development was informed. Zeller's (1995) narrative case report approach was influential, along with the work of Krieger (1984), Wolf (1973) and Stake (1978) (as reported by Dhunpath, 2000).

1) Immersion in data: A considerable period was devoted to the researcher immersing themselves in the textual data as a precursor to organised textual analysis. Transcripts were re-read repeatedly, and the interview recordings listened to multiple times.
2) Scene by scene construction: Zeller (1995) calls for the locating of discrete life periods in text, as constructed by the speaker. Each transcript was coded for reference to distinguished time periods and large sections of text extracted and organised into each life period.
3) Detail: Wolf (1973) states that unique detail should be identified in the text. Story speakers will give "status life" indicators, found in such detail, which provide insight into how they understand themselves. Such close attention to detail offers "powerful representations of individuals and

their social milieu" (Stake, 1978). To note and preserve detail each constructed scene was read and re-read with line-by-line coding (as described by Smith, Larkin and Flowers, 2008).

4) Character through dialogue: Zeller (1995) asserts that a narrative case report can only claim authenticity and a feeling of reality "by rendering the character through full reports of dialogue" (Zeller, 1995: 80). Following step three, prominent sections of the speaker's dialogue were chosen and arranged to form the basis of the narrative case report. Quotations were chosen that were highly representative of important detail and that could be arranged to convey a sense of scene construction and story history to the reader. The speaker's language style and mannerisms were retained without editing to represent their identity and authenticity.

5) Mutual shaping: "Mutual shaping" refers to the full and necessary inclusion of the speaker in the narrative case study development (Zeller, 1995). Close involvement of participants in the shaping of the narrative allows researchers to "banish the indifference often generated by samples, treatments and faceless subjects" (Witherall and Noddings, 1991: 280). Mutual shaping was exacted through a back-and-forth exchange throughout data analysis activity. This is detailed as follows:
   - Scene construction shared and developed in response to the speaker's views
   - Details shared and developed in response to the speaker's views
   - Dialogue extracts shared and developed in response to the speaker's views
   - Final textual narrative case report shared and further developed in response to the speaker's views

Ethical considerations

Ethical permission was sought from and granted by the researcher's institution. Identifying parts of the speaker's story have been omitted due to sensitivity of the emotional content they hold for them and to mitigate the risk of identification. Informed consent and right to withdraw were crucial ethical elements of the study and the speaker was reminded of their right to withdraw without penalty right up until the point of data being published.

Educational narrative story

Scene one: Childhood experiences of neurodiversity

Rebecca had always felt that there was something different about her. Different from her peers and even different from her family. She always thought that there may be a reason; Rebecca and her family always suspected she had dyslexia.

As a child, it had seemed that even her most basic bodily functions were different to others; heat and pain affected her uniquely. This made routine experiences emotionally heightened. For example, she remembers how traumatising even a GP appointment and injection were for her. After the injection, she was suddenly confused, emotionally lost:

> "I thought, 'I don't know who I am, and I don't know what's happened, but something awful has happened.' I didn't know what had happened to me, and all of a sudden, there was a ringing, and I heard them talking, and they said, 'Are you OK?'.

And I asked, 'What's the ringing?'

They replied, 'We pressed the panic alarm. Who are you here with?'

'My mum', but I didn't know who my mum was. I knew I had a mum, but I didn't know who she was until she walked in, and then I realised.

I passed out a lot when I was younger, but that was the worst. I didn't even see anything (blood, needles) so that was the weirdest for me. I think maybe a lot of it is in my head. I'm not good with pain, and I know that, and obviously with my dyspraxia, she [Disability Assessor at university] explained that was why when I get too hot, I pass out. She said I'm really oversensitive to heat and oversensitive to pain, so I can do that (light tap), and that will hurt me. It feels like my body is bruised all over.

That event, at the time, I just thought that was just me being really weird and a bit quirky and whatever, but she [Disability Assessor at university] explained, 'No, that's dyspraxia'. I said to myself, 'Oh, you weren't that special OK' *laughs*. A lot of the stuff she said, I said to myself, 'Oh, I do that', and I didn't realise that was a part of that.

I don't really want it as a label, I just wanted to know what it was because I knew something wasn't right. I knew I was either really weird and had all these things. As we always suspected dyslexia or dyscalculia, because my maths is completely awful. Peers/classmates would get the answer of 10 and I'd get 4,050, and they couldn't understand; 'How did she get that answer?!'

We didn't really know what dyspraxia was until I got diagnosed with it here [at university], and then it was the realisation. So the fainting makes sense now, the pain and the heat and everything, oh OK, that makes sense now".

Scene two: **Mental health needs arise aged 16**

As she grew older, Rebecca's heightened emotional experiences persisted and evolved. They became pervasive, occurring every day. She felt sad all the time and started to get anxious. This exacerbated how different she felt to others. She saw others being OK with life and thought, *"I've got this problem and well, like, no one else has this problem. Like, 'What's wrong with me?'"* There seemed to be no explanation. The confusion she'd always felt about who she was deepened. Family members intervened:

"I think I was 15 or 16, I think. I don't even know how it started. I just remember crying to my mum and saying something's, something's not right. She kind of forced me to go to the doctors, and I couldn't talk because I don't. Even if I was ill, had a cold or something – not that I'd go to the doctors for a cold – but I always would be sat there, and I couldn't start off. If my mum started off the conversation when I was younger, she could talk, then I could talk, but with that I thought, I don't want to talk. I don't wanna. I don't wanna do anything about it. I don't want to talk about it because that admits I have a 'problem'".

These new difficulties and experiences confused Rebecca. She had a view of herself as a positive person and was beginning to not feel like herself anymore. She found that it was *"really upsetting at first, to be that's not me. I'm so, I'm so positive. Who is this?"* Yet, Rebecca always found a desire to cope. Seeking strategies became a means for finding out about herself. She learnt that she could be humorous:

> "I don't even remember the jokes. It's just, I think I've always been a jokey person. But, at that time, that was obviously a mask for me. I thought I'll just make jokes then".

At this point in her life, despite the confusion and emotional pain, Rebecca knew her ambitions. Whilst others made decisions for her and detailed what she would and wouldn't be able to do, she internally rallied against them:

> "I've always thought 'I'm gonna prove you wrong'. Even my teachers at school were always thinking, 'You're not gonna do anything. You're not gonna amount to anything' and stuff. I'm of the mindset, OK that's your opinion. Good luck. I'm doing things that people thought I couldn't do".

Scene three: College and career decisions

When she left school Rebecca felt she had to decide quickly on what she wanted to do with her life. She felt a lack of knowledge about the world of training and work. She found that the difficulties she'd experienced at school transferred into her college course training to be a hairdresser. Her view of herself and her abilities was further challenged:

> "I just felt stupid when I was doing the hairdressing. I've been taught to do this, but I still can't properly do this. I still can't get the science of it. If someone just said oh here's the colour put it on, mix it up, whatever. I'd think, OK cool, and I could do the actual foils, but I couldn't, grasp the science of if the hair's this colour, and they want to get it to this colour, so this is what I need to do, kinda thing".

Rebecca left hairdressing and said to herself, "*Oh, I'll go and ended up somehow working in care*". Then gained a role as a learning support assistant. Whilst initially working in this role, her mental well-being improved, but then she continued to experience high anxiety and low mood. This too left her feeling adrift and that she needed to find a work or study as a solution that would allow her to be herself and follow her desires, which had not gone away. She enjoyed the work but again experienced forces that seemed outside of her control:

- Despite her mental health improving for "*quite a bit*", she remembers "*I did have a breakdown, I didn't go into work for a week*". This was unlike Rebecca, as "*I'm very much of the mindset, let's go into work, let's do this. Well, with that job I especially though, 'I love it lets go in, I was excited to go in every day'*".
- Despite these challenges Rebecca continued to push herself to think about her options and make her own choices. She decided to go to university. She once again heard the voices of others telling her that she wouldn't be able to do it and that it was a bad idea, but deep down, she felt she knew herself:

> "When I initially said to my parents, I'm going to university, they were against the idea, asking, 'What are you doing?' as this was all out of the blue for them, and there was no diagnosis at this

point. My mom was actually, and my Auntie, were really concerned that I was just going to do a year and then either I would drop out or something bad would happen, mental health wise. I've always been really determined. Such as, when I started driving, they were unsure, and I thought, 'Oh, I will'. It might take me longer, and it took me longer than all my friends, and I cried on the test and stuff. I somehow passed...but I've always pushed through whatever. Whether it's social or education or whatever it is".

Scene four: First year at university

University was an opportunity for Rebecca to try again and to prove to others that she could do it. It seemed to be a significant move as it was *"all very new and weird"* and *"just a really completely different experience"*. Initially, her stress increased, but then she received a diagnosis of dyspraxia and dyslexia through the university assessment centre. This provided her with hope and helped her make sense of her past, but obtaining the right support remained complicated and continued to impact her mental health. Support for students can be accessed through government funding, such as the disabled students' allowance (DSA), which is designed to help meet the needs of learners with disabilities.

This funding goes to the university and can be used to access assistive technologies, study skills tutors/mentors and/or mental health tutors/mentors for counselling. Rebecca remembers the difficulties of attaining this mental health support when *"they [the university] messaged finance who messed it up; they've reached capacity here so we will put you through to a town over an hour away"*. She tried to fight this, explaining, "I'm not going *there*, it's literally a 50-minute session". She felt that depending on the session, she may not be in the right mindset to drive afterwards.

There was then a delay in receiving assistive technology. *"It was week 5 when I got all my equipment and study skills support."* This delay has a resulting effect

"That didn't help, I felt, well, I'm already behind, I can't do anything. It was weird because I hadn't had the support before, but I felt that I couldn't start anything until I've got all this support, and I think that didn't help. That started off the anxiety more. I feel that the depression has 'gone down' a bit, and the anxiety is through the roof; last week, it was probably at its highest".

Scene seven: Studying during extreme events

Rebecca's time at university mirrored her previous educational experiences with others doubting her and her striving to prove them wrong. This was exacerbated by two major events, flooding and the COVID-19 pandemic. She felt that each wider challenge was another opportunity for others to doubt her and for her to change their minds:

"I think when COVID hit, they [parents] were thought 'she's gonna drop out. She's gonna leave this now.' And my perspective was, I've got grades back from a module, and I got a B and an A-, and I was really happy, obviously never getting anywhere near those grades at pretty much any time in my life. I was almost crying. So, I sent them to my parents. And now that they know I have the diagnosis they understand that diagnosis. They're a bit like, 'OK, we kind of get it'. I think my mum has done some further reading into it and stuff, and her attitude is now, 'Oh, you're dyspraxic'".

Rebecca continued to show determination, even if that was simply turning up to lectures when physical barriers stood in her way:

> "And then we had floods, so obviously some of our lectures were cancelled. With one of the lectures, my friend gave me a piggyback over to the other side [of the flood] because it was flooding, and I didn't have Wellies, but we wanted to get to the lecture. I was determined. Obviously, I've always been determined, but in that moment, I thought, 'I just have to get there'".

Scene eight: Final year at university

Despite her persistence, university continued to be tough. The first semester of each year still felt like "*mayhem, just absolute carnage*". She began to realise that perhaps her personal challenges may never entirely go away but that she had shown that she could achieve what she wanted to. As she had always done, she constantly innovated and experimented with ways to cope and continue:

> "I noticed that I was scratching [myself, as a result of anxiety], so having these stress balls worked for so long. And then I thought, no, OK, I need to do something else. I've got hobbies of stuff that I go 100% in on and I'm obsessed with and then I'm think, 'Oh I can't do this, or I'm not that good at it'. I feel I kind of use these hobbies now as more of a strategy. I've started one at the minute, which I'm actually really enjoying and I've – I haven't had any problems with it yet. I've started making clay earrings. I've always found with my dyslexia, even writing an assignment, it's always been that I know what I want to say in here, but I can't get it out. And with drawing, I can visualise so many things in my head, but I can't draw them. So, I was really worried with this; is it gonna actually make me more stressed and more upset and anxious because I can't do it? But, touch wood, it's been really good so far, and I've made some really cool things and I'm going to do this to relax and calm me. So if I am feeling anxious, I find like that's helped, as a strategy, even though it's like a hobby, it's just something different."

Ultimately, Rebecca felt that she had grown and shown she could actualise what she always believed she could be capable of. Towards the end of her final year at university, a key change was that her family had begun to see her talents and believe in her too:

> "[T]hey've adapted as well and have the attitude of 'OK, we didn't think she was going to do this but she's doing this now. She's got further than we thought. She's nearly finished. She's getting better grades than we thought.'"

Rebecca went onto complete her degree and start a Master's degree in Educational Psychology. Having achieved her own learning goals, she managed to navigate the challenges she faced due to neurodiversity and mental health. She adopted a new dream to help those with similar challenges to succeed educationally.

Discussion

An individual's academic self-concept can be determined through expectations for attainment from educators (Martinek and Johnson, 1979). Conversely, this does not mean that an individual has to define their academic self-concept as such. Self-fulfilling prophecy has been a contentious topic in academic research, and while most children may live up to positive or negative expectational prophecies from their educators, some children opt to disregard them, especially the negative expectational predictions (Weinstein, 2016). The fundamental concept of the self as an agentic being and setting one's own educational goals is suggested by Bandura's (2000) research on self-efficacy and agentic resilience.

This process of developing academic self-concept in relation to the views of close others, rather than straight adoption of their perceptions, is apparent in Rebecca's narrative. In earlier story scenes, academic attainment and parental comments influence Rebecca's view of her ability. Yet, it is through action and learning motivation that her agentic self develops. This experience leads to challenges to a self-previous projected onto her and an emergency in her belief that becomes bound with her determination and continuation of her schooling.

Neurodiverse students who integrate with mainstream schooling may face difficulties that their neurotypical peers may not face throughout their educational journey (Zolyomi et al., 2018). Azmitia and Hesser (1993) suggest that children are often subject to educators making comparisons with their peers or their siblings; this can affect their academic self-concept and lead to difficulties with mental health such as anxiety or depression. Khalaila (2015) provided evidence of the association between higher self-concept and higher academic attainment. This correlation was demonstrated to be significantly influenced by anxiety as a self-concept factor; additionally, the influence of intrinsic motivation was also significant (Khalaila, 2015).

Social, emotional and mental health difficulties are often linked to individuals with SpLDs/SEND (Rose et al., 2009), and it is clear to see why children in mainstream may face these difficulties due to the pressures of receiving mainstream education rather than specialised teaching to meet their individual additional needs. Those who receive formal diagnosis later in life, e.g. after completing their academic journey/formal education, are often subject to having negative self-perceptions, low self-esteem and beliefs of stupidity (Jahoda et al., 2010).

There are clear parallels between the outcomes of this research literature and Rebecca's narrative. Whilst Rebecca constructs her mental health as sometimes occurring and existing outside of her neurodiverse learner profile, she also reflects that the two continually entwined and informed the development of each other. At the heart of this reflection, academic self-concept again plays a central role, while her early learning differences are experienced as difficulties attributable to a later diagnosis and thus support. As shown by Khalaila (2015) and (Jahonda et al., 2010) the becoming of an agentic being and independent, determined lifelong learner coincided with adult + diagnosis and receiving of support in higher education.

Conclusion

The stigma of neurodiversity is slowly being reduced within society. Within education, it is being addressed through Continuing Professional Development (CPD) training for educators on SpLDs/SEND and funding to provide access to education through resources (Kidd, 2022). Through providing this accessibility to education, more neurodivergent students are able to reach their full academic potential or as close to this as they can. We believe this has been demonstrated with clarity and depth in this chapter through the use of Rebecca's experiences as a narrative educational history. If diverse learners are identified early in their educational experiences, they can receive appropriate support, which influences educational outcomes and their academic self-concept. It is this wider influence on academic self-concept which is the most powerful. As Rebecca has expressed through her own story, a positive academic self-concept can generate agency and independence producing lifelong deep learning. Arguably, this is what all educators and learners strive for.

Summary points

- The chapter presents a narrative case report of a learner with SEND, exploring their educational history and experiences with specific learning difficulties and mental health needs. It highlights how academic self-concept and agency shape the development of self and learner identity.
- The research adopts a life-history approach, using qualitative methods to provide a nuanced understanding of the learner's experiences. The narrative is presented as a series of chronological life scenes, emphasising the speaker's direct speech to highlight personal experiences.
- The chapter discusses the challenges faced by the learner, including the coexistence of mental health difficulties and SpLDs and how these challenges impacted their educational journey and self-concept.
- The importance of early identification and support for diverse learners is emphasised, as well as the role of educators in fostering a positive academic self-concept and agency.
- The narrative underscores the significance of recognising and valuing the strengths of neurodiversity, and how a positive academic self-concept can generate agency and independence, leading to lifelong, deep learning.

Recommended reading

Hanna, M. and Kaal, A.A. (Eds) (2020) *Narrative and Metaphor in Education: Look Both Ways*. Abingdon: Routledge.

This insightful book explores the crucial role of narrative and metaphor in shaping educational experiences and thinking. Drawing on interdisciplinary perspectives from fields such as linguistics, psychology, and education, it demonstrates how storytelling and metaphor influence teaching methods and the way students understand and engage with learning.

Cockain, A. (2024) *Learning Disability and Everyday Life*. Oxford: Routledge.

This book offers a thought-provoking exploration of the lived experiences of individuals with learning disabilities, focusing on the challenges and complexities they face in their daily lives. The text brings together a range of perspectives to examine how social, cultural, and institutional contexts shape the everyday realities of people with learning disabilities. It emphasises the importance of recognising and understanding the nuanced ways in which individuals with learning disabilities navigate societal expectations, barriers and opportunities.

Sewell, A. (Ed.) (2022) *Diverse Voices in Educational Practice: Professional Learning and Education*. Abingdon: Routledge.

This book offers a comprehensive exploration of the importance of diversity in educational practice, particularly in professional learning and development. It brings together a range of voices and perspectives to examine how educators can foster inclusivity and respond to the diverse needs of their students. It emphasises the value of recognising and addressing different cultural, social, and personal experiences within the classroom.

References

Azmitia, M. and Hesser, J. (1993) Why siblings are important agents of cognitive development: A comparison of siblings and peers. *Child development*, 64(2), pp. 430–444.

Bandura, A. (2000) Self-efficacy: The foundation of agency. *Control of human behavior, mental processes, and consciousness: Essays in honor of the 60th birthday of August Flammer*, 16.

Dhunpath, R. (2000) Life history methodology: 'Narradigm' regained. *International Journal of Qualitative Studies in Education*, 13(5), pp. 543–551.

Glazzard, J., and Dale, K. (2013) Trainee teachers with dyslexia: personal narratives of resilience. *Journal of Research in Special Educational Needs*, 13(1), pp. 26–37.

Goodson, I. and Sikes, P. (2001) *Life History Research in Educational Settings: Learning from Lives*. Buckingham: Open University Press.

Jahoda, A., Wilson, A., Stalker, K. and Cairney, A. (2010) Living with stigma and the self-perceptions of people with mild intellectual disabilities. *Journal of Social Issues*, 66(3), pp. 521–534.

Khalaila, R. (2015) The relationship between academic self-concept, intrinsic motivation, test anxiety, and academic achievement among nursing students: Mediating and moderating effects. *Nurse Education Today*, 35(3), pp. 432–438.

Kidd, D.E. (2022) Neurodivergence, Embodiment, Empowerment, Pathography: Expressions from the Margins. *Practicing Anthropology*, 44(4), pp. 31–37.

Krieger, S. (1984) Fiction and Social Science. *Studies in Symbolic Interaction*, 5, pp. 269–287.

Martinek, T. J. and Johnson, S. B. (1979) Teacher expectations: Effects on dyadic interactions and self-concept in elementary age children. *Research quarterly. American alliance for Health, Physical Education, Recreation and Dance*, 50(1), pp. 60–70.

McAdams, D.P. (2001) The psychology of life stories. *Review of General Psychology*, 5(2), pp. 100–122.

Rose, R., Howley, M., Fergusson, A. and Jament, J. (2009) Mental Health and SEN: Mental health and special educational needs: exploring a complex relationship. *British Journal of Special Education*, 36(1), pp. 3–8.

Sewell, A. (2020) Introducing Specific Learning Difficulties. In A. Sewell and J. Smith *Introduction to Special Educational Needs, Disability and Inclusion: A Student's Guide*. London: Sage.

Sewell, A. (2022) Understanding and supporting learners with specific learning difficulties from a neurodiversity perspective: A narrative synthesis. *British Journal of Special Education*, 49, pp. 1–22.

Sewell, A. and Park, J. (2021) A three-factor model of educational practice considerations for teaching neurodiverse learners from a strengths-based perspective. *Support for Learning*, 36(4), pp. 678–694.

Smith, J.A., Larkin, M. and Flowers, P. (2008) *Doing Interpretative Phenomenological Analysis: A Practical Guide to Method and Application*. London: Sage.

Stake, R. (1978) The Case Study Method in Social Inquiry. *Educational Researcher*, 7, pp. 6–8.

Weinstein, R.S. (2016) Children's awareness of differential treatment: Toward a contextual understanding of teacher expectancy effects. In S. Trusz and P. Bąbel *Interpersonal and Intrapersonal Expectancies*. Abingdon: Routledge.

Witherall, C. and Noddings, N. (Eds) (1991) *Stories Lives Tell: Narratives and Dialogue in Education*. New York: Teachers College Press.

Wolf, T. (1973) *The New Journalism*. New York: Harper and Row.

Zeller, N. (1995) Narrative Strategies for Case Reports In. Hatch, J. A., and Wisniewski, R. (Eds.) *Life History and Narrarive*. London: The Falmer Press.

Zolyomi, A., Ross, A.S., Bhattacharya, A., Milne, L. and Munson, S.A., (2018), April. Values, identity, and social translucence: Neurodiverse student teams in higher education. In *Proceedings of the 2018 Chi Conference on Human Factors in Computing Systems* (pp. 1–13).

8 Epistemic injustice and the silencing of student voices

Jeremiah Adebolajo Olusola

Vignette from a PhD research project

In the Autumn of 2022, during my ethnographic immersion amongst a group of British Muslim converts, I questioned Emma, a then 42-year-old part-time accountant, about her experiences within higher education (HE) and her subsequent decision to home school her children. She notes,

> I'm all for education, but I dropped out of uni[versity] myself. I'm basically a pretty religious Muslim chick in a niqab (face veil). I don't shake hands with men, and I don't really free-mix (socialise with non-related males). I don't drink. I don't smoke, and I'm pretty sure most of my views about gender and stuff don't fit into uni[versity] life. It just ain't the place for me. I don't want my kids to go through all that yet, either…. On top of that…I'm a white revert (convert), and it's just not that easy to get heard when you're talking about…Islam and Muslims and stuff, if you're not Asian. Do you know what I mean?

Emma's response offers a fascinating insight into a personal sense of disempowerment experienced within HE. It alludes to both a tension she felt between her personal religious sensibilities and the perceived cultures of university life. Furthermore, it is expressive of a type of marginality that arose due to the interaction between Emma's racial and religious identifications. As I found in my doctoral research (Olusola, 2024), Emma's experience of education is broadly representative of the experiences of many "visible" and "practising" Muslim students who consider the university campus to be a prohibitive environment for their religious subjectivity.

This chapter critically interrogates the socio-political dimensions of being a "practising" Muslim within contemporary educational settings and examines the capacity of student representation systems to capture the voices of such learners. As well as addressing the contemporary rhetoric of diversity, inclusion and widening participation within conceptions of learner voice, the chapter draws attention to the subtle ways in which representation systems can disguise inequalities that are deeply entrenched in the cultures and structures of HE.

Introduction and context

Student academic representation (SAR) is one of the most commonly evoked conceptions of learner voice in HE. Generally, it involves eliciting students' input in educational decision-making via self-nominated or elected (usually untrained) students who represent the metaphorical "voice" of a larger student body within an institution. These representatives engage with pre-existing institutional systems, like Students' Unions (SU), with the aim of informing institutional governance (Winter et al., 2024). This conceptualisation of learner voice is widely accepted to be a desirable phenomenon, one which has been entrenched into HE institutions nationwide over the past two decades and integrated into core institutional expectations and guidelines for ensuring effective student participation (Bols, 2020).

While varying approaches to student academic representation exist, including engaging students as collaborators and consultants in research or pedagogical development, understandings of SAR generally position student representatives as speaking for, or on behalf of, other students. Theoretically, then, this is a manifestation of representative democracy which endows students with agency in the decisions that impact their education. While it is possible for student representation to take on far "thicker" and more direct models of democracy – such as in "The Citizen School" in the city of Porto Alegre, Brazil, where "the entire school community elects the principal by direct vote" (Gandin and Apple, 2002: 34) – it is the far less direct model of student representation that has become the phenomenon commonly referred to as "learner voice" in the United Kingdom, which is the focus of my reflections in this chapter.

Learner voice, in this sense, is primarily limited to those structures and mechanisms that allow institutions to garner student feedback and engagement at both local and national levels and ostensibly advance participatory democratic practices in education. Importantly, however, it has also served to meet the increasingly formalised financial and institutional imperatives linked to institutional investment, reputation and league table standings (Freeman, 2016). These unavoidably political dimensions of learner voice generate questions about the motivations and capabilities of SARs to capture the voices of minority and marginalised students: Are some types of learner voices inevitably privileged through these systems? What are the structural barriers to engagement within these systems and how might those barriers be broken down?

There is a growing body of literature marking Muslim learners as especially marginalised within the post-9/11 British educational context (Revell and Bryan, 2018; Shain, 2021; Zempi and Tripli, 2023), making this group a salient lens through which to explore these questions. Through this exploration, the reader is invited to reflect upon those learners whose voices may not be well represented within SAR systems, the reasons for this lack of representation, and how it may constitute a form of "epistemic injustice".

Pause for thought

Reflecting on the discussion so far in this chapter, consider:

Whether you think that more direct forms of democracy, like the one in The Citizen School, are a positive or negative thing.
Do they give universities more legitimacy to make decisions about learners' education?
How might the connection between SARs and institutional imperatives like investment and reputation hinder the ability to capture the learner voice.
Are there any social groups in your context whose voices may not be well represented in SARs in your institution, and why?

What is epistemic injustice?

Before engaging more fully with the questions I have raise so far, it is necessary to clearly define what is meant by "epistemic injustice" within this chapter, and how it relates to marginalised groups in educational settings. Linguistically, the word "epistemic" can be defined as "relating to knowledge or the study of knowledge" (Cambridge Dictionary, n.d.). Epistemic injustice, therefore, refers to the exclusion or marginalisation of a group/s from participation in the practices, systems and structures that define and construct knowledge (Fricker, 2007). Here, I will delimit the focus of my discussion on epistemic injustice to the experiences of Muslim students who feel the need to self-censor or self-silence in educational spaces, resulting in an inability to utilise their "learner voice" or count themselves "among those who have the knowledge and the position to shape what counts as education" (Cook-Sather, 2002: 3). Fricker (2007), in her book *Epistemic Injustice: Power and the ethics of knowing*, articulates forms of epistemic injustice which occur when the voices of marginalised groups are distorted or unheard due to negative views about the identity of that group. Her description of epistemic injustice aligns with Langton's (1993) concept of "locutionary silencing" in which "members of a powerless group may be silent because they are intimidated, or because they believe that no one will listen" (p. 315). Both of these forms of epistemic injustice resonate closely with Emma's statement, *"I…don't fit into uni[versity] life… it's just not that easy to get heard when you're talking about…Islam and Muslims and stuff"*. Given the growing body of literature in the field of education, which suggests that many Muslim students feel similarly marginalised within HE institutions, it seems apposite to reflect upon the extent to which SAR systems are alive to the perspectives of this marginalised group and truly reflect the collective learner voice.

Whose voice(s)?

At this point, it may be helpful to problematise the terminology of *"the* learner voice" itself. Without careful reflection, the phrase constructs a rather stylised image of a homogenous student perspective and, by extension, experience. This image is reflected in Emma's statement, *"I'm pretty sure most of my views about gender and stuff don't fit into uni*[versity] *life [she chuckles]. It just ain't the place for me"*. The image of a singular perspective among the student body clearly belies the diversity of experience(s) and voice(s) found among student populations in British educational institutions. However, despite increased diversity in the student population in Britain (OfS, 2022), there is evidence to suggest that inequitable structures remain in place. My doctoral research, for example, indicates that some students perceive entering an education system with a fixed cultural reality is so at odds with their religious subjectivity that their voices cannot be properly included as part of "the" learner voice.

Indeed, proponents of a more hardened secularist position demarcate public spaces like universities the domain of "the secular", making the claim that public articulations of religion are antithetical to the post-enlightenment endeavour of the modern university (Asad et al., 2013; Chambers, 2010). Some scholars have suggested that this view of publicly articulated religion is shared by contemporary multiculturalist outlooks in Britain (Sealy, 2021; Modood, 2013). Furthermore, some of those scholars make the unsettling inference that this view arises from a moral panic surrounding the role of Islam as a social entity that extends beyond private religious ritual (Modood, 2013; Sealy, 2021). However, a consideration of religion as a protected characteristic under UK law, which is therefore to be afforded the same legal protections as, for instance, disability, gender, race and sexuality, helps us to identify the inherent problem in this outlook. If, on the one hand, public displays of various identity characteristics are to be celebrated as a mark of Britain's diversity and evidence of inclusivity within multicultural systems, attention must be paid to any differences in the treatment of religion as an identity characteristic. This reasoning seems to align with the values espoused by British universities, as documented within the Quality Assurance Agency for Higher Education's (QAA, 2018) student engagement guidance:

> Providers recognise and respond to the diversity of their student body in the design and delivery of student engagement, partnership working and representation processes: Providers ensure that approaches to student engagement and representation are designed to include the diversity of their student body, identifying and removing barriers to participation, to ensure that the full diversity of student voices can contribute to enhancement and assurance activities. Consideration is given to students' modes of study, the composition and demographic of the student population, and the different backgrounds that students have, to ensure effective engagement and representation.
>
> (p. 5)

Therefore, Muslim students who maintain their beliefs and identities within public educational settings should find themselves heard, represented and celebrated within this definition of student inclusion. Despite this, students like Emma do not find this to be the case. To interrogate the reasons for this, it is useful to deliberate on the role of three intersecting concepts: neoliberalism, secularism and multiculturalism.

Pause for thought

Can you think of an example of epistemic injustice that has occurred in any public institution that you are aware of?

Should all of the protected characteristics be treated equally in the university setting?

Are descriptors like "the learner voice" exclusionary? Can you think of another way to define student representation systems?

Neoliberalism

It may not be immediately obvious how discussions about including religious students' voices in academic representation systems intersects with the economic terms within which neoliberalism can be understood. While competing definitions of neoliberalism exist, the term generally refers to an economic school of thought that favours free-market capitalism. With one of the key corollaries of attending university being the prospect of graduates generating wealth within the economy by attaining higher paying employment, neoliberalism's influence on the direction of the education sector has predictably increased. One of the ways in which this has manifested in universities is in the tendency to conceive of students as consumers (Tight, 2013). This reconfigures the voices of learners as quantifiable through such things as student experience and satisfaction data. This mode of quantification and subsequent marketisation of learner voice has impacted representation systems like SUs in new ways also. It has been suggested, for example, that rather than SUs taking on the shape of egalitarian public squares and spaces for political expression, they are instead now "mediated through commercial interests" (Andersson et al., 2012: 505). This has, in turn, led to a propensity to "promote hedonistic cultures associated with sex and drinking" as part of a normative student culture (p. 507). It is within this contextual backdrop that the religious Muslim student, who may choose not to engage in that culture, emerges as "other". In this way, the influence of neoliberalism may cultivate an inhospitable environment for those students who sit outside of the "normative"; defined by Anderson et al. as "white, middle class secular students" (p. 512).

Secularism

The secular normativity in education remains a much-debated topic. Unresolved contentions surrounding the role of secularity within universities have resulted in observations about the ways in which educational policies and practices speak about, rather than to, religious learners – and in particular Muslim learners. The implementation of the Prevent Duty (HMG, 2021) in educational settings has perhaps received the most attention in that regard (Busher and Jerome, 2020; Miah, 2017), with some suggesting that the policy's regulatory gaze serves to uniquely criminalise features of Islamic theology (Olusola, 2023; Revell, 2012). It has also been suggested that the types of students privileged by SAR systems are those that have the time, money and social leverage to engage with the (often unpaid) schemes that exist to capture learner voice (Marquis et al., 2018; Mercer-Mapstone et al., 2021). This becomes particularly relevant in light of the research indicating that Muslim students have disproportionately less time, money and social leverage than the general student population (see Stevenson et al., 2017).

In spite of these exclusionary factors, there has been little sustained scholarly focus upon the influence of secularism in limiting the types of voices captured and listened to within educational settings. Modood makes use of the rather contentious term "radical secularism" to highlight an important distinction between a hostile stance taken towards publicly articulated religion and a stance of neutrality taken towards others' public expressions of faith. These differing forms of secularism are also distinguished by Habermas (2008), who names the more hostile view of public religious expression "secularist" and the more neutral viewpoint "secularism". The "secularist" position, which treats public expressions of religion as incongruent with modern educational institutions may insist that Muslim students' requests for such things as voluntary gender-segregated spaces, alcohol-free spaces and particular sartorial allowances are culturally and politically unreasonable; it advocates for the privatisation of religion and calls for restrictions on the accommodation of religious demands in public spaces. As alluded to earlier, this stance would appear incongruent with the educational values of "identifying and removing barriers to participation, to ensure that the full diversity of student voices can contribute to enhancement and assurance activities" (QAA, 2018: 5). A number of high-profile cases in the post-9/11 period offer examples of how contestations surrounding inclusion and secular thinking have played out in contemporary educational contexts.

Case study

Consider the short vignette about Emma presented at the beginning of the chapter. To what extent do the events in the following case study reflect Emma's concerns about HE in the United Kingdom?

In the spring of 2013, the Islamic Education and Research Academy (iERA) held an event at University College London (UCL), entitled *Islam and Atheism: Which Makes More Sense?*

The event was a debate between Professor Lawrence Krauss, an eminent atheist, and Hamza Tzortzis, a British convert Muslim and lecturer on Islam. During the event, Professor Krauss reported seeing attendees being assigned seats in an effort to facilitate gender segregation. This caused him to walk out of the event, citing his unwillingness to be involved in events that enforced segregation. It was reported that while Krauss was persuaded to resume the event with segregated seating no longer being facilitated, iERA were subsequently banned from future involvement in UCL campus events. It was determined that the group's intention to uphold their right to voluntary gender-segregated seating was "contrary to UCL's ethos" (Batty, 2013). iERA's then head of public relations, who denied enforcing segregated seating, insisted that non-segregated seating was available and offered, as was male and female segregated seating, to accommodate the religious needs of those who preferred voluntary gender-segregated seating. iERA summarised the point of contention in the following way, "We understood that we could not enforce separate seating, but we could facilitate it". Richard Dawkins, on the other hand, described gender segregation at the event as "sexual apartheid" (Batty, 2013). Amidst the public debate, a number of high-profile figures, including then Prime Minister David Cameron, expressed support for the decision of UCL.

However, the obvious complexities that exist between the rights of the university to insist upon non-gender-segregated seating, and the religious freedoms of students to request voluntary gender-segregated seating as an expression of their Muslim identity, caused the advocacy group, Universities UK (UUK) to seek legal advice. UUK eventually published guidance to universities on this issue, which stated, "[I]f neither women nor men were disadvantaged and a non-segregated seating area were also provided, it might in the specific circumstances of the case, be appropriate for the university to agree to the request" (Burns 2013). This non-prescriptive, non-binding guidance was met with student protests and condemnation from politicians on both sides of the political aisle who condemned the guidance as "pandering to extremism" (Weaver, 2013). Despite the complexities involved in this case, the mainstream media and leading politicians in Britain at the time found themselves in alignment with the prominent secularist position of Dawkins, who frequently argues against the influence religion in the public sphere. This level of cultural and political pressure, which included an intervention from the Prime Minister, eventually led UUK to withdraw the guidance pending review.

Pause for thought

Considering the case study and reflecting on the forms of secularism discussed earlier, how might you respond to the following questions:

Should we consider the university campus in Britain to be an exclusively "secularist" space?
Do you think that the legal protection for the freedom of religion can be reconciled with the role of the university to secure gender equality and safe spaces on campus?
Is it possible to design a policy which upholds the freedom of religion and religious expression at the same time as protecting gender equality?
How would you have chosen to handle the case at UCL?

Multiculturalism: Competing conceptualisations

The case study above exemplifies one of the ways in which the needs of religious students may intersect with the perceived cultural norms of the university campus. Within a multicultural legal and social framework, both the right to religious expression and the right to gender equality are enshrined as protected characteristics. Practically, however, at times in which the social demands of religious subjects come into conflict with more traditionally liberal gender values, the demands made on the basis of religion have often been subordinated. This reveals something about the dominance of liberal secular discourse in multicultural society. Systems designed to capture the learner voice are informed by the same politics of multiculturalism. Contentions like the one in the case study highlight competing conceptualisations of inclusivity in multicultural theory. Two such conceptualisations are relevant to this chapter's discussion of religious accommodation.

This first conceptualisation of inclusivity describes what has been touched upon in relation to the "secularist" position: a reading of inclusivity that is predicated on the toleration of religious practices in private spaces but unaccommodating of social demands made based on religion in the public sphere. This type of inclusivity may reject demands for such things as gender-segregated spaces to accommodate religious requirements. Notably, however, the same oppositions are not often raised in relation to other gender-segregated spaces that remain part of contemporary British life (e.g. single sex schools, single sex members clubs, associations, gyms and changing rooms). This inconsistency may be seen to evidence a theoretical opposition, not to the issue of gender segregation itself, but to the social demands of religious subjects. My research indicates that some religious students recognise this inconsistency and perceive the difference in treatment as unjust. The forms of epistemic injustice which result from this may manifest amongst learners in various ways: through learners' perceived inability to voice transgressive opinions related to religion, the felt need to self-silence in order to avoid the statutory reach of policies like Prevent and the belief amongst certain students that they will not be able to effect change within the fixed cultural reality of their educational institutions (Olusola, 2023).

A second conceptualisation of inclusivity within multicultural theory replaces notions of toleration with that of recognition and hospitality (Schilbrack, 2020; Chaplin, 2011). This model approves of religious expression in private and public settings, seeking to accommodate the social demands made on the basis of religion within both realms. This form of inclusivity celebrates the ability of pluralistic societies to listen to the voices of religious citizens as a mark of diversity and equality. For the purposes of our discussion, we will distinguish between these two models of inclusivity by calling the first "inclusion through toleration" and the second "inclusion through accommodation".

While both of these forms of inclusivity are recognisable within multicultural societies (see "Research in Focus"), it may be argued that "inclusion through accommodation" represents a deeper form of pluralism. Applied to the systems and cultures of UK universities, this reading of inclusivity may avoid the epistemic injustices and "locutionary silencing" experienced by some marginalised learners.

Research in focus

The accommodation of religion takes on significantly different forms in various Western liberal democracies. For example, the constitutional notion of secularism in France – Laïcité – is vastly different to secularism in the British context. Similarly, the role of religion in the United States differs in important ways from the role of religion in British and France. The statuses of religiosity and secularity in each of these multicultural societies have important implications for the freedoms that religious citizens enjoy and the ways in which they are included and excluded in those contexts. The following research outputs provide insights into varying ways in which secularism, religious subjectivity and multiculturalism intersect within France, the United Kingdom and the United States:

Jansen, Y. (2013). *Secularism, assimilation and the crisis of multiculturalism: French modernist legacies* (Vol. 63). Amsterdam University Press.

Modood, T., and Ahmad, F. (2007). British Muslim Perspectives on Multiculturalism. *Theory, Culture and Society*, 24(2), 187–213.

Weiner, I. A. (2014). Calling Everyone to Pray: Pluralism, Secularism, and the Adhān in Hamtramck, Michigan. *Anthropological Quarterly*, 87(4), 1049–1077.

Consider what these countries' competing notions of religious accommodation might mean for learner voices in their respective educational settings.

Reimagining learner voice

Broadly speaking, an "inclusion through accommodation" model is espoused by public institutions in the United Kingdom. Nonetheless, differing views about the role of the modern university continue to create tensions related to inclusion and religion. The rather liminal position of UK universities as neither wholly public nor wholly private further complicates the matter. Their dependency on private funding makes them particularly susceptible to marketisation and the neoliberal impulses discussed earlier, which can play a role in excluding non-normative voices. In this regard, Reay (2017) argues that the mechanisms designed to capture the learner voice frequently account for the "neoliberal vocabulary of aspiration, ambition, choice and self-efficacy" while overlooking the priorities and agendas of less enfranchised learners whose concerns centre around things such as colonial injustice, generational social stability and enacting "a project of retrospective healing" (pp. 112–113). This would indicate that part of the solution to the marginalisation and epistemic injustices highlighted in this chapter may be a reimagining of the systems and mechanisms designed to capture learners' voices. This reimagining would emphasise not only the commercialised interests that appeal to the "individualized project of upward mobility" (p. 113) but also the social ambitions and educational concerns that are important to learners on the margins. This would better speak to the role of the modern university as an egalitarian public square which upholds social values like decolonisation, debate, equality, diversity and the democratisation of knowledge. Indeed, there appears to be an increasing appetite amongst modern university learners to see those values embedded in institutional structures (Shain, 2021).

Any conception of the university as an institution that prepares the next generation of citizenry to enter a pluralistic world, must, it seems, be mindful of mechanisms of racialisation and marginalisation. Within reimagined systems, SAR would be configured to hear the voices of a wider range of learners, finding ways to include the agendas and social aspirations of "the other". It may even be argued that these changes embody less of a reimagining and more of a "restoration" of the previous status and reputation of universities as progressive spaces for socio-political activism.

Conclusion

This chapter has addressed limitations in the capacity of SAR systems to capture the voices of more marginalised learners in HE settings. It has examined the interactions between neoliberalism, secularism and multiculturalism and the influences of these structures on the experiences of some Muslim learners. The chapter identifies a tendency for SAR systems to homogenise "the" learner perspective by projecting neoliberal assumptions onto measurements of success and satisfaction. As the introductory vignette indicates, these assumptions can make it difficult for the needs and social demands of some religious subjects to be recognised and accommodated, resulting in forms of epistemic injustice.

Taking account of the growing diversity in British HE settings and the increased appetite amongst the student body to address critical theoretical concerns such as decoloniality, this chapter advocates for a reimagining of learner voice. Furthermore, this chapter argues that in order for public institutions like the university to uphold the values they espouse, they must endeavour to treat the public social demands of religious students in the same way as any other identity group protected under the Equality Act 2010. While it may not always be easy to navigate the legal, cultural and political tensions that exist in public spaces, there appears to be room for more expansive models of inclusivity to take root on the modern university campus.

Summary points

- SAR systems are a commonly evoked conceptualisation of learner voice in the United Kingdom.
- The combined influences of neoliberalism, secularism and multiculturalism within educational settings in the United Kingdom mean that SAR systems tend to privilege particular categories of students.
- Research indicates that the voices of "non-normative" learners are typically marginalised by representation systems like Students Unions.
- The especially political dimensions of being a visible Muslim in contemporary Britain means that some Muslim students experience forms of epistemic injustice.
- While universities espouse models of inclusivity which seek to equally accommodate the protected characteristics in the public realm, work is needed to challenge exclusionary structures.
- Mechanisms designed to capture learner voice must be reimagined to account for the motivations, agendas and concerns of less enfranchised learners whose voices may be excluded.

Recommended reading

Bhandar, B. (2009) The Ties That Bind: Multiculturalism and Secularism Reconsidered. *Journal of Law and Society*, *36*(3), pp. 301–326.

The article expands this chapter's disscission about the differences and similarities in the ways secularism and multiculturalism govern difference, particularly as it relates to religion.

Lowe, T., and El Hakim, Y. (Eds.) (2020) *A handbook for student engagement in higher education: Theory and practice*. Abingdon: Routledge.

This book provides insight into the role student engagement systems can play in the successes of students, bringing into sharper relief the impact of marginalisation that this chapter describes.

For an extended discussion on the plurality of secular perspectives, see the following book:

Berg-Sørensen, A. (2013) *Contesting secularism: comparative perspectives*. 1st ed. Surrey: Ashgate.

References

Andersson, J., Sadgrove, J., and Valentine, G. (2012) Consuming campus: geographies of encounter at a British university. *Social and Cultural Geography*, 13(5), pp. 501–515.

Asad, T., Brown, W., Butler, J., and Mahmood, S. (2013) *Is Critique Secular?: Blasphemy, Injury, and Free Speech*. New York: Fordham University Press. Available at: https://escholarship.org/uc/item/84q9c6ft (Accessed 20 July 2024).

Batty, D. (2013) UCL bans Islamic group from campus in row over segregated seating. *The Guardian*, 15 March 2013, sec. World news. Available at: https://www.theguardian.com/world/2013/mar/15/ucl-bans-islamic-group-over-segregation. (Accessed 25 July 2024).

Bols, A. (2020) The changing nature and importance of student representation. In T. Lowe and Y. El Hakim (Eds) *A handbook for student engagement in higher education: Theory and practice*. Abingdon: Routledge.

Burns, J. (2013, December 12) University segregation advice may need court ruling. *BBC News*. Available at: https://www.bbc.co.uk/news/education-25353882 (Accessed July 20 2024).

Busher, J., and Jerome, L. (2020) *The Prevent Duty in Education: Impact, Enactment and Implications*. Cham: Springer International Publishing AG.

Cambridge Dictionary. (n.d.) Epistemic. In dictionary.cambridge.org. Available at: https://dictionary.cambridge.org/dictionary/english/epistemic# (Accessed July 25 2024).

Chambers, S. (2010) Secularism Minus Exclusion: Developing a Religious-Friendly Idea of Public Reason. *The Good Society*, 19(2), pp. 16–21. Available at: https://doi.org/10.5325/goodsociety.19.2.0016 (Accessed 25 July 2024).

Chaplin, J. (2011) *Multiculturalism: A Christian Revival*. London: Theos.

Cook-Sather, A. (2002) Authorizing Students' Perspectives: Toward trust, dialogue, and change in education. *Educational Researcher*, 31(4), pp. 3–14. Available at: https://doi.org/10.3102/0013189X031004003 (Accessed 15 June 2024).

Freeman, R. (2016) Is Student Voice Necessarily Empowering? Problematising student voice as a form of higher education governance. *Higher Education Research and Development*, 35(4), pp. 859–862. Available at: https://doi.org/10.1080/07294360.2016.1172764 (Accessed 26 July 2024).

Fricker, M. (2007) *Epistemic Injustice: Power and the ethics of knowing*. Oxford: Oxford University Press.

Gandin, L. A., and Apple, M. W. (2002) Can Education Challenge Neo-Liberalism? The Citizen School and the Struggle for Democracy in Porto Alegre, Brazil. *Social Justice*, 29(4), pp. 26–40. Available at: https://www.jstor.org/stable/29768145 (Accessed 25 July 2024).

Habermas, J. (2008) Notes on a Post-Secular Society. Signandsight.com. Available at: https://www.signandsight.com/features/1714.html (Accessed 02 October 2023).

HM Government (HMG). (2021) *Statutory guidance: Revised Prevent duty guidance: for England and Wales*. London: HM Government.

Langton, R. (1993) Speech Acts and Unspeakable Acts. *Philosophy and Public Affairs*, 22(4), pp. 293–330.

Marquis, E., Jayaratnam, A., Mishra, A. and Rybkina, K. (2018) 'I feel like some students are better connected': Students' perspectives on applying for extracurricular partnership opportunities, *International Journal for Students as Partners*, 2(1), pp. 64–81. Available at: doi: https://doi.org/10.15173/ijsap.v2i1.3300 (Accessed 19 July 2024).

Mercer-Mapstone, L., Islam, M. and Reid, T. (2021) Are We Just Engaging 'the usual suspects'? Challenges in and practical strategies for supporting equity and diversity in student–staff partnership initiatives, *Teaching in Higher Education*, 26(2), pp. 227–245.

Miah, S. (2017) *Muslims, Schooling and Security - Trojan Horse, Prevent and Racial Politics*. London: Palgrave Macmillan, Springer.

Modood, T. (2013) Muslims, religious equality and secularism. In A. Berg-Sørensen (Ed), *Contesting secularism*. Surry: Ashgate.

Office for Students (OfS). (2022) Equality, diversity and student characteristics data (OfS 2022.29). Available at: https://www.officeforstudents.org.uk/media/7137/ofs2022_29.pdf (Accessed 26 July 2024).

Olusola, J. O. A. (2023) Muslim converts as a heuristic device for postsecular thinking: agonism as an alternative approach. *Journal of Religious Education*, 71(3), pp. 297–313.

Olusola, J. (2024) *A Critical Exploration of British Millennial Muslim Converts' Identities, Conversion Narratives and Educational Experiences* [Unpublished doctoral thesis]. University of Worcester.

Quality Assurance Agency (QAA). (2018) UK Quality Code for Higher Education, Advice and Guidance: Student Engagement. *UK Standing Committee for Quality Assessment*. Online. Available at: https://www.qaa.ac.uk/docs/qaa/quality-code/advice-and-guidance-student-engagement.pdf?sfvrsn=6224c181_3 (Accessed 26 July 2024).

Reay, D. (2017) *Miseducation: Inequality, Education and the Working Classes*. Bristol: Policy Press.

Revell, L. (2012) *Islam and Education: The manipulation and misrepresentation of a religion*. London: Trentham Books.

Revell, L., and Bryan, H. (2018) *Fundamental British Values in Education: Radicalisation, National Identity and Britishness*. Bingley: Emerald Publishing Limited.

Schilbrack, K. (2020) Hospitality and the ethics of religious diversity. *Religious Studies*, 56(1), pp. 64–79. Available at: https://doi.org/10.1017/S0034412519000209 (Accessed 18 July 2024).

Sealy, T. K. (2021) *Religiosity and Recognition: Multiculturalism and British Converts to Islam*. Cham: Palgrave Macmillan.

Shain, F. (2021) Navigating the unequal education space in post-9/11 England: British Muslim girls talk about their educational aspirations and future expectations. *Educational Philosophy and Theory*, 53(3), pp. 270–287.

Stevenson, J., Demack, S., Stiell, B., Abdi, M., Clarkson, L., Ghaffar, F., and Hassan, S. (2017) The Social Mobility Challenges Faced by Young Muslims. *Social Mobility Commission*. Available at: https://assets.publishing.service.gov.uk/government/uploads/system/uploads/attachment_data/file/642220/Young_Muslims_SMC.pdf (Accessed 05 October 2023).

Tight, M. (2013) Students: Customers, clients or pawns? *Higher Education Policy*, 26(3), pp. 291–307. Available at: https://doi.org/10.1057/hep.2013.2 (Accessed 15 July 2024).

Weaver, M. (2013 December 13) Michael Gove: university gender segregation is 'pandering to extremism'. *The Guardian*. Available at: https://www.theguardian.com/politics/2013/dec/13/michael-gove-university-gender-segregation (Accessed 25 July 2024).

Winter, J., Turner, R., Webb, O., Valle, L. D., and Benwell, C. (2024) Student academic representation in the UK: An exploration of recruitment, training, and impacts. *Higher Education Quarterly*, 00, e12548. Available at: https://doi.org/10.1111/hequ.12548 (Accessed 25 July 2024).

Zempi, I., and Tripli, A. (2023) Listening to Muslim Students' Voices on the Prevent Duty in British Universities: A Qualitative Study. *Education, Citizenship and Social Justice*, 18(2), pp. 230–245.

9 From voice and systemic action

Addressing race and racism in a teacher education programme

Elena Lengthorn, Rebecca Davidge and Rachael Moore

The authors of this chapter, in their exploration of issues of racism in teacher education, have chosen to use Campbell-Stephens' (2020) expression of "Global Majority" as a collective term for Black, Asian, Brown, dual-heritage, those indigenous to the global south and/or those who have been racialised as "ethnic minorities". Campbell-Stephens coined the phrase as a result of her work in developing school leadership and suggests it is a phrase that speaks to and encourages a sense of belonging to the Global Majority, with the aforementioned groups constituting 80 per cent of the world's population.

Vignette 1

This is an anonymous monograph to protect the contributing student teacher and the placement school. The contributor was a career changer who was training to be a secondary school teacher via the Post Graduate Certificate of Education (PGCE) route, an intensive nine-month programme.

> When I applied for my PGCE at university I had never thought about being a Black teacher. My aim was to inspire children and teach a subject that I love. For about two weeks I was living in bliss being at university, meeting new people and getting to know my subject.
>
> This euphoria ended almost immediately as soon as I began my first school placement. In the department, I was the only Black and gay person, and almost straightaway I was treated as "other". I tried to integrate, but it was a difficult battle, and every day, I felt I struggled to fit in.
>
> In the entire school, including pupils, sixth form and staff, there were four Black people including me. I felt like an alien and an outcast, both in and out of the classroom. The lesson plans did not show any representation other than White people. In RE lessons, Jesus and God were embodied as White figures and depicted as "good and clean".
>
> I observed lessons about extremism and terrorism: they consisted of Islamists or far-right groups' views of Islamophobia. The lesson included the aftermath of a Black Muslim who killed a White soldier.
>
> When I questioned some of the material used in the lesson plans, such as not having a picture of a Black Jesus, I was met with *"I do not like you changing the lessons because you'll get it wrong"*.

> At my first placement I felt physically sick with nerves; I was not sleeping and dreaded every day. I cried all the time because I did not blend in, I had nobody to relate to, and many of the staff and students showed me I was not welcome with microaggressions, stereotypical generalisations and disrespectful comments.

This student teacher shared her experiences and concerns with the university and was subsequently withdrawn from the placement. The student successfully, and happily, completed the rest of the course in supportive partnership schools. They are now an established and respected teacher in a school in the West Midlands where they feel their Black identity is celebrated.

Aisha Thomas (2022) argues that representation in education is crucial and reminds us that many young Global Majority children are surrounded by White people in power. Educators need to understand what representation means to them (Thomas, 2022: 3), before attempting to make changes in the classroom. Inspired by Du Bois' theory of double consciousness (1903, cited by Thomas 2022: 3), which argued that women see themselves through a gender and race lens, Thomas (2022) encourages educators to consider a triple consciousness approach. We have three aspects of ourselves to reflect on:

1. The person you are at home.
2. The person you are at work.
3. The person you are expected to be in education.

In taking time to think about our own identity, we can authentically begin to journey towards inclusive and anti-racist practices in school, and this will positively impact the lives of the young people we encounter. The student teacher in this vignette had not considered what being a Global Majority teacher might mean to them, in the classroom, prior to their training. Their experiences, outlined in Vignette 1, led to significant reflection amongst the staff in our teacher training programme. Through a prolonged time of contemplation, training and discussion, influenced by this student's experiences, the "Commonwealth Awareness Initiative" (CAI) – a collaborative staff and student project to explore the Commonwealth and racism in Secondary Education, transformed our colleagues both personally and professionally.

Introduction

The CAI innovation was born out of reflection, initially by the humanities tutors from the University of Worcester Institute of Education PGCE Secondary team, of our educational responsibility following the murder of George Floyd and the subsequent community and global prominent re-emergence of the Black Lives Matter (BLM) movement. Embryonic plans were galvanised following a freedom of information (FoI) request that asked a number of our PGCE colleagues to report on the anti-racist content of their courses. This led the humanities team to explore their own professional development and complete the Bristol University "Decolonising Education: From Theory to Practice" Continuing Professional Development (CPD) course (https://www.futurelearn.com/courses/decolonising-education-from-theory-to-practice).

This learning, alongside our awareness of a re-energised national focus on racial discrimination in education (Stewart-Hall, 2021; NASUWT, 2021), galvanised our early motivation to extend and open the invitation to develop professionally to the entire PGCE secondary staff team. A timely approach was made to department leaders requesting an opportunity to engage all secondary subject colleagues, initially through allocated time in a team meeting with the key concepts of decolonisation, democratising and diversifying. This proposition was well received and expanded into the development of a series of three CPD workshops on these critical themes that PGCE colleagues could opt into:

Workshop 1: An introduction to decolonisation (March 2021)
Workshop 2: The concepts of White privilege and allyship (May 2021)
Workshop 3: Commonwealth explained (October 2021)

These optional CPD sessions were well attended, enabling colleagues to engage with current research (Diangelo, 2018; Rabiger, 2020; Rabinger, 2021), scholarship and in undertaking an individual and collective evaluation of their own subject-based experiences and practices.

The sessions were also offered as a support mechanism to engage PGCE subject leaders in extending their scholarly activity into writing through a peer-supported and accessible process, to develop work on these themes (decolonising, democratising and diversifying) with their student teachers and in-service school mentors. Their work in this area would be published in a magazine to be shared with local schools, in time to support them in exploring these crucial topics in advance of the Commonwealth Games (the summer of 2022).

The project was underpinned through the exploration of the inspirational text *Empireland*, by Satnam Sanghera, by members of the PGCE team (Sanghera, 2021). This invaluable stimulus material was incorporated into the CPD (either to be read or engaged with via the Channel 4 series "Empire State of Mind"). Connecting with *Empireland* enabled them, a group of educated, White middle-class, tutors to come face-to-face with and acknowledge their uninformed pre-conceptions of Empire. Colleagues reflected that they were confronted with how little they actually knew. The book took them on a learning journey which included a clearer understanding of the past, present and possible future impacts of the British Empire, as well as its potential evolution and legacy in the form of the Commonwealth.

The design of the CAI, in spacing the workshops across two academic terms meant, helpfully, that our reflections continued over many months and stimulated rich discussions on the history of the Commonwealth, White privilege, the role of allyship, our perspectives on the world and our responses to inequality and injustice. Our responsibilities as teacher educators to support student teachers and in-service colleagues in exploring these topics was clear.

CPD attending colleagues were encouraged to consider their next steps in building on these experiences and made visible commitments, in a shared online space, pledging responses from further reading to curriculum change and changes in practice with regard to their use of language and pedagogical approaches. All of the subject-specific lesson activities and resources that were created were made available, via the magazine, through a series of QR codes, supporting all our partnership schools (and beyond) with teaching about the Commonwealth in the lead-up to the Commonwealth Games. The magazine can be accessed here: https://www.worcester.ac.uk/documents/UWPGSEC-Commonwealth-Edition.pdf.

Methods and methodology

This CAI involved three distinct development sessions for colleagues focusing on (i) the Commonwealth, (ii) educator identity in relation to our own subject area and lived experiences and (iii) the development of practical resources to reflect a transformed curriculum. These development sessions involved 12 self-selected participants, staff from the Secondary Education team, for these voluntary opportunities. It was decided that doing anonymous online questionnaires with as many of the participants as possible would provide valuable data to help us address the aims of the project – namely, the success of the community of practice in bringing about systemic change, and the extent to which the development sessions gave confidence to the participants to develop a more diverse curriculum.

Semi-structured interviews were conducted with fewer participants as we aimed for more depth and richer data, with five participants providing detailed responses. The outcomes of this process led to current and future teachers (student teachers) being able to adapt their curriculum to teach about Commonwealth and antiracism, diversity and representation in their own classrooms and communities. The student teachers also had an increased knowledge and confidence in taking these vital issues into their own ways of working.

We chose to use an interpretivist paradigm, as we believed this methodological viewpoint to be the most suitable to our research focus rather than using a positivist paradigm. This is because an interpretivist approach recognises that human experience is not a fixed structure and is given meaning by the individuals themselves (Denscombe, 2014; Lowing, 2011). We were concerned with our participants' experiences and took a constructivist approach, as we saw our understanding of decolonising was constructed through our interactions (Hamilton and Corbett-Whittier, 2013).

The methodology we chose was phenomenological, as defined by Creely (2016), as understanding participants from the inside, because we interviewed PGCE tutors who were members of our own department. There are pros and cons of exploring an insider perspective, and we acknowledged the potential conflicts of interest involved in applying insider approaches (Cohen, Manion and Morrison, 2007). We recognised that there was a potential issue of authenticity regarding the truthfulness of participants' responses, as they may seek to give what they perceive is the right answer. But as the team had been working together on decolonising the curriculum for several months, we established an environment of trust and practised authentic conversations. However, being inside also afforded benefits for participant and researcher such as there was no power play. The researchers were not line managers and there was a democratised structure of participants. As such, relationships were based on long term interdependence, professionalism and confidence.

We drew on the work of Fairclough (1995) and Mullet (2018) to provide a framework in interpreting the data our colleagues had provided. Critical discourse analysis (CDA) provided a structure for discussing power relations, injustice and inequality (Mullet, 2018). This approach was most appropriate when interpreting colleagues' reflections on decolonising their curriculum as "CDA is a useful approach for educational researchers who explore connections between educational practices and social contexts" (p. 117). Mullet observes that CDA procedures give opportunity for interpretation of these social contexts which aligned with the aims of our project. Fairclough's (1995) method of discourse analysis consists of three features which we found helpful in framing the process of our interpretation of the data. He described these dimensions of discourse analysis as (1) description (text analysis), (2) interpretation (processing analysis) and (3) explanation (social analysis). Researcher analysis of the interview transcripts defined the responses of the contributors in order to explore the process by means of which the interview responses were produced: e.g., how the interviews were delivered. Finally, a social analysis provided the socio-historic (situational, institutional, societal) conditions that govern the lens on life (Fairclough, 1995: 97–98).

Participants' personal and professional reflections

Our colleagues were impacted in different ways and to different degrees by taking part in this project. Their collective experience of engaging in a journey of deeper understanding of the challenges staff and pupils face in schools with regards to racism are, however, shared. The personal impact was varied, and this was evidenced through the degree to which both their attitude and actions were affected. The impact of this project, on transforming practice, varied because our colleagues began the process from different starting points due to their personal and professional interests and experiences. As educators, the authors and participants are well versed in the importance of inclusivity and acceptance of difference. However, this project also shone a light on the significance of the need for a deeper understanding of the inherent racism and "othering" that can occur when decolonisation and an anti-racist approach is neglected. Colleagues acknowledged that prior to this project, they had not really understood the history surrounding Britain's involvement in the transatlantic slave trade, the experience of the Global Majority in Britain and the legacy that this has had on the multicultural nation that we have become today. This legacy continues to affect the experiences of both the student teachers, staff and pupils of our partnership schools. One colleague explained that they were only able to begin this journey of deep reflection once they were honest about their lack of understanding and their own naivety:

"I was able to be honest and not pretend about what I understood about racism and diversity".

This acknowledgement enables an openness which is essential in the transformation of action. This naivety was echoed in the shared recognition of a lack of confidence when discussing and teaching student teachers about decolonisation and an anti-racist curriculum. Colleagues shared with us their anxieties surrounding the use of appropriate language, terms and content, which often lead to hesitancy in developing their curriculums. The project enabled our colleagues to share their anxieties in a *"safe-space"* and in turn allowed them to develop a confidence when discussing issues of racism and decolonisation with their student teachers and beyond. Most powerfully, the project led to colleagues *"seeing the world differently"*, seeing differences and acknowledging the power and privilege that we have as not only educators but also individuals.

The initiative also created an opportunity for colleagues to reflect on their curriculum approaches to decolonisation and anti-racist education. The sessions highlighted to them that more time and space was required in order to fully explore the issues that arose during the initiative. It was acknowledged by our colleagues that through our work with our student teachers, we had the potential to impact many hundreds of staff and students in schools. This awareness of our privileged position added weight to the importance of our staff's confidence in their inclusive and representative curriculums. Colleagues reflected that, historically, issues surrounding racism, race, and prejudice had been included in their curriculums, but the breadth and depth of this varied between subjects.

Colleagues acknowledged that there was an inconsistency of approach and that this was largely down to the confidence and understanding of the individual. The sessions delivered through the CAI enabled participants to enhance their provision through their increased understanding of the needs of the curriculum to provide a thorough exploration of an anti-racist approach, leading one colleague to teach this conclusion:

> "As an educator, it has changed my mindset about the purpose of curriculum and the aim of education".

This is not to say that some educators had not already undertaken the development of their curriculums and addressing inequalities and racism prior to the project. However, it did encourage a *"reframing"* of how to approach certain aspects for some. It is not true to say that, for all, their identity as a teacher educator changed dramatically, but it has confirmed and given time and permission to talk more about an anti-racist curriculum. One of the key developments of this project was that it encouraged the team to give more time to focus on decolonisation and antiracism in their sessions. One colleague reflected on how discussions surrounding race were rich, and there was an openness regarding interactions and communications as a result with Global Majority trainees which had not happened prior to this initiative. This reflected the increased confidence of our colleagues to lead and encourage an in-depth and open discussion about race within their teaching.

An area of the curriculum that has been directly impacted by the initiative is within the professional studies course, the backbone of the PGCE programme, and delivered to trainees in all subjects. Diversity has been included in the curriculum for the last seven years and has continually evolved and developed as a result of the changing needs of the pupils in our partnership schools. However, this has not always been a curriculum that has been well received by all student teachers, with comments about the course not being truly representative or inclusive in terms of diversity. Following on from the initiative and the curriculum developments made in regard to decolonisation and antiracism, the programme is now more inclusive and representative of the trainees, staff and pupils in partnership schools. A leading tutor for professional studies reflected,

> "We have to keep adding to the narrative and it has to keep developing. We will include decolonising and be aware of diversifying in every session we do".

This continual development and reflection being an outcome of increased awareness of colleagues that curriculum changes are essential when considering a truly inclusive curriculum.

The CAI project was led by staff who had all been through a system British schooling but had also taught within British schools for many years. Our colleagues, however, had many different personal backgrounds and experiences, which meant that they approached the project with varying degrees of understanding and with different perspectives. As White middle-class educators working in a predominately White demographic, we were very aware of the importance of reflecting on our own privilege and experiences whilst embarking on this project.

> "As a White woman we don't understand the challenges we make assumptions about students all the time".

These reflections confirmed the importance of raising the prominence of antiracism and decolonisation in transforming our curriculum. When interviewing our colleagues, it was evident that personal lived experiences formed the basis of their approach to the writing of their articles and resources. There was an awareness that we are all products of society and, therefore, our perspectives were shaped by the impact of socio-historic environments. Colleagues spoke freely about their own personal situations and how these had shaped their thinking about creating an anti-racist curriculum. Colleagues who would identify as having a protected characteristic found the project to be an opportunity to reflect on their own experiences of being a minority and therefore mused that they were "*more likely to see other peoples' differences perhaps*". This gave them increased confidence in the approach that they were taking with redeveloping their curriculums.

Pause for reflection

There are questions provided, beneath the vignette, to prompt reflection.

Vignette 2

Sharing a lived experience: an anonymous contribution to protect a student teacher and placement school.

My experience of being a Black educator

The Black teacher experience is multifaceted. I feel that I am required, inadvertently, to challenge any injustices that relate to identity or ethnicity. Despite this, I also feel that I am a symbol of hope for students who are in the minority. By working in school, I give them a voice because I am present, and my voice is heard.

I have experienced moments of unease, also known as microaggressions. Often, this has had an undertone of unchallenged unconscious bias from the aggressor. But I think this is due to their curiosity. Through my assimilation, these experiences have become rarer. I do question, though, why must I assimilate? I have reflected and would answer – to build a channel for better dialogue.

A recent experience expresses this: after a lesson featuring the film *The Help*, students approached me outraged that a teacher would say the "N" word. I knew that they meant well by telling me, but I started thinking *I wasn't there; why didn't they challenge it? Why was it my duty to do something about this?*

I found myself mediating between the teacher and the pupils because I am the Black representative. Situations like this are awkward. I spoke to the colleague in question about what had happened. They apologised and gave a context. We discussed steps to approach the next lesson. We agreed the battle wasn't between us but between the polarised views students could develop about a White teacher and a Black teacher.

The toughest struggle of being a Black educator for me is managing how best to impact and influence the school community whilst keeping my authentic, unique Black identity.

Self-reflection questions

1. Whose responsibility is it to tackle racist incidents in schools?
2. How can schools best address systemic racism?
3. At what point should children be taught about racial literacy, if at all?
4. How does it feel to you to reflect on the differences between the experiences of White or Global Majority teachers?
5. Do you think truly anti-racist education is achievable?
6. What training do you think teachers would need in order to embed anti-racist education in schools?

Conclusion

The CAI project was motivated by a combination of social and cultural events and, most significantly, in response to student voice of a racist lived experience of student teachers. The model of triple consciousness by Thomas (2022) helped frame the approach to exploring antiracism and decolonisation through personal, professional and educational aspects. Knowing about the racist experiences of our student teachers allowed us to activate a process of exploration, learning, reflection and adaptation of our approaches to decolonising our teacher education curriculum. Data from participants revealed they responded by increasing representation and diversity in their curriculum planning, and continue to explore the impact of colonisation on what they teach beginning teachers. In some cases, this work has been transformational:

> For us, as a team, it's [CAI] been like a therapy. We've had some difficult conversations and some hard-hitting sessions, but there's been a supportive place to go. I've never reflected as well on how I see people before. I feel like I'm on a journey. My identity as an educator has fundamentally changed, and now I don't look at people the same. I have a deeper connection with people.

This chapter revealed how a student found their voice to share their experience of racism which led to the impact on staff's ability to learn. It explored how the staff were learners who, through reflexivity, responded to the student's voice. Staff learnt to adapt curriculum planning to increase representation, diversity and to explore the impact of colonisation on what is taught. The staff learning journey was analysed, and the impact on wider student learning experience was explored.

In moving forward and planning next steps, we have been influenced by the Ethical Global Issues Pedagogy Framework, developed by Pashby and Sund (2019). This framework is positioned as an acronym – HEADSUP – that serve as reminders and prompts:

- Hegemony – Justifying superiority and supporting domination which can be unseen
- Ethnocentrism – Projecting one view as universal and unknowingly being limited by one's worldview
- Ahistoricism – Forgetting historical legacies and complicities
- Depoliticization – Disregarding power inequalities and ideological roots of analyses and proposals Salvationism Framing help as the burden of the fittest
- Uncomplicated – Solutions Offering easy and simple solutions that do not require systemic change

- Paternalism – Seeking affirmation of authority/superiority through the provision of help and the infantilisation of recipients, including putting young people in the Global North in the position to solve the problems of others.

In light of this, we think it would be pertinent for Initial Teacher Education (ITE) providers, beyond transformations to their curriculum, to explore the antiracism practices and policies in their partnership schools, exploring how they are disseminated and monitored. ITE providers need to consider how they can ensure that there are fundamental changes to how they work to ensure an anti-racist approach is embedded throughout their practice, approaches, and understanding of a truly inclusive experience for all.

The authors would like to thank the participants for sharing their transformational experiences through the CAI project, as well as the authentic vignette contributions from trainee teachers that influenced our curriculum redevelopment.

Summary points

- The chapter discusses how a student's experience of racism led to significant changes in a teacher education programme, emphasising the importance of reflexivity among staff to adapt curriculum planning to increase representation and diversity.
- The authors use the term "Global Majority" to refer to Black, Asian, Brown, dual-heritage and indigenous people, highlighting the need for a sense of belonging and representation in education.
- The chapter details the CAI, which included workshops on decolonisation, White privilege, and allyship, aimed at transforming the curriculum and increasing staff confidence in addressing racism and diversity.
- The initiative encouraged staff to reflect on their own identities and privileges, leading to a deeper understanding of the historical and ongoing impacts of racism and colonisation on education.
- The chapter concludes with the importance of continuous development and reflection in creating an inclusive and anti-racist curriculum, emphasising the need for systemic change in teacher education programmes to support diverse learners effectively.

Further reading

These particular publications were seminal in our understanding and framing of transforming our curriculums, especially in discussions around appropriate language and tacking these issues in a largely White domain space.

Thomas, A. (2022) Representation matters: Becoming an anti-racist educator. London: Bloomsbury.

This book is written to provide a framework for those working in education to help reconsider representation and what this might mean for staff and students. Thomas's (a former teacher) work contains many personal encounters, experiences and perspectives. It includes reflections on diversifying the curriculum, how to challenge racism, interpreting the Equality Act 2010 and consideration of what language to use when talking about race. In the first section of her book, Thomas asks us to reflect and review. She argues the first step to increasing representation is to reflect on our own core beliefs and values, and what has influenced us through our lives. The second section is encouraging the reader to listen to a range of voices represented in education, such as young people, staff, parents and carers, and to decentre from a White lens of education. The last section of the book helps the reader to create an action plan – strategies to move forward in creating anti-racist education in your own context. These include considering legal frameworks, challenging overt and covert racism and decolonising curriculums.

Sanghera, S. (2021) Empireland: How imperialism has shaped modern Britain. London: Viking.

This book challenges readers to see imperialism not only as a legacy of past times and its dark history but also as an explanation for why Britain looks like it does in the modern era. Sanghera is a journalist and writer born in Wolverhampton to Punjabi immigrant parents. His heritage, childhood and upbringing provide a fascinating, and at times humorous, look at the British Empire. He reveals a contradiction and tension felt by many Brits – why an empire that dominated a large area of the world is often overlooked on schools' curriculums. When being British is a cause for proud identity for some and a shameful legacy for others, Sanghera's book encourages us to look carefully at our history and see how modern Britain emerged in order that we can understand who we are and what unites us.

Diangelo, R. (2019) White fragility: Why it's so hard to talk to white people about race. Boston, MA: Beacon Press.

Diangelo can easily make a White reader quickly uncomfortable, but she presents these awkward truths to demonstrate that racism is not confined to "bad people"; on the contrary, she illuminates the ways White people intentionally, or unintentionally, cause racial hurt and offence. Diangelo reveals in the book that the notion of "White fragility" (a term she coined in 2011) serves to uphold the system of White supremacy. Persevering with these feelings of unease though will allow the reader to start having honest conversations, listen to each other and begin to respond with more humility and authenticity. We are encouraged to see the truth – that it is time for all White people to take responsibility for renouncing White supremacy.

References

Campbell-Stephens, R. (2020) *Global Majority; Decolonising the language and Reframing the Conversation about Race*. Leeds Beckett University. Available online: https://www.leedsbeckett.ac.uk/-/media/files/schools/school-of-education/final-leeds-beckett-1102-global-majority.pdf (Accessed: 2 August 2023).
Cohen, L., Manion, L. and Morrison, K. (2007) Research Methods in Education. Available at https://gtu.ge/Agro-Lib/RESEARCH%20METHOD%20COHEN%20ok.pdf. (Accessed: 2 December, 2021).
Creely, E. (2016) 'Understanding things from within'. A Husserlian phenomenological approach to doing educational research and inquiring about learning. *International Journal of Research & Method in Education*, 13(1) pp. 1–19. Available at: https://doi.org/10.1080/1743727X.2016.1182482?journalCode=cwse20. (Accessed 2 December, 2021).
Denscombe, M. (2014) *The good research guide: For small scale research projects*. Maidenhead: Open University Press.
Diangelo, R. (2018) *White Fragility*. Boston, MA: Beacon Press.
Fairclough, N. (1995) *Critical discourse analysis: the critical study of Language*. London: Routledge.
Hamilton, L. and Corbett-Whittier, C. (2013) *Using Case Study in Education Research*. London: Sage Publications.
Lowing, K. (2011) Educational research and enquiry: qualitative and quantitative approaches. *British Journal of Educational Studies*. 59(3), pp. 350–351.
Mullet, D. R. (2018) A General Critical Discourse Analysis Framework for Educational Research. *Journal of Advanced Academics*, 29(2), pp. 116–142.
NASUWT (2021) "Leading the Change for Black Teachers." *Teaching Today. NASUWT Members Magazine*. London: NASUWT.
Pashby, K. and Sund, L. (2019) Teaching for sustainable development through ethical global issues pedagogy: A resource for secondary teachers. Available at: https://www.mmu.ac.uk/sites/default/files/2023-02/Ethical-Global-Issues-English.pdf (Accessed 7 August 2023).
Rabiger, P. (2020) Why I am talking to white people about race. Available at: https://tenpencemore.wordpress.com/2020/02/01/why-i-am-talking-to-white-people-about-race/amp/?__twitter_impression=true (Accessed 2 August 2023).

Rabinger, P. (2021) The white ally and the fight for racial justice. Available at: https://tenpencemore.wordpress.com/2021/02/27/the-white-ally-and-the-fight-for-racial-justice/ (Accessed 2 August 2023).

Sanghera, S. (2021) *Empireland: How Imperialism has shaped modern Britain.* London: Viking.

Stewart-Hall, C. (2021) Why white teachers must learn to talk about race in schools: The problem unpacked. Available at https://equitablecoaching.com/why-white-teachers-must-learn-to-talk-about-race-in-schools-the-problem-unpacked/ (Accessed 3 August 2023).

Thomas, A. (2022) *Representation Matters: Becoming an anti-racist educator.* London: Bloomsbury.

10 Learner voice and the placement experience

Engineering a map of prison-education interactions

Emily Davis and Simon Taylor

> **Vignette**
>
> I feel it is fundamental to note that as my placement progressed, I experienced a shift in how I approached and processed the discussions and observations I had in this context. This reorientation was inspired by observing the ways in which the education and prison systems intersected, and is noteworthy because it greatly informed the themes discussed in this summary.
>
> I have come to understand that approaching this placement experience with the question "What is prison education?" gave limited scope to discuss much beyond descriptive answers of what education contractors and government policy aim to deliver, and in doing so downplayed the interaction between education and the prison context. By asking instead "How is education delivered in a prison context?" We bring this relationship between Prison and Education to the fore, and the discussion is now opened up to larger philosophical and political questions, including how the purpose and practices of a "total institution" affect the way education is delivered by teachers and experienced by learners. (Reflective Journal) (Davis, 2022: 1)

Within education studies, perhaps uniquely for education-based courses, students explore the foundation subjects of sociology, psychology, history and the philosophy of education plus the development of critical thinking skills. A central thread of social justice runs throughout everything the staff and students do, and we adopt a questioning approach as we explore the impact of policy and ideology on different contexts for learning. This is all excellent preparation for the work experience placement element of the course. The approach has built-in flexibility for students (and staff) to try new things and pursue their own interests, whether they be working in alternative provision or with vulnerable or excluded learners. The following analysis was developed by the student through observations, reflective questions and the freedom to interact with learners in different ways.

Introduction

This chapter takes an ecological view of the prison-education context to explore how egalitarian and humanising educational experiences might be best achieved within the complex microcosm of

DOI: 10.4324/9781003406334-10

competing prison and education philosophies and practices. From this relationship focused perspective, we re-envisage the prison teacher role as a "pedagogue of process" (Freire, 2005) who engineers educational experiences using the pre-existing infrastructure of prison-education interactions, such as those between peers.

Chapter context: Trade-off to pay-off

In order to gain access to the prison and the people within in it, I anticipated having to engage with the prison's values and practices. To do so, I assumed, I would have to leave at the door my own beliefs in the egalitarian and humanising purpose of education, and the values that underpin them. I perceived this as a trade-off: values for access, a sentiment commonly expressed by prison educators (Ginsberg, 2019: Wilson and Reuss 2000: 2012: Davidson, 1995) and best epitomised by Peterson (2019: 181) when she laments,

> [I]n order to maintain the fragile relationships that allow us to continue this unprecedented program...to offer whatever transformation it may bring to those who are incarcerated, I must keep my critique to myself, follow the rules.

I realised, however, this was not a trade-off at all. Being granted the privilege of entering the prison context meant I was able to engage with and learn from the people inside. The pay-off for suspending my own ideals were the lessons learnt and subsequently explored in this chapter. In doing so, I heed the words of philosopher Jiddu Krishnamurti (1976) that "learning is the very essence of humility" (no page) and embraced this revelation as an example of Davis and Michael's (2016) call for academia to "get over ourselves" (p. 147) and to learn from and support those on the inside.

> It was my belief that the delivery of egalitarian and humanising education would be marred by the teaching staff's obligation to practice within the parameters of the prison's values and practices. Such a belief rests on the assumption that the sole bearers of this type of education were the education staff themselves. Positioning the teacher like this makes them the gatekeepers of one type of education or another, the type depending solely on the teacher's ability to maintain and balance prison relationships. This perspective, viewed through an oversimplified and polarised frame of the prison-education context, renders the potential for egalitarian and humanising education severely limited, causing us to seek a more creative and nuanced understanding of this environment. (Student Reflective Vignette)
>
> (Davis, 2023: 1)

In an attempt to develop this creative and nuanced understanding, we turn to Neal and Neal's (2013) reconceptualisation of Bronfenbrenner's (1977) ecologies of human development (See Figures 10.1 and 10.2). This framework is useful because it provides a visual map of the prison-education context. It depicts prison and education as two separate yet overlapping contexts, showing the overlapping boundaries of each, and with it the intersecting structure and staff inter-relationships between the two. As a result, one is able to trace the directional flow of philosophical and political agendas across this overlap and through these structure and staff interactions. It provides a road map of interactions, if you will. A cacophony of different agendas, values, priorities and practices

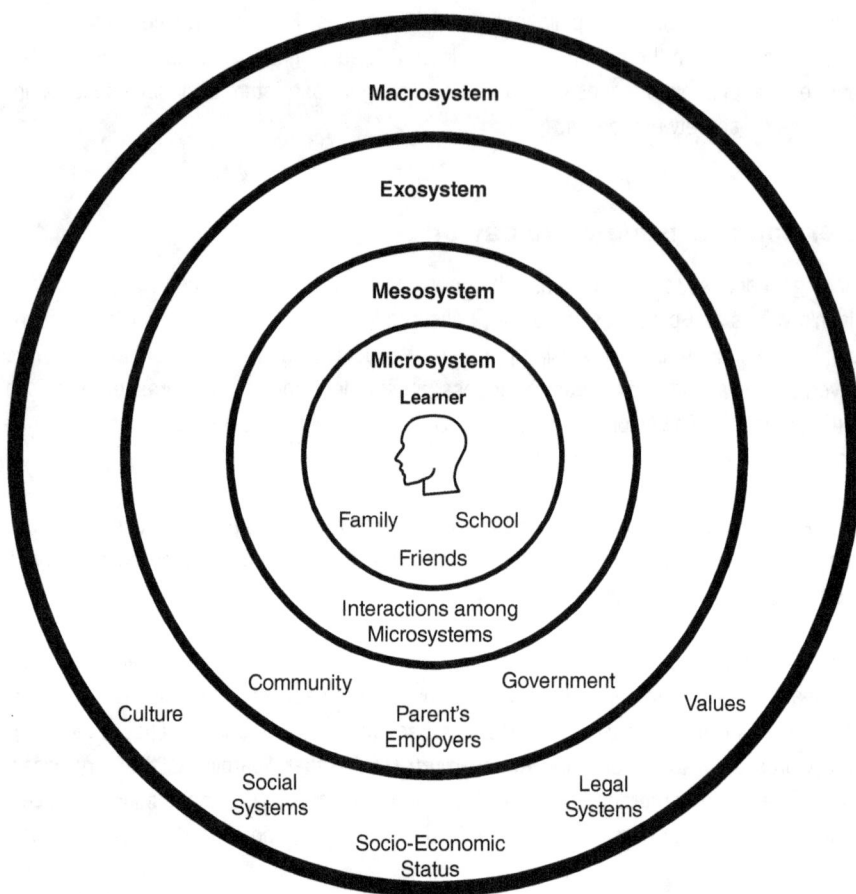

Figure 10.1 Nested ecologies surrounding the individual, and the contextual influences they include. Adapted from Bronfenbrenner (1977)

all taking different routes throughout the overlapping prison- education context via different structures and people intersections but all arriving at the same place: the learner. Tracing education and prison agendas across this map illuminates networks of interactions and flows of power that could be creatively utilised to facilitate egalitarian and humanising educational experiences within the confines of prison values and practices. Recognising these interactions is one thing, but harnessing the educational potential of these interactions is another. Doing so raises questions about how we actually go about providing education in prison and who else might step into the role of teacher. Such is the focus of this chapter.

Prison education: A punishment-security-freedom paradox

The "Prison Education Paradox" (Lackey, 2019: Wilson and Reuss 2000: 2012: Davidson 1995) is a conundrum that has dominated philosophical and political debates about education in prison. It points out the undeniable difficulty, and perhaps even impossibility, of merging together seemingly polarising priorities, purposes, values and practices of prison and education, and the different philosophies that guide them, and expecting both to work to their full potential.

Learner voice and the placement experience 105

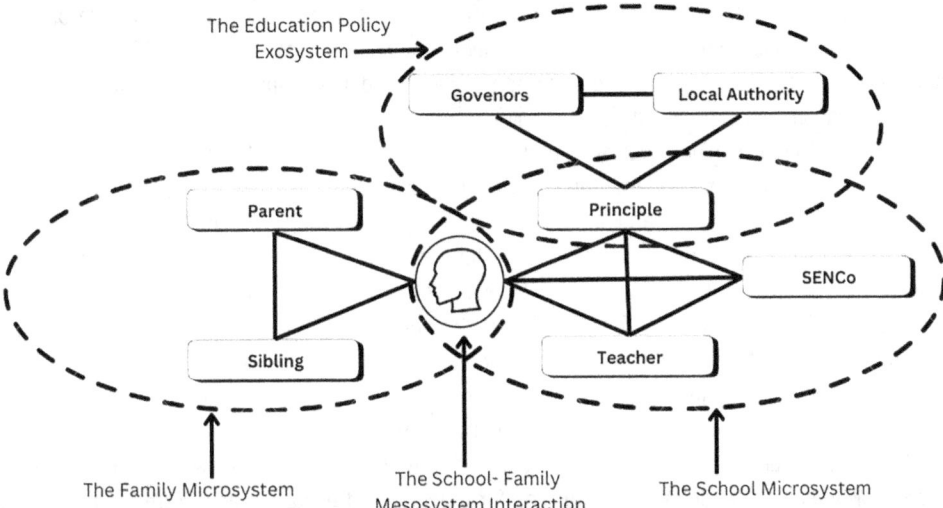

Figure 10.2 Networked ecologies surrounding the individual, emphasising the social interactions within and between each system and the individual they surround. Adapted from Neal and Neal (2013)

Prison educator Jennifer Lackey (2019) summarises the conflict between prison and education philosophies into three paradoxical strands:

1. Prison can be a dehumanising space, whilst education is deeply humanising.
2. Prison can be a place of stagnation, whilst education is deeply transformative.
3. Prison can be a place of isolation, whilst education is community building.

Described as the process of becoming more fully human, humanisation increases the critical consciousness of one's own humanity and the humanity of others in the pursuit of liberation from oppressive political, social and economic systems. It is transformative of the individual, the community, and the world around them, and can only be achieved in solidarity together (Freire, 2005). Conversely, dehumanisation occurs when one's humanity has been taken or distorted. It occurs as the result of an unjust order that engenders domination and alienation, and "fails to recognise others as persons" (Freire, 2005: 55), instead regarding them as a "pathology of the healthy society" (p. 74.) When the purpose of education is humanisation, transformation and community building, it is being guided by a philosophy of collective freedom. This type of education stives to democratise learning and redistribute the power imbalances between teacher and students. It is dialogical and collaborative in nature, demanding mutual trust, respect and criticality from teacher and student alike.

Compare this now with the prison context. Previous UK government white papers from the Ministry of Justice (MoJ) on prison reform (MoJ, 2016; MoJ, 2012) list three purposes of the prison system. The first is punishment, primarily through deprivation of liberty. Indeed, the minister for prisons, James Timpson, in 2024 went as far to say that the UK prison system had become "addicted to punishment" (Guru-Murthy, 2024, 20: 28s). Second is maintaining safety and order so as to protect the public. This is achieved through high-level, ubiquitous surveillance and security practices often likened to that of a panopticon (Collins, 1995: 56). Third is reform, to address and prevent the underlying causes of offending behaviour, freeing offenders from their life of crime. The

106 *Learner Voices, Perspectives, and Positionings*

relationship between each is dynamic. The reports show them to be mutually supportive of each other: i.e. safety and order creates an environment conducive to reform. Wilson (2000: 10) notes that outside, political and public discourse often "oscillates" between these agendas influencing the role of education as a mechanism for either living or control.

Consigned to maintaining order and safety, the UK prison system is dominated by an omnipresence of risk management. It permeates every aspect of the prison system and prisoner identity is constantly being constructed and judged in accordance with the degree of risk they pose. To conceptualise learners in this way pathologises and therefore dehumanises. It reduces their education to a "risk bureaucracy" that focuses on cultivating compliance and reduction of risk rather than humanisation (O'Brien et al., 2022: 687–688.) High-level security and surveillance create practical constraints that limit the freedom and flexibility needed for effective learning. Combined restrictions on prisoner movement and resources limits the free flow of information and constrains teacher-learner interactions to classroom hours only (Thomas, 1995: 38).

Whether education is purposed with producing measurable changes in (risk-based) behaviour, or employability and job readiness opportunities for the sake of freeing learners from a future life of crime, learning is often couched between functionalist and panoptic agendas (Collins, 1995) which creates standardised curricula and practice that emphasise "clear cut correctional dimensions of learning" (Collins, 1995: 56.) When guided by these prison agendas, education becomes accommodating of high-level surveillance and acts as an integral system to the panopticon (Collins, 1995).

Prison ideology and agendas filter down into staff-learner relationships, influencing the educational interactions between them in a multifaceted way. Not only in terms of quantity and quality of communication but also in how learners are perceived and managed, which maintains hierarchical positions and the distortion of their humanisation.

The prison-education paradox mapped onto ecological systems

To get to grips with this prison-education paradox and how it effects the learner, we will employ a visualisation of Bronfenbrenner's (1977) and Neal and Neal's (2013) ecological perspectives. In brief, Bronfenbrenner argued that human development is influenced by the multiple environments an individual is both directly and indirectly connected to. Specifically, development is shaped by the contextual factors within each environment and their interaction with one another and the individual. These environments were visualised as nested ecologies and categorised according to their proximity to the individual and the type of contextual influences they house (Figure 10.1). Of key relevance to this discussion is Bronfenbrenner's acknowledgement that the interactions *between* these environments and the individuals within them also affect development, not just the environments themselves. He coined the term for these cross-environment connections: "the mesosystem".

The mesosystem and how it interacts with other systems was developed further by Neal and Neal (2013) who re-envisaged the original ecologies as networked rather than nested environments (Figure 10.2). They placed greater primacy on the social interactions within and between settings, insisting that it is the social interactions that determine how the different systems relate to each other. Their focus on the interconnected nature of these relationships as a dynamic network helps to clearly visualise and therefore better understand the cross-ecological interactions between the prison and education contexts and how they are directly or indirectly connected to the learner.

Figure 10.3 applies this model to the prison and education contexts, depicting their microsystems and exosystems, the people and departments found in each and their direct and indirect

Learner voice and the placement experience 107

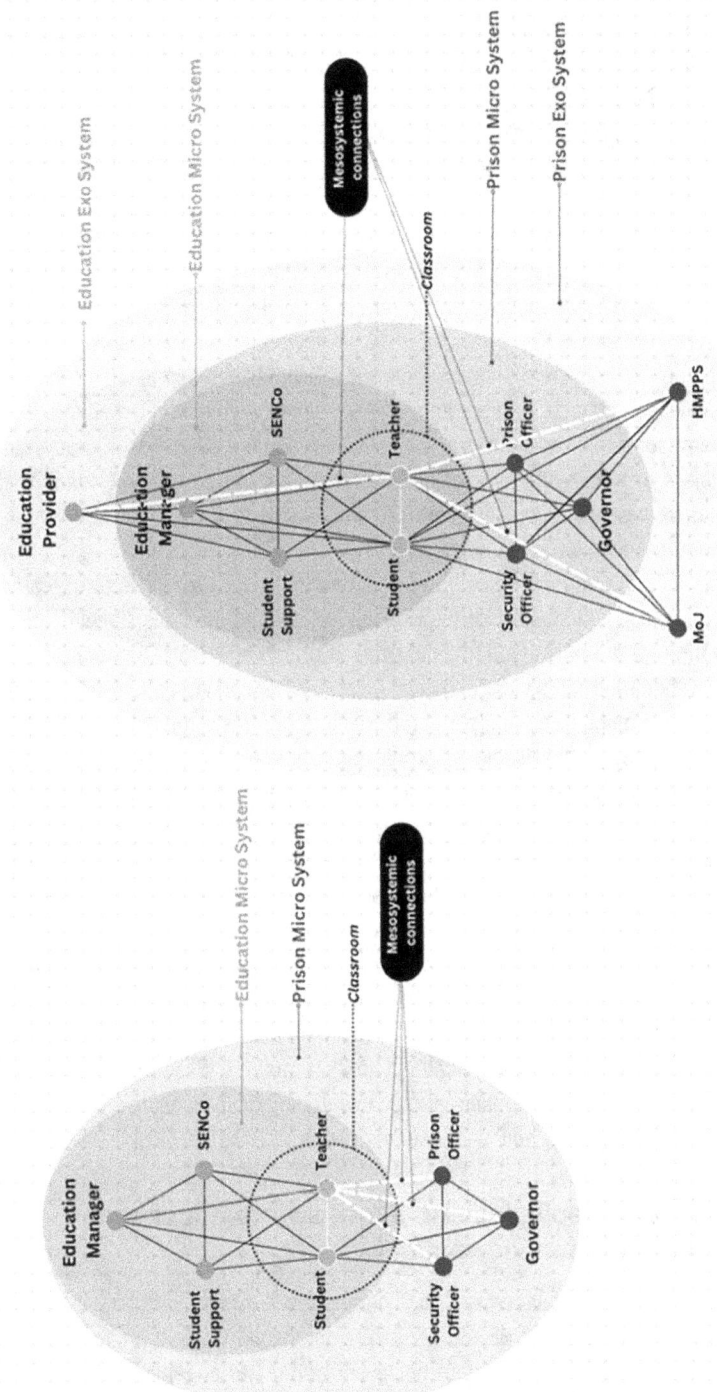

Figure 10.3 A developing networked model of prison and education contexts showing their microsystems and exosystems (Source: Davis, 2023)

connections to each other. The education microsystem houses teachers, student support and other typical front-line education staff but sits within the prison microsystem, thus creating interactions with front-line prison staff as depicted by the connecting lines. Moving outwards into the exosystems, we encounter the prison's overarching agendas and policies from government departments such as the MoJ and His Majesty's Prisons and Probation Service (HMPPS). Because the education microsystem is housed within the prison's microsystem, it is automatically enveloped by the prison's exosystem too. This is where we encounter a mesosystemic interaction, an indirect connection depicted by the dotted white line between front-line education staff such as the teacher and broader prison-specific agendas and policy issued by crime and justice government departments.

Figure 10.4 introduces the education and prison macrosystems with associated philosophies and values. Again, because the education microsystem is set within the prison's microsystem, and therefore its exosystem, education front-line staff are also enveloped by the prison's macrosystem as well, creating another mesosystemic connection but this time between teaching staff and the prison ideologies and values. What is of great importance to note here is that because education is positioned within the prison's microsystem, every individual within the education microsystem interacts with and is subject to both systems simultaneously, prison and education. This is unlike the prison's front-line staff who only occupy and therefore are subject to the policies and values of the prison's systems, not the education's system.

This model shows it is the prison's values and agendas that shape all aspects of learner-staff interactions in this context. The influence of the prison's values and agendas travel across ecologies, disseminated through the purpose and limitations of prison and education staff interactions with each other and with learners. Policy agendas and acceptable working behaviours stipulated by MoJ and HMPPS that form much of compulsory staff training, creates a mesosystemic connection between HMPPS and the teacher that seeks to promote the prison's moral and political ideologies and their subsequent agendas. The way that these ideologies and agendas are enacted is in the way policy conceptualises learners and defines the nature and limitations of their interactions with staff. Figure 10.5 illustrates this: prison ideology and agendas are disseminated from the prison macrosystem along the mesosystemic connections between the government departments in the prison exosystem and the teacher in both the education and prison microsystems. These ideologies and agendas are then passed from the teacher to the student through teacher-student interactions. When internalised and enacted by the teacher these ideologies and agendas characterise their teacher-learner relationships and are experienced as the Prison Education Paradox. In the following section, we examine what kind of conceptualisations and interactions these cross-system connections create for learners, before finally looking at how this ecological perspective might offer ways to circumvent potential limitations on educational experiences.

The filtering of prison ideologies and agendas into education: The effects of cross-system interactions

From the "omnipresence of risk management" that permeates the prison context stems HMPPS' Counter Corruption Policy (MoJ and HMPPS, 2022.) It sets out the working parameters for prisoner/staff relationships in order to protect staff from being corrupted into engaging in criminal activity. Protection from corruption is integral to maintaining safety and security for everyone, which in turn enables the prisons to reform prisoners. Just as O' Brein et al. (2022) explained, this policy requires staff to manage prisoners according to their risk of corrupting staff (MoJ and HMPPS, 2022: 5.)

Learner voice and the placement experience 109

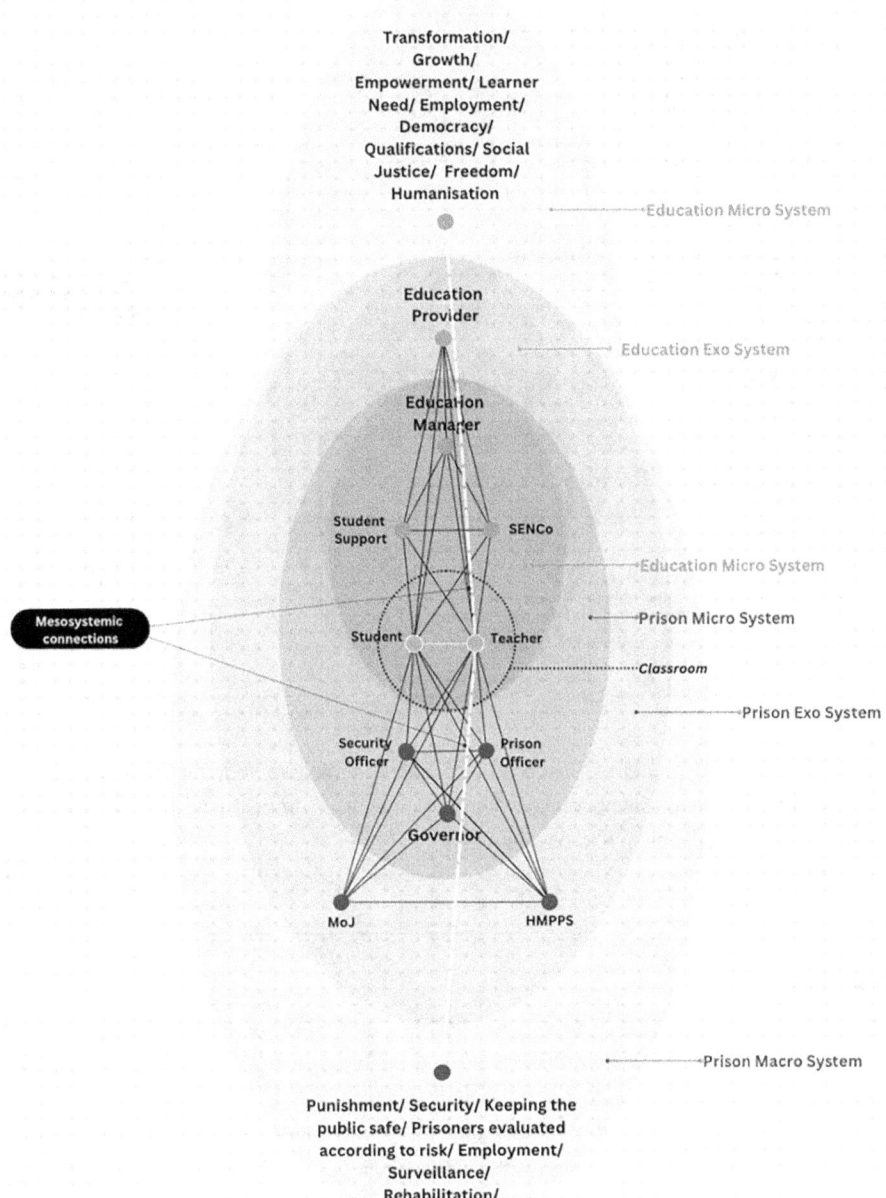

Figure 10.4 Networked model of prison and education contexts including macrosystem
(Source: Davis, 2023)

Those assessed as being such a risk are identified as "potential corruptor" and "robustly managed" (p. 8.). Deemed by policy as a necessary perspective for maintaining safety and order, but by Freirean standards, it is a term that pathologises and therefore dehumanises. Regardless of one's own philosophical stance, as a policy strategy, it applies "robustly" to the teacher/student relationship.

110 Learner Voices, Perspectives, and Positionings

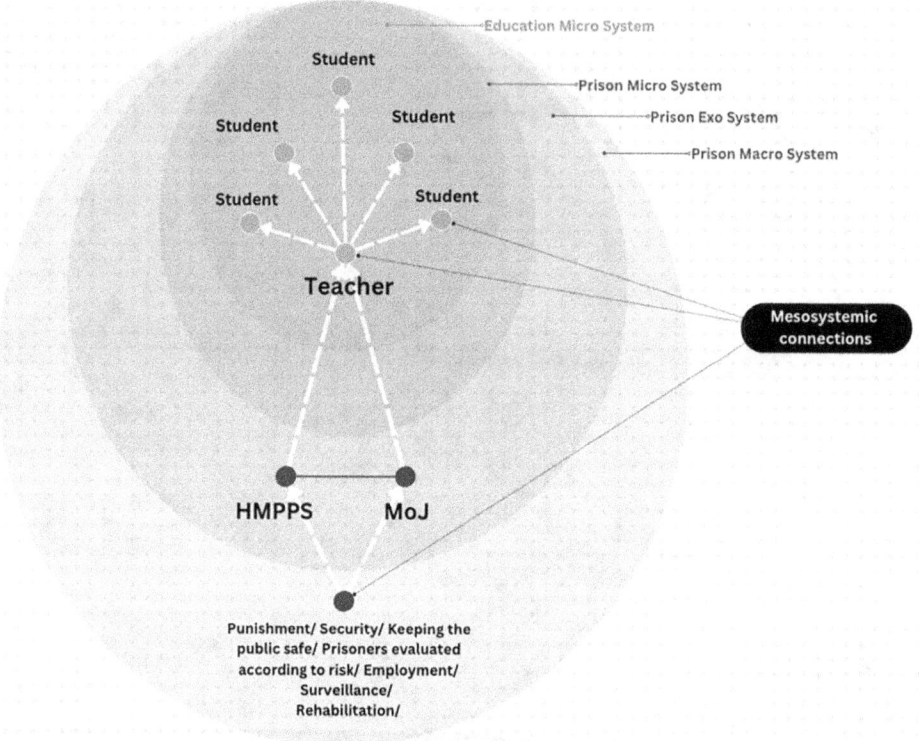

Figure 10.5 Networked model of prison and education ecologies showing the dissemination of prison agenda along mesosystemic connections from prison macrosystem to students in education microsystem

(*Source:* Davis, 2023)

> **Vignette**
>
> *When speaking of how best to safeguard one's self against being corrupted by a prisoner, security and counter corruption officers advised those of us in training, "you must always think the worst." They explained it is possible for a prisoner to use interactions with staff as an opportunity to manipulate them into engaging in criminal activity. The officers explained it was important for the sake of everyone's safety, resident (prisoner), and staff, to "remember where you are working and who you are working with." For me, this highlighted the dichotomy of building relationships and rapport in a context where, to quote prison educator Alison Reuss, "Mistrust and suspicion frequently underpin any form of social interaction" (2000:2012: 30), and in the "worst case scenario" thinking is an essential part of best practise.*
>
> *(Students Reflective Journal; Davis, 2022)*

Mutual trust, respect and openness towards students is not a position unique to Freire's philosophy of humanising education. A major tenant of fellow humanist Carl Rogers' (1957) work applied to teacher-student relationships is his concept of unconditional positive regard (UPR). UPR involves valuing the student unconditionally, refusing to place on them conditions of worth whereby their value and treatment is determined by their level of conformity and behaviour. It is an attitude that supports autonomy rather than control and enables the student to express themselves without judgement or criticism (Klipfel and Breecher-Cook, 2017: 96).

It is clear to see how embodying UPR, and the mutual trust, respect and openness it supports, becomes problematic in a context where suspicion, thinking the worst and risk characterise the teacher-student relationship as part of best working practice. The act of perceiving and managing learners according to risk and "potential corruptor" status, whilst deemed a safeguarding necessity by security and safety focused policy, is to enact "conditions of worth" whereby the learner's value and staff relationships are mediated by their behaviour and level of conformity.

To judge the honesty and intentions of a learner's expression and interactions with staff, to adjust one's trust, acceptance and openness towards a prison learner depending on those judgements whilst simultaneously embodying UPR seems a contradiction difficult to avoid. Such is the prison-education paradox. This can be understood from an ecological perspective in Figure 10.4 where the teacher is subject to mesosystemic connections to both prison agenda and education philosophy simultaneously.

Figure 10.5 shows how this construction and dissemination of risk and scepticism occurs from an ecological perspective. Prison and public safety agendas in the macrosystem mandate high-level security and order. Under this mandate, safety agendas are conceptualised into risk management and counter corruption policy at the exosystem level. The policy is then transmitted to staff through training and enacted within their prisoner-staff relationships in the overlapping prison and education microsystems. This mesosystemic connection between overarching prison agendas, teachers and students shapes learning interactions whereby teachers are expected to construct, assess, respond to and manage prison learners according to risk.

Ginsberg (2019) acknowledges that prisoners are compelled to identify as prisoners continuously on a minute-by-minute basis. We can see from Figures 10.3–10.5 this is partly because they permanently live within the prison microsystem and are unable to leave it. But also, because the microsystems they inhabit are informed by punitive and security-focused agendas and practices from the prisons exo- and macrosystems, of which all clearly conceptualise and delineate the prisoner/non-prisoner (staff) binary. When the teacher-learner relationship is characterised by these prisoner/non-prisoner binaries, Ginsberg notes that we create an identity divide that cannot be crossed, which makes pursuing a commonality impossible and increases teacher-learner power disparities. This limits the capacity for democratised and collaborative learning necessary for humanising, transformative and community building education.

Pause for thought

Tension between punitive, high security and educative contexts can manifest in the teacher-student relationship in prisons. There is often a call for staff to "think the worst" in their students in order to safeguard themselves, other staff and the wider community. This contrasts with educational literature that advocates for UPR (Carl Rodgers) and humanisation (Paolo Freire).

Reflective Questions

1. How could this perspective, as experienced by a key worker, create a partial barrier to them being able to provide effective education programmes on a prison house block, for example?
2. What strategies might help prison educators to reconcile these different concerns?
3. How could a move towards commonly accepted "good educational practice" avoid feeling like a step away from "good prison practice"?

Filtering education ideologies and agendas into prison: Using cross-system interactions to our advantage

Ginsberg (2019) insists that to cross the identity divide between prison teacher and prison learner and the power imbalances inherent within, educators need to find ways to democratise learning interactions. To achieve this, we propose utilising a different network of interactions and in doing so reimagining who and what the teacher role involves. Peer-peer relationships are a pre-existing network of potential learning interactions that are not limited by the same type of mesosystemic connections with risk management and panopticon agendas that problematise the traditional prison teacher-learner relationship.

In her report for HM Inspectorate of Probation, Gill Buck (2021: 5-7) acknowledges the democratic and egalitarian potential of peer mentorship in offender learning, quoting Freire's own words that a mentor's task is fundamentally liberatory, believing in the autonomy, freedom and development of their mentee. It is an empowering and relationship-based approach to learning that shifts away from pathologising to focus on strengths and support. In the St Giles Trust's (2017) review of their prison-based peer advisory programme, it is the capacity for peers to build trust and have open conversations without judgement or, in other words, demonstrate UPR, in a context where this is often problematised, that is central to successful learning and support. Noteworthy is the report's mention that the mentors' UPR is vital and yet only achievable because they are *not* staff (p. 14). This suggests peer mentors are able to embody educational philosophies connected to humanisation and can bring to learning interactions humanising qualities that the teacher cannot. This is because peers occupy a different ecological position to the traditional prisoner teacher. The peer mentor/mentee is not subject to the same paradoxical prison-education mesosystemic interactions discussed earlier that give rise to the complexities and limitations inherent within the traditional prison teacher-learner relationship. Additionally, as both reports suggest, by occupying the same ecological space within the prison environment, peers share similar microsystem and mesosystem experiences. These shared experiences often help scaffold learning from a relational, experiential and practical point of view. In this scenario, teaching staff work with peer mentors on planning the organising and delivery of material and support, assisting with the learning process between peers rather than direct instruction.

Compared to teachers, peers don't have the same obligation to policy that conceptualises and manages one another according to risk or reform, and so their learning does not have to be built around "clear cut correctional dimensions of learning" (Collins, 1995: 56). Speaking from the context of learner-fashioned and learner-governed education programmes, Davis and Michaels (2016) say it is precisely the capacity for the learners to define their own educative purpose, that is both free from the restraint of the prison's definitions of rehabilitation and notions of being rehabilitated, that makes these educational experiences so impactful. Davis and Michaels use the term "peer-to-peer educators" (ibid.: 146) and explain these incarcerated teachers facilitate reading and writing groups and further study access courses and collaborations between incarcerated, writers, artists, political and historical analysts. They write books, pamphlets, resources, legislation, course curricula and policy. The fact that they are not classed as academics and have accrued their knowledge through non-traditional avenues does not make them any less teachers. They urge non-incarcerated teachers to listen to and engage with incarcerated teachers. To commit themselves to "intentional, insistent, deep collaboration" (p. 147) to help maintain education's humanising potential and steer it away from the panopticon, and risk-based rehabilitative indoctrination.

We propose that to engage in "intentional, insistent, deep collaboration" is to enact what Freire (2005) describes as directing and facilitating the process of knowing and learning rather than directing the students themselves. It is about collaborating to create an environment where learners can question, explore, reflect, act, teach and gain agency over their learning. Effective pedagogy is not so dependent on a teacher's knowledge or delivery of course material, but on their interactional skills and their ability to "resist, defuse, and mediate" the tensions within the prison context (Thomas, 1995: 30).

As shown in Figure 10.6, diverting the flow of prison ideology and agenda away from educational interactions by creatively utilising a peer network system is about enabling and facilitation, not about violation of power because that simply is not possible, and many will argue it is unethical in a prison context. As a pedagogue of process, you engineer and support learning interactions among pre-existing networks that will *enable* learners to engage meaningfully with humanising education. This is what (Wilson and Reuss 2000: 2012) explain as facilitating a form of empowerment least likely to conflict with and most likely to flourish within the context of prison education. That is, a version of empowerment that is about enabling and giving ability rather than giving power to authority.

Conclusion

It is neither the place nor the purpose of this discussion to judge the purposes and ethics of prison structures or those who work so compassionately and diligently within them. To impose a binary of good vs bad, or right vs wrong is naive, inaccurate and unhelpful. Instead, this discussion illuminates the reality of prison education and provides the reader with a road map of how best to meaningfully negotiate it.

The prison-education context has been simplified and mapped on to an ecological framework to better convey to the reader that this environment is a microcosm of different interactions. Each interaction is connected to different agendas that when amalgamated create and shape educational experiences. The stretch of these interactions is far-reaching and grounded in a multiplicity of philosophical, political and economic debates and values.

Through this ecological perspective, we have shown *how* paradoxical values and agendas of freedom, security, and punishment filter through the prison-education environment through structure-staff-learner interactions. This paradox is experienced in the purposes and limitations of risk-based relationships imposed on teachers and learners. When entering the prison-education

114 *Learner Voices, Perspectives, and Positionings*

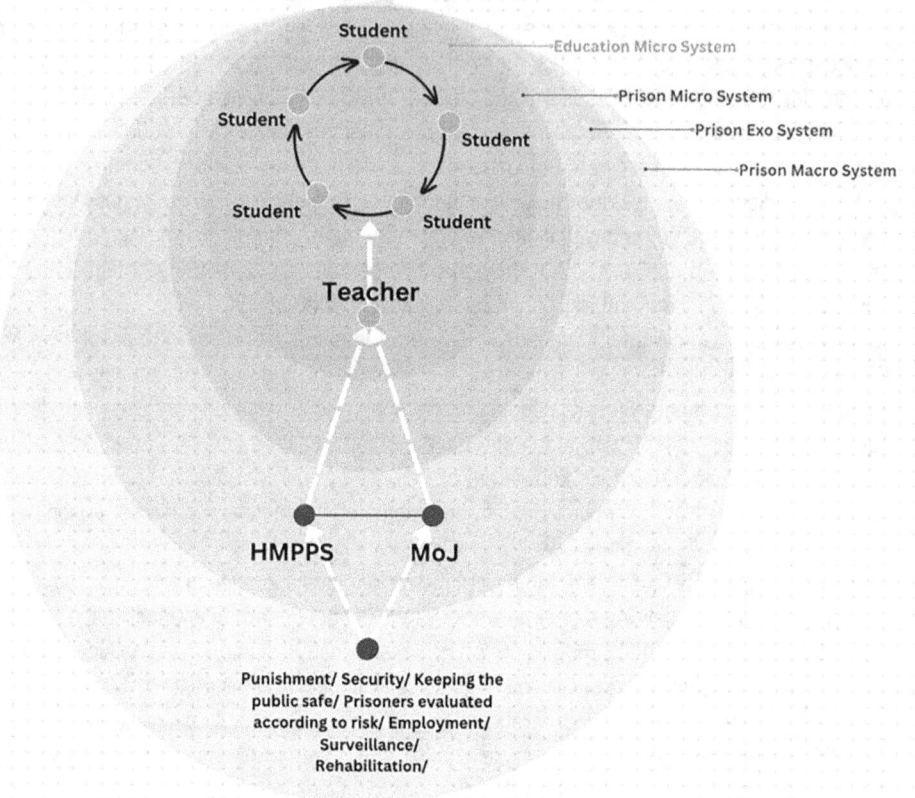

Figure 10.6 Shows the disruption of prison macrosystem influence on learning when teachers facilitate learning between peers
(*Source:* Davis, 2023)

context, it is your prerogative to have an awareness of the whole map. This awareness will help orientate yourself in relation to the wider landscape, where you are, what sort of difficulties might impede your educational ventures, where and why they are likely to occur and where they have come from.

Perhaps more importantly, it offers a guide for navigating humanising education in context where this is problematised, practically, politically, and ethically.

Summary points

- There exists a paradox within prison-education systems between the dehumanising elements of incarceration and punishment, and the liberatory elements of education
- Educators in prisons need to try and reconcile two competing ideas: from "thinking the worst" and managing risk, to trust and "UPR" for their learners

- The role of the peer mentor is essential to humanise the teacher-prisoner relationship; shared experiences can help to scaffold learning
- We need to consider the complex interactions that take place when mapping the ecological space of the prison and systems of education
- These interactions in prisons can be empowering if teachers can facilitate peer-to-peer learning and provide meaningful engagement with the humanising elements of education

Further reading

Inside out prison exchange project

This project provides higher education courses whereby the classroom consists of both incarcerated "inside" students and non-incarcerated "outside" students learning together in a prison setting. Content and instruction are non-hierarchical, non-directive and dialogical so as to emphasise collaborative peer learning. Students are encouraged to share their experiences and perspectives as experts in the material at hand.

This is a condensed exploration of the philosophy and methodology of the project in one chapter.

Pompa, L., (2010) Breaking down the walls: Inside-out learning and the pedagogy of transformation. In S. J. Hartnett *Challenging the Prison-Industrial Complex*. University of Illinois Press.

Have a listen to the projects podcast. Listen to Episode 1 for overview of the project, Episode 8 for an Inside student's experience, and Episode 11 for an Outside student's experience. https://podcasts.apple.com/ca/podcast/the-inside-out-podcast/id1192245507

Prison newspapers

The *San Quentin News* began as an inmate-produced newspaper in California, USA, and has evolved to include a podcast, community forum and news channel. Inmate journalists and editors work together to report on prison life and how it is affected by the wider political, cultural and economic landscape on the outside. The forum hosts conversations between inmates, prosecutors, district attorneys, judges, police officers, teachers and politicians on matters related to prison reform and social justice.

An NPR Newscast interview with *San Quentin* journalists (4 minutes) https://www.npr.org/2024/06/12/nx-s1-4947579/prison-newspapers-growth-journalism-inmates
A POLOTICO article reviewing *San Quentin News* journalism in the relation to social justice, prison reform and prisoner rehabilitation. https://www.politico.com/news/magazine/2020/06/25/criminal-justice-prison-conditions-san-quentin-media-335709
An example of a *San Quentin News* broadcast (11 minutes) https://www.youtube.com/watch?v=5rdHdOhTV14
Ear Hustle podcast, created and produced in San Quentin Prison https://www.earhustlesq.com/

Art publication

STIR Magazine is an art publication designed and edited by a group of long-term prisoners in HMP Shotts, Scotland. With a focus on creativity, self-expression and the use of high-quality graphic design equipment, the editorial team set the theme for each issue, collect inmate-produced artwork from across seven prisons and curate them into the finished publication.

STIR Magazine https://www.sps.gov.uk/about-us/partnership/stir-magazine

St Giles Trust Peer Advisor Programme

The St Giles Trust Peer Advisor Programme is a level 3 or 4 qualification in Information, Advice and Guidance, active across 30 prisons in the UK. It gives inmates the skills, knowledge and experience to offer practical and emotional support to their incarcerated peers.

St Giles evaluative report on their Prison Peer Advisor Programme. https://www.stgilestrust.org.uk/our-impact/evaluations-of-our-work/peer-advice/prison-peer-advice/

References

Bronfenbrenner, U. (1977) Towards an experimental ecology of human development. *American Psychologist*, 32(7), 513–531.

Buck, G. (2021) Mentoring and Peer Mentoring Available at: https://www.justiceinspectorates.gov.uk/hmiprobation/wp-content/uploads/sites/5/2021/04/Academic-Insights-mentoring-and-peer-mentoring.pdf (Accessed 16 October 2024).

Collins, M. (1995) Shades of the Prison House: Adult Literacy and the Correctional Ethos. In H. S. Davidson *Schooling in a total institution: Critical perspectives on prison education*. London: Bergin and Garvey .

Davidson, H.S. (1995) *Schooling in a total institution: Critical perspectives on prison education*. London: Bergin and Garvey.

Davis, E. (2022) Reflective Summary. Assignment for *EDST2123, BA (Hons) Education Studies*, Worcester: University of Worcester, Unpublished.

Davis, E. (2023) Engineering A Map of Prison-Education Interactions. *Assignment for EDST3128, BA (Hons) Education Studies*, University of Worcester, Unpublished.

Davis, S.W. and Michaels, B. (2016) Ripping off some room for people to "breathe together". Peer-to-peer education in prison. *Social Justice (San Francisco, Calif.)*, 42(2), pp. 146–158.

Freire, P. (2005) *Pedagogy of the oppressed, 30th anniversary*. New York, Bloomsbury Academic.

Ginsburg, R. (2019) 'The Perils of Transformation Talk in Higher Education in Prison', in Ginsberg R, *Critical Perspectives on Teaching in Prison: Students and Instructions on Pedagogy Behind the Wall*, Routledge, New York.

Guru-Murthy, K. (2024) Ways To Change The World, [Podcast], 29 February, available at: https://www.youtube.com/watch?v=W2jRUqE4fK8 (Accessed: 21 September 2024).

Klipfel, K.M., and Brecher Cook D., (2017) *Learner-Centered Pedagogy: Principles and Practice*. 1st edn. Chicago, American Library Association.

Krishnamurti, J. (1976) *Krishnamurtis Notebook*, Krishnamurti Foundation Trust, UK, Available at: https://www.perlego.com/book/976182 (Accessed: 12 September 2024).

Lackey, J. (2019) The Prison Education Paradox, available at: https://www.ted.com/talks/jennifer_lackey_the_prison_education_paradox, (Accessed: 21 September 2024).

Ministry of Justice, (2012) Prisons Strategy White Paper, available at: https://assets.publishing.service.gov.uk/government/uploads/system/uploads/attachment_data/file/1038765/prisons-strategy-white-paper.pdf, (Accessed: 21 September 2024).

Ministry of Justice, (2016) Prison Safety and Reform, available at: https://assets.publishing.service.gov.uk/government/uploads/system/uploads/attachment_data/file/565014/cm-9350-prison-safety-and-reform-_web_.pdf , (Accessed: 21 September 2024).

Ministry of Justice and HMPPS, (2022) Counter Corruption and Reporting Wrong Doing Policy Framework, available at: https://assets.publishing.service.gov.uk/media/627b8d308fa8f57d7fe4e147/counter-corruption-pf.pdf (Accessed: 21 September 2024).

Neal, J. and Neal, Z. (2013) Nested or Networked? Future Directions for ecological systems theory, *Social Development*, 22(4), pp. 722–737, available at: doi: 10.1111/sode.12018

O'Brien, K. et al. (2022) 'Education as the practice of freedom?' - prison education and the pandemic, *Educational review (Birmingham)*, 74(3), pp. 685–703.

Peterson, T. (2019) 'Healing Pedagogy from the Inside Out: The Paradox of Liberatory Education in Prison', in Ginsberg R, *Critical perspectives on Teaching in prison: Students and Instructions on Pedagogy Behind the Wall*, New York, Routledge, pp 175–187.

Reuss, A., (2000:2012) 'The Researcher's Tale', in Wilson, D., and Reuss, A., *Prisone(er) Education: Stories of Change and Transformation*, United Kingdom, Waterside Press.

Rogers, C.R. (1957) 'The necessary and sufficient conditions of therapeutic personality change', *Journal of consulting psychology*, 21(2), pp. 95–103.

St Giles Trust (2017) St Giles' Peer Advisory Model, Available at: https://www.stgilestrust.org.uk/app/uploads/2021/06/pdf_The-Peer-Advisor-Model-in-Prisons-final-final-1.pdf

Thomas, (1995) 'The Ironies of Prison Education', in Davidson H.S., *Schooling in a total institution: Critical perspectives on prison education*, London, Bergin and Garvey.

Wilson, D., & Reuss, A. (Eds.). (2000:2012) *Prison (er) education: Stories of change and transformation*. Waterside Press.

11 Global voices
Empowering students for world-class education

Madeleine Findon and Rabiat Malik

Introduction

Why then the world's mine oyster, Which I with sword will open.
– Shakespeare, The Merry Wives of Windsor, 1602

Over time, Shakespeare's phrase has come to represent a cliché: that opportunities are out there for the taking. When coupled with the notion of learning, we are also reminded of the much older phrase "pearls of wisdom", thus underlining the idea that great potential may be found through engaging with the world beyond our doorstep. This is something that international students are highly aware of, travelling around the globe in search of knowledge and experience that will transform lives. In recent years, internationalisation has become a major feature of higher education, bringing with it new opportunities for students and their universities. However, this chapter argues that the voice of international students is yet to be fully heard in the process, meaning that the full potential of internationalisation has not yet been realised. The chapter explores this issue as a co-constructed endeavour between two individuals with different experiences of internationalised higher education.

Rabiat is a Nigerian international postgraduate student at the University of Worcester, United Kingdom, currently exploring the fascinating world of Early Childhood Education and Special Educational Needs (SEN) through an MA programme. This is her first experience as an international student having lived, worked, and studied only in her home country until now. This is also her first experience of writing for a wider audience, amplifying her voice further than ever before. Maddy is currently a Senior Lecturer on the MA that Rabiat is studying, having worked as an academic over the last decade at several internationalised institutions. She is British and was also once, briefly, an international student in Barcelona. For Rabiat, getting the opportunity to study abroad was one that she believed would change her life in many ways as, the United Kingdom offers opportunities for cutting-edge education, which is highly valued and would open doors to career opportunities worldwide. For Maddy, study abroad was something that would enable her to integrate further into her chosen country at the time; while helping to ensure a more interesting CV should she ever return to the United Kingdom.

These highly personal motivations are a microcosm of a wider sectoral interest in international study and engagement, and are reflected by universities themselves, which have their own global ambitions. These institutions, including those here in the United Kingdom, value international connections, resources, influence and prestige in the eyes of the globe – many pursuing "world-class" status (Altbach, 2004; Page and Chahboun, 2019). Utilising the lenses of their research and personal experiences, the authors maintain that learner voice is integral in securing the process of adaptation, for international students and their universities, that is a necessary precondition to ensure the academic achievements students are seeking, as well as securing the institutional reputation that is essential to the continued success of British universities.

As a concept, learner voice is one that has been explored extensively elsewhere in this book. In this chapter we focus on particular issues that concern how the voice of international students can be heard in UK universities. It has been noted that while there may be a growing body of literature regarding international students' experiences, very little of it represents the perspectives of students themselves. We seek, therefore, ways to "de-mute" (Page and Chahboun, 2019: 872) these voices. The phrase, "world-class" is one that emerges persistently in the discourses around higher education, first coined (or problematised) in 2004 by Altbach who suggested that it was a fuzzily defined basis used to claim respect and standing on the global stage. We suggest that perhaps this is a misunderstanding of what "world-class" should represent, particularly in the context of discussions about international students' experiences. In this chapter, we wish to subvert the phrase, preferring it to represent a vision of practice that truly enables students and institutions around the world to benefit from the interchange of culture, learning and experiences.

This conceptual reinterpretation has come about as a result of Maddy's experiences working with and listening to the experiences of international students, including Rabiat. Both authors would suggest that there has often been a mismatch between the global impact universities want and the extent to which they genuinely engage with the people who will contribute to their international reputations. Reflecting on the characteristics of "world-class" university education, and the process of obtaining that status, it seems that the concept needs to be rethought in order to ensure that internationalisation can reach its full potential for all involved. The concept of learner voice as a catalyst for change has extensive precedents: in discussing educational revolution, Paulo Freire (1970) stated that, "Dialogue with the people is radically necessary" (101): dialogue being a process where all parties may speak and be listened to. In thinking about how to revolutionise practices to meet our definition of 'world-class', this chapter will focus on the relationship between learner voice and adaptation, de-muting learner voice, and a vision for the future of "world-classness" in universities.

Learner voice for adaptation

Successful adaptation, or adjustment, matters to international students and to their universities: it is a protective factor for the success of international students and increases the likelihood that those students will recommend their university to prospective students (see research cited by Malay, Otten and Coelen, 2023). This impact alone suggests that the onus to adjust lies not just with international students but with their universities too. Owing to the particular challenges and narratives framed around them, it has been argued by researchers such as Tavares (2021) that universities should consider international students as falling within the remit of their commitment to equity, diversity and inclusion (EDI), though it is not clear the extent to which this call has been acted upon. Before we look at how adaptation can be supported through learner voice, however, let us begin with some context about the process of internationalisation in relation to universities in the UK.

An analysis of the opening quotation of this chapter in the context of Shakespeare's original dialogue reveals a much darker intent than its popular usage would suggest, one that perhaps surfaces a tension in the journey of internationalisation that is being undertaken by UK universities. To open an oyster is a forceful act, the contents are taken and/or consumed. Who, or what is being consumed in the process of internationalisation? At the time of writing this chapter, the United Kingdom retains its position as a popular destination for international students, seeking the same benefits that inspired the authors to make their own journeys abroad. It is also true that the United Kingdom needs international students. As a result of rising inflation, teaching home undergraduates is currently a loss maker; meanwhile, based on figures from 2021/22 "every nine EU students and every 11 non-EU students generate £1m worth of net economic impact for the UK economy over the duration of their studies" (Cannings, Halterbeck and Conlon, 2023: v).

Economic benefits aside, it is vital to also recognise the enrichment to culture and learning that takes place wherever international exchange takes place. As noted across a variety of sectors, diversity is a necessary precondition for development, owing to creative processes being catalysed by the cross-fertilisation of different ideas and perspectives (meme change: Csikszentmihalyi, 2014). The presence of international students in our universities has the potential to enhance the experiences and intellectual development of all students and staff, fostering new forms of knowledge and innovative practices. Sadly, the reality is that this outcome is nearer to being a "long-standing myth" (Knight, 2011: 14) than a reality, with international students being more likely to experience marginalisation and racial or ethnic tensions than feeling a part of a vibrant, global academic community.

This failure to fully realise the potential of internationalisation is a shame for a variety of reasons. It demonstrates a lack of respect, care and hospitality on the part of universities, which is damaging to the well-being of international students, as well as reflecting badly on the reputation of universities. Where international students are listened to, providing them with opportunities to join and contribute to the community, the process of adaptation becomes much easier. Rabiat comments:

> Navigating the university was difficult at first, but as I began to engage with my tutors during classes I started to become comfortable. Being part of the student representative team helped me develop a feeling of belonging as I felt I was part of the community. Additionally, locating a prayer room for my faith, and connecting with my fellow international students' group showed me that I was not alone and I gained a sense of belonging.

We argue in this chapter that, for the real benefits of internationalisation to be realised, we must build a co-constructive, rather than co-consuming model of internationalised higher education, which necessitates listening to the voices of our global learners. Nonetheless, the process of including international students in the UK higher education system has not been without its challenges. The path to internationalisation in UK universities has been uneven, with several surges in numbers of international applications, political narratives around foreign nationals and policy changes that have complicated the transition to life in the UK for many, and questions around the preparedness of UK systems for these cohorts.

While all students may arguably face a period of adjustment in embarking upon a new programme of study, the greater range of variables experienced by international students can make this process harder. Adjustment (or adaptation) is both a psychological and sociocultural process (Bierwiaczonek and Waldzus, 2016 in Malay, Otten and Coelen, 2023), which for international students can include getting used to a range of differences in social norms, cultural beliefs about study, pedagogical/andragogical approaches, assessment methods and learning styles, as well as finding their feet in terms of accommodation, employment and official requirements. Rabiat's own experience mirrors this: "As international students, the way we are used to studying is completely different to what we are presented with here in the UK".

Neither is the adjustment process for international students a homogeneous experience, Malay, Otten and Coelen (2023) highlight those levels of Cultural Distance (variance in cultural values) and Cultural Intelligence (ability to adapt and operate across diverse cultural environments) of international students are recognised to have an impact upon the rate of adjustment. Staff and students on our programme have observed that prior academic experiences can vary from country to country, meaning that some students have a greater hill to climb in terms of adjusting to academic norms and expectations. As Rabiat observes:

Student voices are of varying degree, just as Jones (2017) described: even students from the same country can have varying experiences due to individual backgrounds and prior exposure to the learning environment. What one perceives as a challenge will not appear the same for another, thereby putting more pressure on the institution as they make an attempt at listening to learners and to make adjustments. However, these adjustments are essential for the smooth running of the programme so that all international students enjoy a positive experience throughout their study.

As has been noted elsewhere in this book, recognition of the value of learner voice in establishing quality education has been growing in recent years, chipping away at the notion that it is the *educators*, not the learners, who hold the answers. Regarding higher education, Cook-Sather wrote in 2002, "There is something fundamentally amiss about building and rebuilding an entire system without consulting at any point those it is ostensibly designed to serve" (p. 3). Cook-Sather (2002) goes on to suggest that listening to learner voice is an essential tool for higher education institutions (HEI) in the processes of reform and improvement, noting its role in evaluating change, moving discussions and action forward. She further highlights a range of research that identifies benefits for teaching such as ensuring conceptual understanding, accessibility of methods and greater participation. Into this picture the role of the voices of international students must now be considered. Given the inevitable march of internationalisation, those voices are more important than ever as universities seek to adapt. Altbach (2004) stated that "world-classness" is conferred by the judgement of others. Newspapers and league tables aside, given the importance of the international student to the institution, perhaps they should be the arbiters of world-class status?

We can clearly see that listening to the voices of international students is of enormous benefit to institutions, but what of students themselves? As highlighted earlier, international students face greater challenges in terms of adjustment and adaptation, many of which can be alleviated by universities when they listen to the voices of those students. Some initial research carried out with international students on our programme identified these challenges as including accommodation, orientation/induction, academic skills and financial instability (Findon, Mahama and Ojo, 2025). Reporting on this research means that the university can begin to target these issues. Interestingly, Cook-Sather (2002) noted that the process of being listened to can also be empowering for students, encouraging them to engage and share their views further, which may better prepare students for the world in which they find themselves after graduating. However, it appears that international voices are not yet being listened to, or sufficiently acted upon, which leads to frustration on the part of those students. Rabiat notes:

> We can give kudos to my university in their efforts to make students voices heard, we have never had any doubt about the media put in place, our concerns are mostly about the effectiveness of the said media.

In the next section of this chapter, we would like to think about what effective strategies for listening to student voice could look like.

Pause for thought

1. Have you, or would you like to study abroad?
2. What are or would be the key benefits or challenges be for you?
3. What might a "vibrant, global academic community" look like in your university?

De-muting the voices of international students

Since Cook-Sather's (2002) seminal article, many of those working in higher education will have noticed an increase in strategies designed to facilitate student voice i.e. student staff liaison committees, student surveys etc. However, as highlighted by Rabiat in the previous section, questions remain about the efficacy of those channels. Paulo Freire notes, "Many political and educational plans have failed because their authors designed them according to their own personal views of reality, never once taking into account…to whom their programme was ostensibly directed" (Freire, 1970: 67). This observation is very much reflected in the dearth of material Page and Chahboun (2019) could locate that centred on the perspectives of international students themselves. A change in approach is clearly necessary, but as Freire (1970: 27) also says, "no reality transforms itself". For him, change requires a critical engagement of all stakeholders in the process. Thus, to truly "de-mute" the voices of international students, a co-creative process involving hard thinking and informed action must take place.

Critical engagement must begin with an honest appraisal of the realities of the situation: Freire (1970) observes that people do not usually appreciate the true extent to which they hold, or do not hold, the power and what the impacts of their position might be. Furthermore, it is also important to critically consider of the aims and intentions of all involved in the proposed change. Universities are hierarchical systems, described as reminiscent of medieval guilds (Ben-David and Zloczower, 1962) and frequently exclusionary (Settles et al., 2021). What is sometimes skirted around in the drive to facilitate international student voices is the role that institutional racism can play in muting them. Though discussions of racism often come freighted with uncomfortable emotions, it is important to confront the unseen, or unrecognised, processes that may be hindering change. Institutional racism is defined by Macpherson (1999) as

> [t]The collective failure to provide an appropriate and professional service to people because of their colour, culture or ethnic origin. It can be seen or detected in the processes, attitudes and behaviour, which amount to discrimination through unwitting prejudice, ignorance, thoughtlessness and racist stereotyping, which disadvantage minority ethnic people.
>
> (para 6.34)

Though most universities in the UK would view themselves as progressive and are often caricatured that way in the press and public discourse, tradition and privilege feature significantly in the DNA of these institutions, meaning that modes of thinking and processes may go unchallenged (also affecting staff: e.g. Settles et al., 2021). For all the rhetoric around the benefits of internationalisation, international students themselves are often framed in terms of the challenges that they present to the institution (Ye, 2018 in Tavares, 2021). Through no fault of their own, international students may need support with language, their communication style may be different, and they are often unsure how to engage with the teaching and learning. Tavares (2021) describes international students as facing "unique issues of discrimination on the basis of their othered institutional status" (p. 1553). Furthermore, the institutions' practices are framed as "right", with the onus being upon the students to adapt, betraying a colonial mindset (as per Grande, 2018). The point being that listening requires a basic sense of respect to be in place: it must be understood that a voice is worth listening to.

Arguably, humanisation is a helpful principle to work with. Often, the issues around internationalisation fall into the trap of painting a dichotomous picture, placing individuals onto opposing sides of "us" and "them". This tendency is a characteristic example of "othering", which Said (2016): 332 described as "the continuous interpretation and reinterpretation of their differences from 'us'". Where this takes place, we fail to see each other as people, which can lead to a misrecognition of their intentions and values. With thanks to Freire (1970), we understand that the majority of the work of humanisation is the responsibility of universities which, as the architects of the educational structures in which international students find themselves, are the party with the greatest share of the power. Universities then need to take steps towards understanding their international students as people, and how they experience those educational structures. By beginning to treat the students humanly, they will become humanised themselves in the eyes of students.

So, what does it mean to treat students humanly? Let us start with Rabiat's important observation about the variances between individuals under the label "international student". Clearly, ceasing to consider international students as a homogeneous "blob" is a necessary step. As we can see from the work of Malay, Otten and Coelen (2023) cited earlier in this chapter, international students are a diverse group: our own programme currently includes students from Nigeria, India, Ghana, the United States of America and Pakistan. Steps taken towards de-muting international student voice, therefore, need to consider the varying degrees of Cultural Distance that may be at play and avoid the trap of normative-Western thinking. Furthermore, it needs to be recognised that country of origin is not the only mark of diversity: the same characteristics of age, gender, disability, subject experience that mark the home student population are also present within the international one, intersecting with their national identity in different ways. We know that channels for student voice can, in general, be beset by issues around exclusion and privilege and so require active development of inclusive mechanisms (Matthews and Dollinger, 2022). For international students, the intersection of national identity with a characteristic such as gender or social status, for example, may further complicate access to these channels where they require engaging in activity that is too far removed from internalised modes of engagement.

De-muting the voices of international students requires some thinking about the methods that are used. Rabiat explores this more fully:

> Traditional feedback and survey methods often fall short in capturing the experiences and perspectives of international students. Cultural differences, language barriers, and academic expectations can significantly impact their responses. The traditional feedback mechanism for

student voice often operates within a structured framework known as the "feedback loop" (Young and Jerome, 2020). It typically involves students providing feedback through surveys or evaluations, which are then collected and analysed by university staff. The findings and resulting actions are subsequently communicated back to students, ideally closing the loop. However, this approach has several limitations. One is the survey structure which needs improving to include in-person feedback giving students the opportunity to give open-ended answers. Another limitation is focusing on satisfaction on the part of the schools. Like "oh, at least we listen", rather than fostering genuine dialogue between the student and staff. This can lead to a perception that students are simply voicing complaints rather than engaging in meaningful discussions about their educational experiences. This has been experienced by students from my cohort: the number of times we tried to talk about the issues we were faced with, it started to look like we were complaining, as the people we were talking to could not do anything in earnest and still needed to talk to a higher authority, creating red tape on the way.

For the most part, my experience in the university has been positive as concerns raised during my early experiences about assignment structure were resolved and better assignment support and scaffolding were provided. This led to a larger proportion of students passing, which was welcome. In addition, prompt assignment feedback further enabled students' success as we were able to apply the learning to our subsequent assignments. Discussing incorporating the "student voice" in curriculum development, Brooman, Darwent and Pimor (2014) suggest aligning the redesign process more closely with student feedback so that a more inclusive curriculum can be achieved. Following my experiences, although the way the programme is designed is good, not enough has been done yet to ensure student voices are highlighted. At the end of each semester, surveys are submitted regarding the courses and curriculum, and course representatives are encouraged to get feedback from their course mates, but to this day the original design remains the same. While there's growing awareness of the importance of student voice in the University, it might not translate directly to an easier experience for current students as they may not be ones to benefit from the change. This frustrates students, making them uninterested in raising their voices, giving feedback or getting involved in any survey.

In terms of the aims and intentions of the parties involved, Page and Chahboun (2019) note that the primary goals of universities and international students regarding internationalisation are not necessarily the same. This is not to say that they must be at odds, but that universities need to be careful that they are not assuming what students want or need (Page and Chahboun, 2019). As discussed earlier, Universities generally prize internationalisation (to varying degrees) for the potential of financial gain, prestige and growth of a globalised culture (Page and Chahboun, 2019, Knight, 2011). International students, on the other hand, prioritise many other benefits of internationalisation: academic achievement, future earning potential, competitiveness and expertise in the field (Page and Chahboun, 2019). Particularly, they have been found to favour social interaction with fellow-nationals, or other international students, over engagement or assimilation with the host-nation and cultural interchange practices, particularly in the early stages of their sojourn (Page and Chahboun, 2019; Knight, 2011). This is an example of priorities diverging: the hoped-for internationalised culture does not emerge as anticipated, which is viewed by universities as a deficit, though it may be no more than an inevitability under current practices or prevailing social discourses (Page and Chahboun, 2019, Knight, 2011) and may simply be an example of international students adopting healthy protective practices in an environment that feels alien and sometimes hostile.

At the end of this section, it seems very clear that, although moves have been made towards de-muting the voice of international students, these frequently appear tokenistic and/or ineffective, leading to disillusionment in the process on both sides. However, this failure to launch is not to say that internationalisation is not the oyster full of pearls that had been hoped for but that the attempts to build internationalised academic environments are yet to be undertaken in the true spirit of co-creation. By critically examining their own structures and ambitions and by genuinely listening to the voice of international students, universities will be able to identify common ground to build on: "an indivisible solidarity between the world and the people" (Freire, 1970: 65). In this way, a truly "world-class" university might be established.

Pause for thought

1. Have you experienced or witnessed examples of institutional racism, particularly in relation to international students?
2. How well do you think student voice activity in your university currently includes international students? Why?
3. Where do think that the common ground between international students and their universities lie?

What could "world-class" look like?

There is always a risk that ambition may wither somewhat in the face of reality. The aim of this section is then not to provide a list of unattainable mandates, but to consider how world-classness can be achieved as a model of a co-creative, rather than co-consuming, internationalised higher education, by examining when and how changes to student voice processes should be implemented. While the focus of this chapter has been on the voices of international students, as with much of the work that has been completed on equality, diversity and inclusion across multiple sectors, these suggestions harm no one, but have the potential to benefit not just the target group, but many others who may have found their voices muted for a variety of reasons.

Let us begin with "when". According to Freire (1970: 101), "The earlier dialogue begins, the more truly revolutionary will the movement be". From this we take two meanings: firstly, that it is important to act now if we want to be able to change the system; secondly, that listening to the voices of international students must take place from the moment they join us. However, universities are perhaps not known for their sense of urgency or ability to respond swiftly to new demands: they are generally quite bureaucratic in nature. Interestingly, while Woodgates (2023) notes that university staff often feel that their institutions are poor at managing change, recent events such as the rapid adaptation to COVID-19 practices have shown that universities actually *do* have the capacity to react quickly. Perhaps the sense of urgency is key here: universities need to view the de-muting of international student voice as a pressing need. At the time of writing, Home Office (2024) data showed that between January and July of that year, the rate of visa application for study purposes was 16 per cent lower than the previous year, for reasons ranging from policy change in the United Kingdom to economic crises abroad. This prospective loss that might act as a spur to improving practices in order to boost recruitment and retention.

The apparent lag between feedback and change was highlighted by Rabiat earlier as a potential driver for disaffection: student suggestions rarely have an impact on their own cohort. This is something that could change if international student voice is de-muted from the very beginning of the programme. As it stands, it is often not until well into the semester, or even later, that processes such staff/student liaison committees and module feedback forms are initiated. A more agile and responsive practice would involve dialogue with international students from induction onwards about their hopes, expectations, needs and experiences. Furthermore, as Cook-Sather (2002) points out, a student body is never static. New "markets" will open up to our agents, who knows where our students may come from in the future? Time, politics and social changes will also exert their own influences over these individuals (Bronfenbrenner and Ceci, 1994), changing their circumstances, needs and ambitions. Dialogue, listening and change are not one-shot events, but ongoing processes: revolutions must keep turning, they should not stop.

In thinking about how processes must change, there are similarities in thinking between radical, big-picture thinkers such as Freire (1970) and those who focus more on the pragmatics of student voice (e.g. Cook-Sather, 2002): reform requires the dismantling of prevailing structures and modes of thinking in order to make way for new and better processes. Specifically, de-muting international student voice needs to move away from approaches that are tokenistic or sublimate the input of students (Cook-Sather, 2002; Matthews and Dollinger, 2022) in order to ensure a meaningful and impactful dialogue can take place, leading to genuine change and improvement. Rabiat notes,

> An example is the student's representative bodies of which I am a member. The opportunity gave me access to students in their element. Our role as students' reps is to ensure we are gathering students feedback, helping us bridge the gap between students and staff in ensuring that diverse voices are represented, giving us firsthand information about students concerns, which we as reps can relate to and bearing in mind that we are part of the same system.

While it is clear that Rabiat has found the student representative mechanism to be a useful one here, it seems there is still work to be done in ensuring that the dialogue gives way to meaningful change and that change is co-created rather than imposed. A way forward here might be ensuring that international students are consulted each time change is proposed that would affect them, and that the feedback and resulting impact of such consultations is recorded and publicly reported. Furthermore, according to the research by Matthews and Dollinger (2022), it is important to distinguish between student representation and student partnership in the fostering of student voice. These activities have very different functions: representation is about voice in the processes of governance, while partnership discourse is more about impact on teaching and learning (Matthews and Dollinger, 2022). The former of these has been codified in UK university practices for some long while, with the latter being a newer addition that might be hoped to address a perceived lack of impact on teaching and learning practice. While representation often involves the student body electing a peer, while partner students are often selected by staff, the problem with both of these practices is that they may end up prioritising the voices of individuals rather than cohorts, particularly "the highly engaged students" (Matthews and Dollinger, 2022: 564). One might also argue here that certain aspects of privilege, similar to those noted by Tavares (2021) as impacting international student success more broadly, would certainly influence whose voices are heard e.g. English as a first language, race, ethnicity, social class and gender.

It therefore seems important that a balance is struck in ensuring both representation and partnership are allowed to flourish, but the onus must be on ensuring that both types of activities allow for a true de-muting to take place. In terms of representation, there are more collective approaches that could be taken – i.e. by looking at the demographics of the group to ensure that a team of students with different backgrounds can work together and that they are trained to facilitate different forums to collect the views of their peers i.e. face-to-face, online, group and individual. Rabiat comments that "We have a mentorship programme, where we pair new international students with existing international students who have survived the system to help facilitate support in assisting student transition into the university". We know that this has facilitated student voice to some extent in that international students have reported needs and challenges through that system that they were unwilling to voice to tutors or the pastoral team, whether through fear, shame or uncertainty. It is the intention to extend the peer mentoring programme across the student body: there is certainly scope to build on this foundation to include a feedback mechanism, with more formalised and far-reaching channels. When thinking about partnership, one benefit of the approach we took is that rather than approaching those students known by the tutor to be engaged and interested, a formalised call for expressions of interest was circulated that allowed for a range of students to respond and signal their intentions in a more private way. This meant that volunteers with a range of profiles put themselves forward, bringing a real wealth of experience with them.

As stated earlier in this chapter, we strongly feel that "world-classness" will be judged by the wider world, not by universities themselves. Universities interact with that wider world in a multitude of ways, but although numbers may stall from time to time, the movement of students through the internationalisation of higher education is now one of the most significant ways in which that interaction occurs. To nurture these relationships, and to fully reap their benefits, universities need to become more agile and adaptable in responding to the voices of international students, as well as establishing processes that ensure that a multitude of voices can be heard, rather than those that are easiest to listen to.

Pause for thought

1. How rapidly do you feel your university is able to respond to issues raised by students? Do you have any sense of why that is?
2. Do you feel that student voice mechanisms in your university are working? Why or why not?
3. Do you think that the voices of all students are listened to equally? Can you identify the quietest voices? How could you amplify them?

Conclusion

Returning once more to themes of oysters and pearls, there is a Chinese proverb (provenance unknown) that begins: "Pearls lie not on the seashore: we have to dive for them". Change is never easy and there is still much work to be done if the goal of world-class listening is to be achieved. Crucially, however, neither Maddy nor Rabiat think that this particular pearl is beyond reach.

International students expend a great deal of energy on the process of adaptation – there is a significant range of challenges that they need to overcome in order to make a success of their sojourn abroad. Adaptation means success for these individuals, opening up wider possibilities ahead of them. Yet each individual success or failure to adapt reflects also on the institution and their processes, marking out their ability to listen, to change and support those students on their journey, securing their reputation as a truly world-class place of learning where all are welcomed and treated as part of the community. It is therefore up to universities to reflect on their practices and engage in meaningful dialogue with international students: listening to global voices is the only way to secure lasting global legacy.

In keeping with the theme of the chapter, the last words belong to Rabiat:

> When our ideas, experiences, and thoughts are valued and taken seriously, it encourages a sense of safety, belonging, and self-worth. Listening to the voices of international students is paramount in creating an empowering and transformative university experience. This, in turn, leads to improved learning outcomes, a feeling of being heard and understood, and a newfound confidence in our ability to make a positive impact on the world a voice at a time.
>
> I encourage my fellow students to embrace the power of their voices by actively participating in discussions on issues that matter to them, getting involved in university communities, and sharing their unique perspectives. I also encourage universities to adopt strategies such as an inclusive curriculum, providing supportive services like peer mentoring, and offering opportunities for student leadership to create an environment where international students feel empowered to express their viewpoints and make significant contributions. By continuously refining our approach, we can create a truly inclusive and supportive learning environment that meets the needs of international students and meets the university's goals.

Summary points

- The true potential of the internationalisation of UK universities is yet to be fully realised.
- Currently, the onus to adapt is generally placed upon international students, rather than their universities.
- The voice of international students is rarely considered in policy, practices and research about them.
- Universities need to critically consider their processes, aims and structures to allow them to listen effectively to the voices of international students.
- By listening to the voices of international students, universities can build a truly world-class environment: one that favours genuine interchange.

Recommended reading

Page, A.G. and Chahboun, S. (2019) Emerging empowerment of international students: How international student literature has shifted to include the students' voices. *Higher Education*, 78, pp. 871–885.

This article argues that the aims of universities in the process of internationalisation often diverge from those of international students themselves, leading to perceived failures when students do not match the expectations of universities. The authors demand that the voices of international students in research are "de-muted", enabling a better understanding of their priorities.

Tavares, V. (2021). Feeling excluded: international students experience equity, diversity and inclusion. *International Journal of Inclusive Education*, 28(8), 1551–1568. https://doi.org/10.1080/13603116.2021.2008536

The authors of this article suggest the perspectives of international students are under-explored in relation to equality, diversity and inclusion. Their own research leads them to conclude that international students commonly experience exclusion and othering.

References

Altbach, P.G. (2004) The Costs and Benefits of World-Class Universities. *Academe*, 90(1), pp. 20–23.
Ben-David, J. and Zloczower, A. (1962) Universities and academic systems in modern societies. *European Journal of Sociology/Archives Européennes de Sociologie*, 3(1), pp. 45–84.
Bronfenbrenner, U. and Ceci, S.J. (1994) Nature-nurture reconceptualized in developmental perspective: A bio-ecological model. *Psychological Review*, 101(4), p. 568.
Brooman, S., Darwent, S. and Pimor, A. (2014) The student voice in higher education curriculum design: Is there value in listening? *Innovations in Education and Teaching International*, 52(6), pp. 663–674. https://doi.org/10.1080/14703297.2014.910128
Cannings, J., Halterbeck, M. and Conlon, G. (2023) *The benefits and costs of international higher education students to the UK economy*. Report for the Higher Education Policy Institute, Universities UK International, and Kaplan International Pathways.
Cook-Sather, A. (2002) Authorizing students' perspectives: Toward trust, dialogue, and change in education. *Educational Researcher*, 31(4), pp. 3–14.
Csikszentmihalyi, M., 2014. The systems model of creativity and its applications. *The Wiley handbook of genius*, pp.533–545.
Findon, M., Mahama, J. and Ojo, O. (2025) *Share Your Voices: Capturing the Perspectives of MA Education International Students*. University of Worcester. Unpublished.
Freire, P. (1970) *Pedagogy of the Oppressed*. London: The Continuum Publishing Company.
Grande, S. (2018) Refusing the university. In S. Grande *Toward what justice?* Abingdon: Routledge.
Home Office (2024) Monthly monitoring of entry clearance visa applications Updated 8 August 2024. Available: https://www.gov.uk/government/statistics/monthly-entry-clearance-visa-applications/monthly-monitoring-of-entry-clearance-visa-applications (Accessed 15 August 2024).
Jones, E. (2017) Problematising and reimagining the notion of 'international student experience'. *Studies in Higher Education*, 42(5), pp. 933–943.
Knight, J. (2011) Five myths about internationalization. *International Higher Education*, (62). Winter 2011 pp. 14–15.
Macpherson, W. (1999) *The Stephen Lawrence Inquiry: Report*. London: Home Office.
Malay, E.D., Otten, S. and Coelen, R.J. (2023) Predicting adjustment of international students: The role of cultural intelligence and perceived cultural distance. *Research in Comparative and International Education*, 18(3), pp. 485–504.
Matthews, K.E. and Dollinger, M. (2022) Student voice in higher education: The importance of distinguishing student representation and student partnership. *Higher Education* 85, pp. 555–570.
Page, A.G. and Chahboun, S. (2019) Emerging empowerment of international students: How international student literature has shifted to include the students' voices. *Higher Education*, 78, pp. 871–885.
Said, E.W. (2016) *Orientalism: Western conceptions of the Orient*. London: Penguin.
Settles, I.H., Jones, M.K., Buchanan, N.T. and Dotson, K. (2021) Epistemic exclusion: Scholar (ly) devaluation that marginalizes faculty of color. *Journal of Diversity in Higher Education*, 14(4), p. 493.
Tavares, V. (2021). Feeling excluded: international students experience equity, diversity and inclusion. *International Journal of Inclusive Education*, 28(8), 1551–1568. https://doi.org/10.1080/13603116.2021.2008536
Woodgates, P. (2023) *Change by Design: How universities should design change initiatives for success*. HEPI.
Young, H. and Jerome, L. (2020) Student voice in higher education: Opening the loop. *British Educational Research Journal*, 46(3), pp.688–705. https://doi.org/10.1002/berj.3603

12 Empowering disabled learners' voices and agency through universal design for learning

Seán Bracken, Alice Hopkins, Anastasia Kennett, Harriet Lawrence, Emma Richardson, Kirsty Wedgbury and Christian T. Wilson

Introduction

This chapter explores the integration of learner voice (LV) and agency within the Universal Design for Learning (UDL) framework to enhance educational experiences for disabled learners. It highlights the critical role of learner involvement in shaping curricula that reflect their diverse needs and perspectives. Drawing on learning experiences of students who assisted in co-organising sessions for an international conference, and further developing lessons learned by seeking their input and reflections regarding the creation of professional development modules for higher education (HE) lecturers, the chapter demonstrates how UDL principles can facilitate inclusive practices that empower learners. The argument put forward in this chapter is that it is necessary to creatively co-design environments where students feel heard and valued, and where they are provided with agency to advocate for their meaningful participation in educational decision-making processes. By sharing personal testimonies of students with diverse learning requirements, the text underscores the transformative impact of inclusive design on learning outcomes. Furthermore, it critiques existing educational policies and practices that often overlook the voices, experiences and agency of marginalised learners, proposing strategies for fostering genuine engagement and collaboration.

Ultimately, the chapter argues for a systemic shift towards inclusive educational practices that truly validates and incorporates the agency of all learners, thereby enriching the learning landscape and promoting equity in HE. The chapter begins by providing a contextual overview, this is followed by an exploration of the notion of LV and its interface with agency, thereafter there is an overview of how the UDL framework may enable greater agency. Finally, the chapter rounds off with the salient lessons learned and an identification of implications for future policy and practices within and beyond the United Kingdom.

Contextual overview

By drawing on a praxis-based and action-oriented case study process (Kemmis and Smith, 2008), a possible pathway is provided for educators and students alike who are interested in overcoming barriers to learning encountered by disabled or other marginalised learners. The case study incorporates three distinct phases carried out over an eight-month period in 2024-2025, which when taken together made an important contribution to a British Council funded project entitled

DOI: 10.4324/9781003406334-12

"Strengthening Inclusion in Higher Education in Indonesia and the UK through Universal Design for Learning". Ethical clearance for the project was secured through our partner Universitas Indonesia.

During Phase 1, in preparation for an international conference focused on UDL (INCLUDE and ICEQ, 2024), two academic colleagues recognised the imperative of incorporating the LV dimension into the planning and realisation of the conference. Following a wider call out to our university, four students who self-identified as having a disability came forward to engage with the challenge. These students worked closely with academics in planning how the conference might be more cognisant of the requirements of disabled learners. These students worked closely with academics in planning how the conference could purposefully embed the requirements of disabled learners from the outset, thus enabling their active participation. The students also pre-planned some sessions primarily focused on sharing students' narratives of their experiences to be featured during the conference. In Phase 2, the students, who are co-authors to this chapter, were also enthusiastically involved in a follow up workshop with three colleagues from Indonesia and others from within the University of Worcester, which informed development of an open-access, online professional enhancement course for HE teachers within and beyond the United Kingdom. Cognisant that the most recent UDL framework 3.0 (CAST, 2024) posited LV very much to the fore while considering application of inclusive design, insights from the co-collaborating learners proved pivotal at this project phase. Finally, Phase 3 involved a meta-reflective analysis of key lessons learned overall and what the implications of these might be for policymakers, students and teachers alike. Aspects of the mutually beneficial and transformative attributes of the learning journey are captured in the call out boxes, such as the first one shared by Anastasia, which illuminate aspects of how the conjoining of the UDL framework with LV agency engendered a sense of empowerment.

Finally, Phase 3 involved a meta-reflective analysis of key lessons learned overall and what the implications of these might be for policymakers, students and teachers alike. Aspects of the mutually beneficial and transformative attributes of the learning journey are captured in the call out boxes, such as the first one shared by Anastasia, which illuminate aspects of how the conjoining of the UDL framework with LV agency engendered a sense of empowerment.

Anastasia's story: A seat at the table to imagine inclusion beyond borders

Representing diverse learners at the Power of Potential Conference and the Indonesian module development project gave me a seat at the table alongside other diverse students. I found the experience welcoming, sympathetic and understanding to my needs. I was given the questions in advance to support my processing speed, and I was able to make notes (either on presentation cards or may laptop) which I took with me, supporting my memory recall. There was a desire to listen to us and to change their module and teaching practices based on our experiences which was both exciting and overwhelming. The people in the room wanted to hear our thoughts, feelings and experiences of being in a HE classroom and they were happy to hear our positive and negative experiences. They provided a space in which academics could learn from diverse students and diverse students could learn from academics. For instance, I increased my learning about diversity and inclusion (within the United Kingdom and on a global scale) at the conference but more intimately on the Indonesian

> project in which we conversed with each other across a table about local, national and international practices. In both instances, we discussed similarities and differences, allowing us to discuss ideas for future strategies that could help to support diverse students across the globe. The biggest impact for me was having a seat at the table, knowing that people wanted to hear my voice. It meant that I and people like me were represented.

As identified by Anastasia, the purposeful application of UDL principles facilitated an **anticipatory inclusive design** (Bracken, 2024) approach assisted in breaking down barriers to learning and participation. Anticipatory inclusive design involves the purposeful reflection and planning for future learning and assessment goals, resources and methods, as well as considering learning spaces and technologies, so that these can be devised to be as flexible and accessible to the greatest extent possible. Collaborating with learners in this process from the outset is a shift from teaching-oriented pedagogy to situating the learning requirements of diverse learners at the heart of the inclusive educational design process (Bovill, Cook-Sather and Felten, 2011).

> **Pause for thought**
>
> Reflecting on the discussion so far in this chapter, consider:
>
> In the previous extract, Anastasia mentions the importance of being heard. To what extent do you feel you have had a "seat at the table" regarding your own educational requirements and ambitions?
>
> What are some of the ways that Anastasia identifies her requirements were met to facilitate her engagement with these projects. How might such strategies be mainstreamed?
>
> What do you believe is significant in terms of Anastasia's story, how might implications for your learning be integrated meaningfully into educational practices across the life course?

Exploring notions of learner voice and agency

The importance of learner voices to inform their agency has been amplified by practitioners right across the learning life course, and increasingly so in HE (Seale, 2009). Arguably, such initiatives have their roots in practices often associated with early years (EY) and primary school philosophies of learning that posit the child as learner at the heart of children's social, cultural and cognitive development. For example, initiatives such as Te Whariki in New Zealand, and the Regio Emelio Approach from Italy, which have highlighted the necessity for curriculum learning to be creatively fashioned by directly integrating young people's experiences, informed by their capabilities and their personal cognitive, as well as their wider cultural contexts (Taylor, 2024). A logical next step in terms of how curriculum could be developed necessitates an authentic and agentic involvement of young people through elicitation of their voices.

Of late, the incorporation of LV has become somewhat mainstreamed within higher education institution (HEI) policy initiatives; this is exemplified for instance in the QAA's (2024) Sector Agreed Principles, the second of which directs

> [p]roviders (to) take deliberate steps to engage students as active partners in assuring and enhancing the quality of the student learning experience. Engagement happens individually and collectively to influence all levels of study and decisionmaking.

Another UK-based agency whose stated goal is to strengthen HE through transglobal collaboration has published a compendium of case studies along with a comprehensive review of relevant literature addressing the key area of student peer learning and support (AdvanceHE, 2024). However, to date, what is noteworthy about such initiatives and their ensuing publications is the relative dearth of direct involvement with, and lack of voice afforded to, the very persons whose interests are supposedly being promoted. So, there is a strong rationale for undertaking research that will reveal ways in which learners' voice and agency can be further strengthened. The authors contend that the UDL framework provides an effective conceptual lens to explore how learners' voice and their experiences might be better revealed through action research.

Threading learner voice and agency through the UDL framework

UDL is encapsulated within a framework that was developed to address the diverse needs of learners in educational settings (CAST, 2024; Rose, 2000). Originating from the principles of inclusive design in architecture, UDL was conceptualised by an interdisciplinary team at Harvard University. This team drew inspiration from Ron Mace's work at the Centre for Universal Design at North Carolina State University, which emphasised creating spaces that accommodate a wide range of users, including those with disabilities. By integrating Mace's inclusive design principles with social constructivist theories from Vygotsky and Dewey, the team formulated UDL to promote educational inclusion (Bracken, 2024).

UDL is built on three core principles: multiple means of engagement, multiple means of representation, and multiple means of action and expression. The first principle, multiple means of engagement, focuses on involving learners by tapping into their interests and motivations. This principle addresses the affective and relational aspects of learning, aiming to recruit learners' interest in the attainment of meaningful and attainable goals. By highlighting the need for authenticity in the curriculum and assessment design process and by involving learners meaningful in that endeavour, students' engagement and motivation throughout the learning process is enhanced. The second principle, multiple means of representation, acknowledges the diverse neurological and linguistic backgrounds of learners. It emphasises providing various ways to present information and content, ensuring that all learners can access and understand the material. This principle supports the scaffolding of learning by offering different organisational schemata, which can be particularly beneficial in leveraging learning technologies and artificial intelligence to enhance educational experiences (Saborío-Taylor, and Rojas-Ramírez, 2024). The third principle, multiple means of action and expression, focuses on the different ways learners can demonstrate their knowledge and skills. It promotes the use of various modes of assessment, allowing learners to express their understanding in ways that resonate with their cognitive, socio-cultural and economic contexts (Hanesworth,

Bracken and Elkington, 2019). This principle also encourages the development of executive functioning skills, helping learners set and achieve realistic goals while reflecting on their learning strategies. The importance of UDL in informing curriculum development lies in its anticipatory approach to learner diversity. Traditional methods, such as curriculum differentiation, often fall short in addressing the complex and intersectional needs of diverse learners. UDL, on the other hand, advocates for designing curricula that inherently consider the variability of learners from the outset. This proactive approach ensures that educational environments are inclusive and accessible to all students rather than retrofitting existing curricula to meet individual needs.

UDL's emphasis on inclusivity and equity aligns with international educational initiatives, such as the Salamanca Statement and Framework for Action (United Nations, 1994), which advocates for integrating all students, including those with special educational needs and disabilities, into mainstream schools. Despite these initiatives, many educational systems still struggle to provide high-quality inclusive education. Reports, such as the one from the Committee on the Rights of Persons with Disabilities (United Nations, 2017), highlight the ongoing challenges in teacher preparedness and curriculum design within the United Kingdom to meet the needs of diverse learners. By adopting UDL, educators can create more inclusive learning environments that cater to the diverse cognitive, physical, and socio-cultural needs of students. This framework not only supports the attainment of appropriate learning outcomes for all learners but also fosters a more equitable and just educational system. As educational changes continue to accelerate, UDL offers a robust and adaptable framework for curriculum development that can help navigate the complexities of learner diversity and ensure that all students can succeed. Critically, in order to do so, and as argued by Christian in the following testimony, all players concerned need to consider the wellbeing and engagement of disabled learners.

Christian's story: Challenging the status quo to amplify disabled learners' voices

One of the most important elements to UDL is engagement. Fundamentally, it's the cornerstone of anything that you want to accomplish. Diverse learners need to be front and centre. We need to be able to feel welcome to share our experiences, to ensure disabled people do have a voice. Disabled people do have an important message and want it to be heard. However, far too often disabled people are not listened to. When disabled people are not listened to, that's when problems occur! Disabled people need to be in the heart of the conversation, because they are the people most likely to effect change regarding disability. I have had many experiences, when teaching has gone above and beyond to help me improve my learning. However, on some occasions educators have not been prepared to ensure teaching practices are inclusive or have refused to accept that teaching practices even should be inclusive. In my experience, this leads to disagreements which are detrimental to learning. For me, attending the UDL conference allowed my voice to be heard in a way it never was before. I felt listened to; I felt like what I had to say mattered! Additionally, with the Indonesian delegates, I got a sense we were really contributing to something special! For far too long, people like me, have not been listened to. We have not been engaged enough. We need to challenge the status quo and think about the teacher – student relationship. Are we excluding the most important people, the learners themselves?

According to Christian's testimony, in this instance, the UDL framework provided a helpful mechanism for enabling his voice to be heard. But it is important to recognise that the UDL framework has been critiqued. There are two major dimensions to the critical observations made regarding UDL, the first is that it lacks a robust evidence base (Boysen, 2024) and secondly, as argued by Seale, Burgstahler and Havel (2022), UDL tends to be exclusionary of other frameworks and models of inclusion. With this in mind, it ought to be acknowledged that as a social construct, there will always be some shortcomings with the frameworks, and consequently, its adoption should be dynamic and adaptive rather than being dogmatic and exclusionary. Ultimately, educators and policymakers have a shared goal to enable accessibility and to promote policies, systems, practices and resources that facilitate a maximisation of learning outcomes for all learners. Adopting a systems approach to tackling exclusionary policies and practices, such as that encouraged by the UDL framework, can only assist in realising that shared goal, but findings should be provisional and judiciously couched.

> **Pause for thought**
>
> While UDL promotes inclusivity, many educational systems still struggle to effectively implement these principles. What barriers exist that prevent the adoption of UDL in learning spaces, and how can they be addressed?
>
> Christian's story highlights the importance of engaging disabled learners in the conversation. How can educators ensure that the voices of all learners, especially those with disabilities, are not only heard but actively shape educational practices?
>
> Critics argue that UDL lacks robust evidence base and may exclude other valuable frameworks. How can educators balance the adoption of UDL with the need for a diverse range of inclusive practices that cater to all learners?
>
> UDL should be seen as a dynamic and adaptive framework rather than a rigid model. In what ways can educators remain flexible and responsive to the evolving needs of their learners while implementing UDL principles?

Insights from the collaborative praxis of UDL implementation

Following inputs to the formation of the conference event and an engagement with the development of the professional development materials for lecturers, the authors held a reflective review of learning that had emerged from these experiences. This entailed of a 90-minute dialogue around core questions that elicited learner and lecturers' views. The session was digitally recorded and analysed to reveal key themes that had been articulated as particularly important by the learners. While ethical dimensions for this follow up activity had been covered by an initial internal approval process, the ongoing consideration of care for self and others recognised that ethicality as practice pervades all phases of enacted research seeing to bring about systems change (Jenlink, 2004).

The shared meta-reflective analysis of experiences identified key insights that had accrued over the eight-month collaborative journey. These included the necessity to posit inclusivity and flexibility at a heart of the curriculum design process. However, these was also recognition that in bringing about such change, individualised initiatives were less likely to be impactful, so formation of communities of praxis were encouraged to better facilitate cross-institutional alliances that could identify and address systemic barriers to engagement. The golden thread to facilitate meaningful change was learner agency and empowerment, these concepts are explored further in the next section.

Incorporating inclusivity and flexibility into curriculum design

The need for inclusive practices in curriculum development was a recurring topic, with students advocating for more flexible and responsive educational structures. There was a shared believe that the UDL, with its emphasis on flexibility of teaching methods, and assessments could provide a shared conceptual basis for bringing about change. By providing the knowledge, skills and capacities for students to co-create course content, or to facilitate the crafting of meaningful learning outcomes that aligned with course objectives, there was a belief that educational experiences would be more aligned with the realities of diverse learning requirements. As articulated by one of the students, "We need to push towards bigger change… creating programmes that reflect our needs", and design-based approaches conjoining flexibility with a shared understanding of what learning was required would be pivotal in enabling that bigger change to become successful.

Designing in such flexibility can be particularly beneficial for neurodiverse learners who may require different approaches to succeed. For example, by making recorded transcripts or videos of shared learning events accessible, there was greater scope to revisit and unpack challenging concepts. Additional strengthening of executive functioning is provided as learners become more reflective and aware of how best to set and attain realistic learning goals. As part of joint goal setting, and to advance the development of inclusive cultures that challenged power structures, students and their teachers became increasingly aware of the potential impact of co-constructing traditionally hegemonic academic endeavours. For instance, by involving disabled learners in the authoring and co-authoring of book chapters, poster presentations and articles on learner journeys, students concerned have a growing capacity to influence wider policies and practices pertaining to inclusion. Overall, the concept that marginalised learners should have a stake in curriculum design and enactment, and that flexibility should be a key attribute of ongoing change processes, chimes with a Freire (1978) sociological approach. Thus, in an age of multiple learner diversities, while re-envisioning the nature of curriculum development, the authors contend that a "one-size-fits-all curriculum" is no longer fit for purpose. One of the key enabling strategies for realising this goal was to put systems in place that encouraged disabled students to have a shared purpose with other disabled learners.

Enabling peer support and community building

Students highlighted the significance of peer support networks in navigating their educational journeys. As one of the students shared, "Having different students being put into groups to share their experiences…is quite a good idea". Over the duration of the project, structured peer support networks helped students feel less isolated and they reflected on the necessity to scale up this approach. Institutions can facilitate this by establishing mentorship programmes where students with disabilities are paired with peers or faculty who understand their challenges. This not only provides emotional support but also practical guidance in navigating academic and social environments.

Learning from this experience, has encouraged the academic authors to consciously advocate for a specific platform for students with diverse needs at all academic events that proport to advance their needs. A basic premise in doing so would be to include collaborating with students to fashion what that platform ought to achieve and for students to pre-determine how they may wish to share their truth with other delegates, whether they might be academics or other students. Indeed, the importance of faculty understanding and supporting students' social and learning requirements was a key theme. Accordingly, one of the students identified, "It's good to have the insight in relation to the professionals". This is because they can assist in navigating ways through official systems and processes which may be mysterious or challenging for students acting alone.

However, as the students observed, not all HE teachers were aware of what their needs might be, so they identified that training was essential for fostering an inclusive environment. Institutions should provide professional development opportunities focused on understanding disability and inclusive teaching practices. This training can equip educators with the skills to adapt their teaching strategies based on meaningful student feedback, creating a more supportive learning atmosphere. As occurred in this project, actually involving the students concerned in the co-creation of professional enhancement programmes would add authenticity to these initiatives and strengthen the agency of learners so that it was more than merely tokenistic. Nonetheless, there is also a recognition that even when there may be a shared commitment to challenging inequities with defined learning spaces, sometimes the wider cultural context falls short and puts barriers in place.

Challenging institutional barriers

During the shared discussions, one of the students expressed a view that "[t]he whole system really is not built for us", thus revealing frustrations with institutional policies or practices that often hinder rather than help students with disabilities. It was one thing to be "invited to have a seat at the table", but what was the difference if the table itself was inaccessible, or worse, the table was inadvertently placed outside the house. Because students are rarely involved in the initial phases of organisational design, many of the systems and processes that are subsequently there for their benefit may in fact create barriers to educational progression. Institutions must critically assess their policies and practices to identify and eliminate barriers to inclusion. This could involve regular reviews of accessibility standards and ensuring that all facilities and resources are compliant with best practices in disability support. Engaging students in these reviews can provide valuable insights into their needs and experiences. This can also be pertinent to the co-construction of physical and social spaces around the campus and the input of students on organising committees where they are consulted on issues related to access, signage, respite spaces and the environment – for example, being asked to share their views about architectural lighting heating and import of biophilic design. In terms of classroom accessibility and the inclusive functionality of equipment, teaching staff need to become more conversant with basic principles of digital accessibility. Increasingly, that will entail recognising and applying the affordances provided by ethical and critically informed uses of artificial intelligence that enable disabled learners ever greater access to the curriculum while enhancing their capacities to strengthen learning outcomes (Almufareh et al., 2024).

Teachers, students and cross campus teams, as well as university leaders, can be encouraged to think of physical and digital spaces as canvases for opportunity that foster inclusion. By asking probing questions, such as does the space welcome ALL people with mobility, sensory, learning, cognitive or socio-cultural requirements? There is ample scope for collaborative groups to embrace and amplify different cultures and contexts utilising UDL by asking, "Who is not at the table?" and perhaps ever more provocatively, "Who has designed the table, and for what purpose"? Steps can then be taken to seek to redress and overcome some of the challenging institutional barriers in place (Richardson, 2024). This might involve for example, conducting an audit of assessment practices and learning from innovative and inclusive ways in which students learning can be captured more emphatically and effectively.

Agency and empowerment

As identified earlier, the consistent notable feature pervading throughout the differing project phases was that of advancing student agency and empowerment. Students emphasised the importance of having their voices heard. Nonetheless, voice itself may be feeble or become subsumed into a cacophony of other more powerful voices unless it is amplified by agency and empowerment. The latter necessary components of voice emerged from a sense that students felt they were making a difference by firstly transforming their own lives while also transforming the perspectives that others, especially academics, may have had of them. And that ultimately, when they collaborated in this way, students and academics working together could alter wider systems and processes. There was a growing realisation for all concerned that the solution finding endeavours were best embarked upon in collaboration with teachers and other stakeholders who may be expert in facilitating and enabling voice to becoming meaningful and impactful. Empowering students to take an active role in their education is crucial. Institutions can support this by creating student-led focus groups where students can share experiences and collaborate on solutions. This approach not only fosters a sense of community but also enhances student engagement and ownership of their learning. Through such meaningful engagement, shared academic and student perspectives can lead to more effective and relevant learning environments. By listening to and integrating student voices, educators can create more meaningful and impactful learning experiences for all. That co-constructed approach is highlighted in Alice's account:

Alice's story: The UDL framework as an enabler for voice and agency

The idea of UDL informed by the student voice is something which captivated me when I first discovered it. Predominantly, my education has been within the mainstream system, and it was only specialised in a school for the blind in the two years prior to coming to university. In the main, the approach to my learning was such that little effort was given into adapting teaching and learning strategies to suit my needs.

I have had minimal experiences of educators taking initiative when it comes to adjusting teaching practises to better my learning. Throughout my education, I have often been required to guide my educators in how best to support me; this had been a difficult process due to a lack of willingness to aid me on the part of many teaching staff. For me, attending the UDL conference with its focus on the LV and its building of a safe and empowering environments for my voice to be heard was revelatory. Additionally, when meeting with the Indonesian delegates, I was fascinated to learn of their varying challenges when it comes to engaging with diverse learners in differing cultural contexts. The alternate approaches taken to develop UDL in an inclusive way while maintaining a focus on student lead practices, and the shaping of educational policies was captivating. The opportunities that I as a learner have been presented with have been enriching. Along with my peers, my voice has been heard and acknowledged when it comes to the advancement of UDL.

Pause for thought

Throughout this section, there is an emphasis on the application of the UDL framework to facilitate learner agency in the curriculum and assessment development process. Mindful of the other chapters in this book, how might this approach be further complemented by adopting additional conceptual frameworks or strategies for action?

The importance of peer supports and community building have been highlighted in this section. From your experiences, what are some of the potential strengths and drawbacks of advancing this idea?

Perhaps one of the greatest challenges might be overcoming more systemic institutional barriers. From your experiences, what might these be and how might they be overcome in time?

The final point in this section identifies the centrality of agency and empowerment. In keeping with the notion of goal setting as identified within the UDL framework, what might be a concrete goal for advancing your own sense of agency within your studies and to enhance your educational journey?

Implications of our experiences for co-development of an inclusive education for all

The learners involved in this project are far from uniform in their learning requirements, what a blind student requires in terms of accessibility may be very different from a student with a cognitive learning impairment, so there could never be a "one-size-fits-all" approach to meeting their needs. Thus, UDL necessitates an appreciation for intersecting diversities of learner identity markers, whether they may be through multiple variabilities in (dis)ability, gender, culture or any other major identifying characteristics (Chu et al., 2013). The universal imperative in the design process is the necessity to provide individuals and groups with the resources, strategies and materials they require to gain equitable access to learning pathways. Whilst doing so, it would be helpful to identify shared ways that barriers to learning can be overcome (Culver et al., 2023). In practical terms, this might involve, for example, reconfiguration of traditional modes of assessment enabling much more flexibility regarding how all students are provided latitude to evidence learning outcomes. This involves being open to innovation and collaborating with key colleagues across the campus to facilitate an inclusive design approach to the actualisation of considerate, and to the greatest extent possible, universally accessible architectural, environmental, social, technological and psychological learning, social and being spaces (Holcombe et al., 2023). A critical driving force within this complex and rewarding interplay is the agency of disabled learners. To some extent, that dynamic interplay of factors is captured in Figure 12.1.

Through adopting a collaborative approach practiced and honed over an eight-month period, the project team have gleaned insights regarding what may be required to scale up these ways of working so that they might become more systems-based with the potential to broaden impact across the wider university. Critically, there is a necessity to frame **LV and agency** at the heart of the process. Given that the affordances of technologies and the ethical use of artificial intelligence have such a liberating role to play for disabled learners, it will be important to secure inputs and advice from colleagues working with **information technologies**. For example, there is ample scope to jointly identify and publicise apps and tips for accessibility and identify how to make virtual

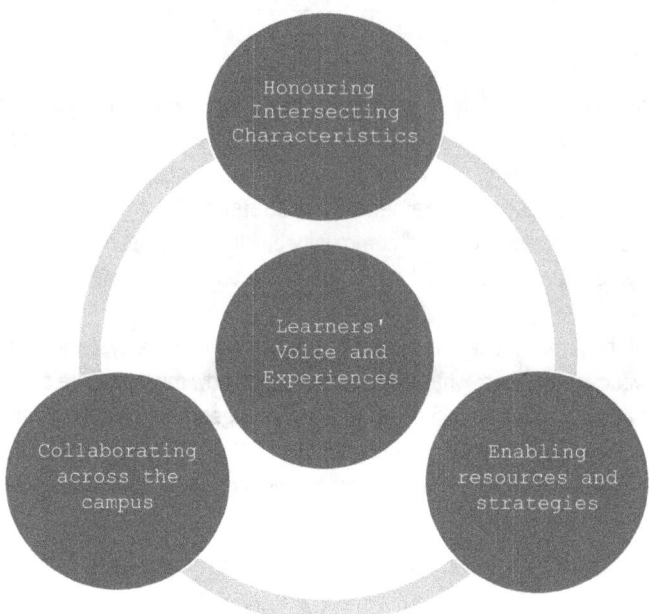

Figure 12.1 Grounding LV praxis and research on principles of UDL

learning environments ever more accessible, simply by providing reading materials and presentations in advance facilitates enhanced accessibility for all learners. Further, it will be beneficial to incorporate advice and collaboration from colleagues in **student services**, as well as liaising with **library and information specialists** to explore aspects of accessibility for reading lists and enhancing accessibility of learning resources. Finally, by reaching out beyond the university confines and **encouraging international research links** in the field of UDL, there is room to grow intellectually and to reflect on, and challenge, one's own cultural positioning within a wider striving towards attainment of educational experiences that, as the Sustainable Development Goal 4.5 aims to,

> [e]liminate gender disparities in education and ensure equal access to all levels of education and vocational training for the vulnerable, including persons with disabilities, indigenous peoples and children in vulnerable situations.
>
> (United Nations, 2015)

In her testimony, Harriet provides a glimpse as to how our shared endeavours may have advanced our understanding as to how such an ambitious goal may well be within our grasp should we have the courage and determination to make it a reality.

Harriet's story: the UDL framework as an enabler for voice and agency

During my education, I often found my voice less acknowledged in traditional settings where a one-size-fits-all approach is the "norm" for meeting students' needs. This experience shaped my interest in UDL, emphasising flexible, student-centred learning experiences. Attending the conference was transformative with the emphasis placed on the learner's voice, allowing me to freely express my thoughts, highlighting the importance of including students in discussions that shape educational policies and practices. I felt empowered, my opinions were valued by educators, emphasising shifts towards more inclusive, student-centred education. Meeting with the Indonesian delegates was another highlight. Engaging with individuals from different cultural backgrounds, discussing shared challenges and opportunities in education was fascinating. The exchange was mutually enriching learning about Indonesia's innovative approaches to UDL. This experience emphasised the learner's voice in driving educational change. It was inspiring to see how our input could contribute to shaping educational strategies. This conference reinforced my belief that students should have active roles defining their education, our perspectives creating more effective learning environments. Integrating student voices, educators can create more meaningful learning experiences for all. For me, early access to educational resources is essential, allowing preparing and engaging with material at my own pace. This approach reduces stress and anxiety, enhancing my participation in class and leading to a more fulfilling learning experience. Assessment techniques that offer multiple ways to demonstrate learning, such as projects and presentations, align with my strengths, encouraging deeper engagement, and providing a more accurate reflection of my learning than traditional exams.

Pause for thought

How can we effectively address the diverse learning needs of students to ensure that a "one-size-fits-all" approach is avoided in education?

In what ways can empowering learners by incorporating their voices and agency into educational practices lead to more meaningful and effective learning experiences?

What collaborative strategies can educators, technology specialists and support services implement to enhance accessibility for all learners, particularly those with disabilities?

Harriet speaks to the necessity to review the ways in which traditional assessments might be reimagined to evidence learning. How might this be achieved in a system where "norming and sorting" behaviours appear to be predominant in shaping educational policy and practice?

Suggest how incorporating international perspectives on UDL could challenge our local understandings and practices, and how reflections might lead to the promotion of greater equity in education?

Conclusion

Consulting and employing student experts as architects of UDL will increase the likelihood that inclusion, dignity and equitable opportunities become effective building foundations for enhancing the physical and socio-cultural fabrics of teaching, assessments, and wider learning communities. A synthesis of the LV transcripts highlights the critical need for inclusive practices in HE that empower students, particularly those with disabilities. By fostering agency, promoting peer support, and challenging institutional barriers, educational institutions can create environments that not only accommodate but celebrate diversity. Engaging students in the design and implementation of their educational experiences is essential for meaningful change, aligning with contemporary research in disability studies and learner engagement. While doing so, where possible and relevant, it is helpful to incorporate an international or transnational dimension to the learning, as this enables academics and students to better contextualise their own and others' interpretations of what it means to appreciate diversity and to strive for equity while realising inclusion through UDL. Further, there is also a recognition that the UDL framework can always only be partial and when applied to generalised cohorts of learners, individualised additional requirements will always be required as complementary measures. However, the concept and practical application of notions of universality are enormously facilitative for learners, service providers, lecturers, as well as for institutional and national policymakers who, by taking proactive measure to facilitate a generalised anticipatory design approach, can thereby provide diverse learners with ever more effective learning and social pathways.

Summary points

- Learners with diverse learning needs are experts by experience of UDL, they are the most fitting architects of their own learning design, but they require facilitative conditions of agency to realise their learning potentials.
- UDL provides a framework for inclusivity in learning environments, however this ought to be applied flexibly and is never a "silver bullet" responding to all students' needs.
- Technology can play a significant role in enhancing learner agency.
- Policy changes are necessary to support inclusive education, and these should be meaningfully and agentively informed by the disabled learners' experiences.
- Incorporating an international dimension to our educational experiences enables scope for widening our experiences and reflecting on our own cultural understandings of inclusion and accessibility for ALL learners.

Recommended reading

Meyer, A., Rose, D. H., and Gordon, D. (2014). *Universal Design for Learning: Theory and Practice*. Boston: CAST Professional Publishing ISBN: 978-0989867405

This text provides a comprehensive overview of UDL principles and their application in educational settings.

Cook-Sather, A., Bovill, C., Felten, P. (2014). *Engaging Students as Partners in Learning and Teaching: A Guide for Faculty*. New York: Jossey Bass ISBN: 9781118434581

This guide explores strategies for involving students in the educational process, emphasising the importance of their voices.

Bracken, S. and Novak, K, (editors) (2019) *Transforming Higher Education through Universal Design for Learning: An International Perspective*. Abingdon: Routledge.

This book provides a comprehensive overview of the applications of UDL in differing HE cultural and geographical contexts.

Acknowledgements

In the first instance, the authors would like to extend our thanks to the British Council for funding this research project. A heartfelt expression of appreciation also goes to our project partners at Universitas Indonesia who, through their dedicated efforts to strengthen inclusive practices, have greatly enriched our understandings of what can be achieved with commitment and compassion. Finally, sincere thanks are due to colleagues within the Inclusion by Design Research Group at the University of Worcester, whose untiring efforts made our international conference and follow up workshops not only possible but also transformative and inspiring.

References

AdvanceHE (2024) Student led peer learning and support, Resources. Available from https://www.advance-he.ac.uk/knowledge-hub/student-led-peer-learning-and-support. (Accessed 22nd September 2024).

Almufareh, M., Kausar, S., Humayun, M., and Tehsin, S. (2024) A conceptual model for inclusive technology: advancing disability inclusion through artificial intelligence. *Journal of Disability Research*, 3(1), 20230060.

Bovill, C., Cook-Sather, A., and Felten, P. (2011) Students as co-creators of teaching approaches, course design, and curricula: implications for academic developers. *International Journal for Academic Development*, 16(2), pp. 133–145.

Boysen, G. A. (2024) A critical analysis of the research evidence behind CAST's universal design for learning guidelines. *Policy Futures in Education*, 22(7) 14782103241255428.

Bracken, S. (2024) Universal design for learning as an enabling framework for equity, diversity, and inclusion. In, *Curriculum in a Changing World. 50 views to celebrate BERA's 50th Anniversary. London: British Education Research Association in association with the British Curriculum Forum*. London: Troubador Publishing.

CAST (2024) The UDL Guidelines. Available online: https://udlguidelines.cast.org/ Accessed 22 October 2024).

Cho, S., Crenshaw, K. W., and McCall, L. (2013) Toward a field of intersectionality studies: Theory, applications, and praxis. *Signs: Journal of women in culture and society*, 38(4), pp. 785–810.

Culver, K. C., Kezar, A., and Koren, E. R. (2023) Improving access and inclusion for VITAL faculty in the scholarship of teaching and learning through sustained professional development programs. *Innovative Higher Education*, 48(6), pp. 1071–1094.

Freire, P. (1978) Pedagogy of the Oppressed. In Beck, J., Jenks, C., Keddie, N. and M. Young (Eds.) *Toward a New Sociology of Education*. London: Transaction Publishers.

Hanesworth, P, Bracken S, and Elkington, S. (2019) A typology for a social justice approach to assessment: learning from universal design and culturally sustaining pedagogy. *Teaching in Higher Education* 24(1), pp. 98–114.

Holcombe, E.M., Kezar, A.J., Ueda, N., and Vigil, D. (2023) Shared equity leadership: Working collectively to change campus cultures. *Journal of Diversity in Higher Education*. https://doi.org/10.1037/dhe0000536

INCLUDE and ICEQ (2024) Power of Potential: Sharing Experiences from Universal Design for Learning Journeys, 26th – 28th June, University of Worcester. Accessed from https://include.wp.worc.ac.uk/conference-details/ 24/11/2024

Jenlink, P. M. (2004) Discourse ethics in the design of educational systems: Considerations for design praxis. *Systems Research and Behavioral Science: The Official Journal of the International Federation for Systems Research*, 21(3), pp. 237–249.

Kemmis, S., and Smith, T. (2008) *Enabling praxis*. Rotterdam: Sense Publishers.

QAA. (2024) UK Quality Code for Higher Education 2024: Sector Agreed Principles. Available online: https://www.qaa.ac.uk/the-quality-code/2024 (Accessed 22 September 2024).

Richardson, E. V., Hopkins, A., Kennett, A., Lawrence, H., Wilson C.T. (2024) Involving Experts by Experience: The Potential for UDL Conferences to Inspire Learners with Diverse Needs (This work is equally co-authored). Poster presentation: The 2nd International UDL Symposium *Including Every Learner: In the school, in the home, in alternative learning setting*. Maynooth, Ireland, September 16th-17th 2024.

Rose, D. (2000) Universal design for learning. *Journal of Special Education Technology*, 15(4), pp. 47–51.

Saborío-Taylor, S., and Rojas-Ramírez, F. (2024) Universal design for learning and artificial intelligence in the digital era: Fostering inclusion and autonomous learning. *International Journal of Professional Development, Learners and Learning*, 6(2), July 2024, ep2408, No Pagination Specified.

Seale, J. (2009) Doing student voice work in higher education: An exploration of the value of participatory methods. *British Educational Research Journal*, 36(6), pp. 995–1015.

Seale, J., Burgstahler. S. and Havel, A. (2022) One model to rule them all, one model to bind them? A critique of the use of accessibility-related models in postsecondary education. *Open Learning: The Journal of Open, Distance and e-Learning*, 37(1), pp. 6–29.

Taylor, S. (2024) *Creativity in the Early Years: Engaging children aged 0-5*. London: SAGE.

United Nations (1994) The Salamanca Statement and Framework for Acton on Special Needs Education: World Conference on Special Needs Education: Access and Quality. Available from: https://www.european-agency.org/sites/default/files/salamanca-statement-and-framework.pdf (Accessed 25 November 2024).

United Nations (2015) *The UN Sustainable Development Goals*. United Nations, New York, 2015. Available at https://www.un.org/sustainabledevelopment/summit/. (Accessed 26 November 2024).

United Nations (2017) Committee on the Rights of Persons with Disabilities: Concluding observations on the initial report of the United Kingdom of Great Britain and Northern Ireland https://www.undocs.org/en/CRPD/C/GBR/CO/1 (Accessed 25 November 2024.)

13 The role of learner voice in producing powerful and sustainable educational change

Marie Stephenson

Introduction

For some time, the field of educational leadership has been dominated by a narrative driven by specific leadership approaches. Ligget (2022: 3) identifies these as transformational leadership, distributed, shared and instructional leadership. Although these constructs offer educational leaders valid ways to frame leadership practice in schools, they don't explicitly reflect what Duncan (2003) describes as *the new leadership*, a deliberate approach grounded by "democratic, humane, and inclusive principles" (p. 468). We need principals with principles, individuals who genuinely acknowledge and understand how to serve as social justice advocates and democratic change makers (Lac and Mansfield, 2018: 39). Leadership practice "must evolve to provide an even more powerful, transformative learning space that better meets students' needs" (Mansfield, 2014: 392), to co-create what Duncan (2003: 470) describes as "transformative classrooms which strengthen their functioning in both school and life". According to Duignan (2006), traditional leadership models reinforce power imbalances between students and school leaders, by failing to consider the dynamic and complex nature of the educational leadership landscape, and an increasingly diverse society (Ward et al., 2014: 333). Educational leaders must be able to respond to a wider range of issues (Kugelmas, 2003; Wang, 2018) and consider contextual challenges at every level (Tamadoni et al., 2024: 124).

Mansfield et al. (2018: 16) who cite Dantley and Tillman (2009) ask leaders to enable a democratic environment which encompasses "multiple voices, identities and perspectives". They further suggest that educational leaders need to better understand the power of their own voices and how they should be used to empower the voices of others. For Brasof and Mansfield (2018: 5), the concept of learner voice is still not a priority and has been overlooked in educational leadership, despite rhetoric to the contrary. The power to affect positive school improvement and educational change has remained firmly in the hands of a range of adults in schools and other educational institutions. Learners have been excluded from decision-making based on outdated views about their ability and maturity to understand and communicate regarding institutional structures and processes when, in fact, they ought to be appreciated "as critics and creators of educational practice" (Cook-Sather, 2020: 182). Today's educational leaders need to deliberately include learners by weaving their voices through the fabric of leadership. According to Cook-Sather (2016: 14) genuine collaboration and co-construction leads to meaningful change and enables learners to understand how they are valued and where they fit into the larger picture.

The notion of voice has been roundly explored in a variety of forms in previous chapters where it has been presented as a complex phenomenon which is *agentic* (Chapters 1 and 3), important for *identify formation* and developing a sense of *belonging* (Chapter 5), crucial for *supporting advocacy* (Chapter 6) and necessary for *ensuring marginalised voices* are heard (Chapters 8, 9, 10 and 11). Its importance is clear (Simmons, 2011: 542), but to hear a voice, we must know *how* to listen.

According to Watson and Barker (1984: 189) "listening is a complex process rather than a singular skill". It is more than a physical act; it is a communicative practice (Johnson and Bechler, 1998). The notion of listening and how to listen properly remains poorly understood (Feuerman, 2008), not just by scholars, but also by educational leaders. Tate (2003) and Feuerman (2008) found that educational leaders were in fact inefficient listeners having rated themselves as good. Indeed, Smith and Piele (2006: 64) reported similar issues in the general population, noting that we use only 25 per cent of our listening capacity. Not only do we think we're good at listening, but it is likely we don't really understand what it is to listen well.

Listening constitutes more than recall and memory or information-processing, it is cognitive and behavioural in nature (Johnson and Bechler, 1998), but also emotional. Waks (2011), reflecting on Dewey's (1938) account of listening describes the process as *immersive*; it must be receptive, aim-directive and constructive, a *total inclusive transaction* in which the results of the conversation pass from one to the other, as "a mutual coordination of means and ends"; as such, the parties "become aligned with respect to action steps and intended results" (Waks, 2011: 195). Through respectful listening information is received from the deliverer where it is transformed to create value (Bonsu, 2019). It involves mental presence and focus, openness and should be non-judgemental. This active engagement involves patience and attention to facilitate feedback and clarification. It is a respectful act designed to determine the collective truth (Duncan, 2003: 471).

Cook-Sather (2016: 10) advises listeners to demonstrate a genuine desire to hear and thus act, rather than indulge, oversimplify, dismiss or demean learner voice by rendering it passive or considering it an embellishment. Or, as Johnson and Bechler (1997) report, they may deceive others by making the right noises or nodding at the right time. We need to be attuned to both what is being said and to what may be left out; this requires great skill, energy and practice (Wasonga and Murphy, 2007).

Pause for thought

How well do you listen?
Do you tune out and begin thinking of your reply before someone is finished speaking?
Can you tell when someone is doing this to you in a conversation?
How does this make you feel?

Bertrand and Rodela (2018) warn us against underestimating learners or viewing them "as victims of injustices or passive recipients or beneficiaries of justice work" (Wang, 2018: 491). Caslin (2022) reminds leaders to examine the roles they play in silencing voices, as "students are capable of greater involvement in their educational decisions" and that although "it is their right to do so" (Quinn and Owen, 2016: 62), this is often rhetoric, not reality.

Fernandez, Heng and Eng (2022: 547) recounted significant challenges for learners regarding "perceptions of immaturity, incompetence, and inexperience" as well as "fears of bias, reprisals, and rejection" when asked to share their views. Indeed, Jones and Bubb (2021) found further issues around learner voice processes, where the channels of participation were too rigid, lacked structure, and created frustration and disappointment for learners when follow-up was limited. Seeking and eliciting students' views has the potential to challenge beliefs and perspectives (Cook-Sather, 2016) and could result in resistance and administrative pushback (Lac and Mansfield, 2018). Tensions lie beneath the surface, which means that educational leaders need to understand the complexities of genuinely enabling student voice.

According to Quinn and Owen (2016) inviting learners to be involved in their own learning experiences requires a shift in traditional power relations. Students are key to educational leadership (Lac and Mansfield, 2018); therefore, these important stakeholders need to be pulled in and engaged rather than left in the margins (Bertrand and Rodela, 2018). Mansfield (2014: 38) notes that leaders have a moral responsibility to redress the balance of power themselves, to "prioritise equity and aim to cultivate student voice", to "deconstruct the realities of student's lives" and critique the landscape for marginalising conditions (Mansfield, 2014: 396). But leaders must also understand the power of their own voices and how to use them to empower the voices of others (Mansfield et al., 2018,). More often than not, it is leaders who are listened too (Feuerman, 2008; Simmons, 2011), and this needs to change (Duncan, 2003). As Quinn and Owen (2016) note, we must create spaces where power can be challenged, where there is opportunity for disagreement, questioning and dialogue because engaging in student voice is messy (Caslin, 2022) and difficult (Ainscow and Messious, 2018). Whilst there have been gains, the ideal remains elusive (Nelson, 2016). The reality is that power imbalances cannot be eradicated; the system and its hierarchies produce and sustain it. But that does not mean that we should not strive to change it.

Whilst it is important that leaders need to see learners in a different way: learners must also change their self-perceptions and develop agency to step forward and be heard. Salisbury (2021: 760) echoes the thoughts of Cook-Sather (2007) and advises us to create ways for learners "to actively participate in the school improvement process as planners, researchers, and implementers"; to empower student voice work. He also asks leaders to support learners as they cultivate their agency by giving them opportunities "to critically assess their social context" (Salisbury, 202: 760) and take ownership of their own identities within their communities. So how can this be done given the very people who often hamper student voice are the very people crucial for its success (Salisbury, 2021)?

Pause for thought

Whose responsibility is this?
What role do you think you have to play in improving education for yourself and others?
How do you think educational leaders can enable this positive change?

Relational leadership is a leadership approach that emphasises the importance of relationships and social interactions; it focuses on the dynamics between school leaders, teachers, students and other stakeholders. It is crucial for enabling student voice because it prioritises trust, collaboration, empathy and open communication, creating an environment where students feel valued and empowered to express their views. Relational leadership encourages collaborative decision-making processes where students are active participants rather than passive recipients (Spillane, Halverson and Diamond, 2001). It is a leadership construct which prioritises interactions, identifies leadership as relational work and gives voice to "distinct perspectives" through "situated activities" over time (Helstad and Møller, 2013: 248).

Møller (2006: 66) explains that a school is "a network of relationships among people, structures and cultures". Hallinger and Truong (2016) agree but note that what is crucial is how these relationships are constructed. For them, relational leadership is a reciprocal process rather than one-way influence; where trust emerges and enables school improvement. Similarly to Wasonga and Murphy (2007) the notion of trust was identified by Stephenson (2017) in her PhD thesis as the most instrumental leadership disposition. For Edwards-Groves and Grootenboer (2021: 264) relational trust was "a fundamental organisational resource in school activity" and "entangled in the social exchanges, mutually understood responsibilities and designations". Stephenson (2017) also noted that the development of reciprocal relationships over time enabled a strong ethical environment and, although like Edwards-Groves and Grootenboer (2021) she found that trust was aligned with respect; she also showed that relational trust allowed values such as fairness and dignity to flourish.

So how might educational leaders build trust to enable student voice given that it is complex and multifaceted, requiring deliberate strategies and approaches? Educational leaders must cultivate an environment where students feel safe, valued and empowered to express their perspectives for fostering meaningful engagement and enhancing educational outcomes. Trust acts as a foundational element in this dynamic, facilitating open communication and collaboration between students and leaders. It is not only an abstract ideal, but a concrete mechanism (Bryk and Schneider, 2003). It is the bedrock of any collaborative relationship, as it promotes transparency, mutual respect, and a willingness to listen to diverse viewpoints. For Czerniawski (2012: 136), it must be "unbounded, reciprocal and philanthropic".

According to Louis and Murphy (2016), to create this type of culture, leaders must be attentive, selfless, and genuine; they must care, as it is the space where affective trust exists. The notion of caring in education is deeply rooted in the philosophical and ethical frameworks that emphasise the moral responsibility of educators to create nurturing environments that support student growth. According to Noddings (2013), a caring educational space is one where students are recognised as unique individuals with distinct needs, aspirations, and perspectives. Caring educational spaces are environments characterised by emotional warmth, mutual respect, trust and empathy (Duncan, 2003). According to Gilligan (1982) the latter is essential to understand and respond to students' emotional needs and is instrumental in fostering a caring environment. These *spaces* prioritise the holistic development of students, attending not only to their cognitive needs but also to their emotional and social well-being, fostering a sense of belonging which encourages students to actively engage in their educational journey, thereby enabling learner voice to emerge.

However, this commitment to caring requires a change in institutional practices and structures (Czerniawski, 2012). One of the most significant changes educational leaders must make is to rethink governance and decision-making processes within their institutions. Traditional governance models often prioritise top-down decision-making, leaving students with limited influence. To demonstrate care for student voice, educational leaders must adopt participatory governance models that actively involve students in decision-making processes. When students have a say in their learning, they are more likely to be engaged, motivated, and successful (Hattie, 2009). According to Fielding (2004), participatory governance empowers students by providing them with a platform to express their opinions, contribute to policy development, and influence institutional practices.

Incorporating students into governance structures can take various forms, such as creating student advisory boards, involving students in curriculum design committees or establishing student representation on school boards and administrative councils. Flutter and Rudduck (2004) emphasise that involving students in decision-making processes not only empowers them but also enriches the decision-making process by incorporating diverse perspectives and insights. By integrating student voice into governance, educational leaders signal their commitment to valuing student perspectives and fostering a collaborative educational environment.

> **Pause for thought**
>
> Can you remember any instances or initiatives where your voice was sought and included?
> Were leaders genuinely interested in what you had to say?
> Was it followed up with action and what was the impact?

Mitra (2018) agrees with Flutter and Rudduck (2004), noting that it is crucial that this is genuine and intentional to avoid learners feeling co-opted through government sanctioned student voice efforts, or impression management tactics (Czerniawski, 2012). After all, learner participation and collaboration ought to be voluntary for the learner where they feel the ability to exercise control over their educational experiences (Hajisoteriou and Sorkos, 2023). Educational leaders must establish authentic relationships with learners and show genuine interest. Lac and Mansfield (2018) advise leaders to prioritise constant interaction and dialogue with learners. Indeed, dialogue is one of the central planks to student voice, without it, there is no communication. It informs relationships, empowers and provides students the opportunity to participate, leading to consultation, resulting in a shift in power relations.

As noted earlier, those in authority positions traditionally hold power and reinforce hierarchies. What we really want to engender is leadership from below (Hatcher, 2005) to provide the ways and means for the redistribution of power, divesting responsibility and transforming students into leaders of their educational experiences. Student voice literature talks about empowerment, but Taylor and Robinson (2009) claim that this is not enough because it does not actually address the *dominant discourse* or acknowledge the context; it falls short of addressing the fact that power is constantly shifting, subjective, relative and value laden. The authors encourage us to explore power as a pluralistic and intricate process to better understand how we should enable student voice.

Noyes (2005) makes an interesting observation in his thematic review regarding the notion of power and pupil voice. He reminds us to think carefully about how we create boundaries for genuine power sharing and negotiation, given students and those that traditionally hold power have different ideas about what is significant to them. This raises questions about whether it is possible to create democratic schools when there are problems around what is being controlled and by whom. To compound matters Mitra (2018) explains that both adults and pupils often resort to their predetermined roles, despite efforts to forge different types of relationships. In this contested territory where clumsy and poorly defined student voice activities may disempower students (Mitra (2018: 479) we are asked to "nurture democratic spaces" by critiquing our educator voices to ensure they do not silence those that need to be heard (Mansfield et al., 2018).

Hajisoteriou and Sorkos (2023) believe that reshaping these relationships has the potential to transform school culture. Wasonga and Murphy (2007) note that *effective* educational leaders do not underestimate the importance of the informal school network as a dynamic and powerful enabler of positive change. Indeed, Mitra (2018) found exactly this in her study regarding the role of student voice for secondary school reform in the United States. However, this was not the case for Jones and Bubb (2021) who reported that, even in ideal conditions, the impact of student voice on school improvement is fraught with a range of issues. They list challenges such as time and resource constraints, and doubts regarding competence – for instance, making safe recommendations, or demonstrating a reluctance to challenge norms. Similar to the views of Mayes, Finneran and Black (2019), there is an assumption that students know how to make school better. But let us be clear, we are not asking them to do this; we are asking them how *we* might make school better for *them*, and this is an important distinction.

> **Pause for thought**
>
> Do you agree with Mayes, Finneran and Black (2019)?
> What would make school "better"?
> Do you think this is challenging for educational leaders too?

So, how do we centre student voice as "a natural part of school culture", where students are positioned as change agents, supported by systems and structures (Lac and Mansfield, 2018: 43)? Brasof and Mansfield (2018: 5) cite Mansfield (2011, 2015), who advocates for "inviting students to participate in the governance of their schools", as it "enables school leaders to learn necessary perspectives about school challenges and ultimately design and build community around effective change strategies". Scholars encourage educational leaders to adopt a range of deliberate strategies which contribute to providing a more equitable, socially just learning environment; these include involving learners in policy change, curriculum reform, culturally relevant pedagogic approaches and in research (Mansfield, 2014).

Welton, Mansfield and Salisbury (2022) advocate the involvement of students in policy discussions and debates to advocate for themselves and their communities. They believe that this neoliberalist and neoconservative approach challenges an increasingly marketised education sector. After all, students are not simply *consumers* of education, it *belongs* to them (Wang, 2018, Jones and Bubb, 2021). Therefore, collaborating in this way enables greater ownership, cutting across the nexus of school hierarchies and operational activities (Wasonga and Murphy, 2007). But, as with all change, there are also challenges: in his study regarding student voice in school safety policies, Hipolito-Delgado (2024) explains how educational leaders can make power sharing difficult; they can give the impression that students voices are being taken seriously when they are not. This creates an illusion of partnership (Hipolito-Delgado, 2024), an appendage to support a preconceived agenda, where suggestions are ignored if they challenge the status quo. Students must not be tokenistic symbols, but authentic participants (Mitra, 2018).

Children and young people have distinctive views about learning, teaching and schooling according to Cook-Sather (2006: 361). Demetriou (2016: 73), writing in Cook-Sather et al. (2016) offers concrete approaches and tools for finding out what students think of their pedagogic experiences and encourage educationalists to be creative. Centring students in this way is co-constructive: it changes what both parties know and understand. Students reported increased feelings of respect, confidence and positivity and appreciated how their views impacted the school and wider community. Teachers also benefited; they changed their views regarding student potential by addressing assumptions about student competence and capability. By embracing these practices, and incorporating these new narratives, teachers can transform their pedagogy (Himeles, 2016). Taylor and Robinson (2009) believe that this type of approach bears the hallmarks of radical pedagogy; it is the embodiment of the centrality of student voice. A *pedagogy of hope*, rather than a *pedagogy of the oppressed* (Freire, 1970).

As noted, there are other strategies used by educational leaders to address the notion of student voice. Student councils have long been a staple of many schools, serving as a platform to elicit the views of students. However, Jones and Bubb (2021) question the efficacy of student councils in their study concerning schools in Norway. There were issues around how council members were selected, who set the agenda and the lack of follow-up action. Students were reluctant to be honest, felt pressurised and that the process was pointless. Mayes et al. (2019: 159) highlight further issues around student representatives, and their skills as mediators of other students' voices, where "children and young people are likewise enmeshed in their own interpersonal relations of power".

Mansfield (2014) suggests that we involve students in our research efforts. It is a powerful approach, and when done well, is transformational, especially if it involves marginalised groups. It provides a formal framework and legitimacy to proceedings; it also fosters leadership, responsibility and ownership. This type of engagement offers students opportunities to seek their own solutions and motivates them to re-engage and expand their educational opportunities (Bland and Atweh, 2007). But as with all student voice initiatives, success is predicated on how these relationships are managed, what topics are chosen to be explored and how research outcomes are addressed; these decisions are traditionally in the behest of those in charge. So how do we ensure that students have a *real* seat at the table?

Working with others is a central tenet of both relational leadership and student voice and is key to enabling culture change and school improvement. It is a skill which requires commitment from all parties with a more equal distribution of power (Wasonga and Murphy, 2007) to create what Mitra (2018) describes as a flat power dynamic for a more inclusive community. We must work hard on creating these cultures because they don't happen by chance (Mitra, 2018). In truth, we find ourselves working against a backdrop of school hierarchies and competing agendas when trying to create genuine collective processes. Wasonga and Murphy (2007) ask leaders not to concern themselves with leadership style when co-creating leadership but to focus on the larger moral context, and the ideals that shape the school community. Over time it becomes invisible (Jones and Hall, 2021) and holistic; it becomes *how we do things around here*.

Pause for thought

To what extent have you been "heard" in your educational journey?
What do you think are the key qualities of a listening leader?
What will *you* take forward from reading this chapter?

Leaders need to possess, nurture, cultivate and practice a range of dispositions. Jarrett, Wasonga and Murphy (2010: 638) summarise the findings of Murphy et al. (2004) and Wasonga and Murphy (2007) advising leaders to work on as "collaboration, active listening, cultural anthropology, egalitarianism, patience, humility, trust/trustworthiness and resilience" or, more simply, develop **awareness**, change **attitudes** and, most importantly, **act** (Celoria, 2016: 206). Effective and transformative educational leaders understand their own behaviours and decision-making processes, which are crucial for promoting an inclusive and collaborative environment. They mediate and moderate reactions and interactions and are attuned to the emotional climate and culture in which they operate. They facilitate better communication and understanding, building relationships and fostering trust at *all* levels with *all* stakeholders.

Conclusion

The listening leader changes attitudes by modelling active listening, setting the standards for communication and participation across the organisation. Leaders need to slow down and develop listening routines which demonstrate care, curiosity and regard, and to tune into the power of perception (Safir, 2017). Learners and others must feel free to express their opinions and ideas without fear, to challenge the status quo and speak out on matters which affect them. Schools must be "safe and productive learning environments" (Brasof and Mansfield, 2018: 5) supported by systems and structures which enable voices to be heard in a genuine, non-tokenistic way. The listening leader must also model and embed democratic principles with staff, educating them on the power and efficacy of student voice by providing Continuing Professional Development (CPD) on active listening, cultural competency and inclusive practice to create school-wide change and improvement that supports student expression.

However, all of this is pointless unless voices are honoured through action. We must go beyond rhetoric and show individuals *how* well they have been heard. Student voice practices are not about gathering input but recognising our learners as capable contributors who bring unique and valuable perspectives. Whilst the type of educational leadership discussed in this chapter can help transform and sustain inclusive cultures, there are also further wide-reaching positive consequences (Mansfield, 2014). When students are *really* heard, they see the power of *their* agency; they understand how to become active, engaged citizens that are unafraid to stand up for what they value; it is *this* that they will carry through their lives and in everything that they do. *They* are the custodians of a more equitable, democratic and inclusive society.

Summary points

- We do not really understand what it is to listen, and this needs to change. Listening is predicated on a set of core principles, these include respect, care, trust and empathy. When attended to, these allow students to feel a sense of belonging and empowerment, which gives them agency in their own educational journeys.
- We all need to develop our listening skills, we must make conscious efforts to do so, as listening well is only achieved through practice. We must form these habits to transform education for all and sustain educational change.
- Educational leaders need to work closely with all stakeholders to build positive and successful relationships. This involves setting the standards for communication and participation across the organisation, where individuals feel free to express their opinions without fear of judgement.

- Educational leaders need to think differently about how and why they are leading in their settings to create more democratic and humane educational spaces which offer students opportunities to be genuinely heard.
- None of the discourse in this chapter will be meaningful unless it is enacted; *your task is to listen well, speak your mind and advocate for the change you want to see.*

Recommended reading

Ainscow, M. and Messiou, K. (2018) Engaging with the views of students to promote inclusion in education, *Journal of Educational Change*, 19(1), pp. 1–17.

This important paper is a culmination of the authors' research over may years. They explain that it is the responsibility of all educators to enter into a dialogue with the most important stakeholder in education: students. They focus primarily on ways to promote inclusion, how these conditions can be created and what leaders need to do to set the inclusive agenda in education. They talk about the hidden voices that are powerful levers for educational change and acknowledge that although there are challenges, they are well worth it to manifest the promise of inclusion.

Cook-Sather, A., Clarke, B., Condon, D., Cushman, K., Demetriou, H., and Easton, L. (2016). *Learning from the Student's Perspective: A sourcebook for effective teaching*, Taylor & Francis Group. ProQuest Ebook Central, https://ebookcentral.proquest.com/lib/worcester/detail.action?docID=4186024.

Alison Cook-Sather is a widely respected and prolific writer on the concept of seeing from the student's perspective. This book is a practical guide for educators who wish to transform cultural, institutional and classroom structures to enable student success. She believes that it is only by learning through students' perspectives and experiences that we can create an engaging and enduring educational environment.

Duncan, K. (2003). Professing educational leadership: The value of listening. *Journal of School Leadership*, 13(4), pp. 464–491.

This work explains the importance of open listening in the classroom, although based in the United States, Duncan highlights the role of leadership in creating the right climate for change. The concept of democratic pedagogy and democratic leadership are thus explored. With this, she asks us to challenge traditional notions of power and the value of shared approaches to enable voices to be genuinely heard. She adopts these practices because she believes she is educating the leaders of the future, and that they will, in turn, recognise and respect others to become the role models we need in education.

References

Ainscow, M. and Messiou, K. (2018) Engaging with the views of students to promote inclusion in education, *Journal of Educational Change*, 19(1), pp. 1–17.
Bertrand, M. and Rodela, K. C. (2018) A Framework for rethinking educational leadership in the margins: Implications for social justice leadership preparation. *Journal of Research on Leadership Education*, 13(1), pp. 10–37.
Bland, D., and Atweh, B. (2007) Students as researchers: engaging students' voices in PAR. *Educational Action research*, 15(3), pp. 337–349.
Bonsu, S. (2019) 'Listen: Communicating in knowledge-based organizations'. *International Journal of Global Business*, 12 (2), pp. 13–24.
Brasof, M. and Mansfield, K.C. (2018) Student voice and school leadership: Introduction. *Journal of Ethical Educational Leadership*, Special Issue 1, pp. 5–8.
Bryk, A.S. and Schneider, B. (2003) Trust in schools: A core resource for school reform. *Educational Leadership*, 60(6), pp. 40–45.
Caslin, M. (2022) We may be listening but are we ready to hear? A reflection on the challenges encountered when seeking to hear the educational experiences of excluded young people within the confines of the English education system. *International Journal of Research & method in Education*, 46(1), pp. 83–97.

Celoria, D. (2016) The preparation of inclusive social justice education leaders. *Educational Leadership and Administration: Teaching and Program Development*, 27, pp. 199–219.

Cook-Sather, A. (2006) Sound, presence, and power: 'Student Voice' in educational research and reform. *Curriculum Inquiry*, 36(4), pp. 359–390.

Cook-Sather, A. (2007) What would happen if we treated students as those with opinions that matter? The Benefits to Principals and Teachers of Supporting Youth Engagement in School. *NASSP Bulletin*, 91(4), pp. 343–362.

Cook-Sather, A., Clarke, B., Condon, D., Cushman, K., Demetriou, H., and Easton, L. (2016) *Learning from the Student's Perspective: A sourcebook for effective teaching*, Taylor & Francis Group. ProQuest Ebook Central, https://ebookcentral.proquest.com/lib/worcester/detail.action?docID=4186024

Cook-Sather, A. (2020) Student voice across contexts: Fostering student agency in today's schools. *Theory into Practice*, 59 (2), pp. 182–191.

Czerniawski, G. (2012) Repositioning trust: A challenge to inauthentic neoliberal uses of pupil voice. *Management in Education*, 26(3), pp. 130–139.

Dantley, M.E., and Tillman, L.C. (2009) Social justice and moral transformative leadership. In C. Marshall & M. Olivia (Eds), *Leadership for social justice: Making revolutions in in education* (2nd ed.). San Francisco, CA: Wiley.

Demetriou, H. (2016) Accessing Students' Perspectives through Three forms of consultation. In A. Cook-Sather, A., Clarke, B., Condon, D., Cushman, K., Demetriou, H., and Easton, L. (Eds) *Learning from the Student's Perspective: A Sourcebook for Effective Teaching*, Taylor & Francis Group. ProQuest eBook Central, https://ebookcentral.proquest.com/lib/worcester/detail.action?docID=4186024.

Dewey. J. (1938) The philosophy of the arts. *LW*, 13, pp. 366–367.

Duignan, P. (2006) *Educational Leadership: Key challenges and ethical tensions*. Cambridge: Cambridge University Press.

Duncan, K. (2003) Professing educational leadership: The value of listening. *Journal of School Leadership*, 13(4), pp. 464–491.

Edwards-Groves, C. and Grootenboer, P. (2021) Conceptualising five dimensions of relational trust: implications for middle leadership. *School Leadership and Management*, 41(3), pp. 260–283.

Fernandez, L., Heng, M.A. and Eng, C. L.K. (2022) Voices on 'voice': A juxtaposition of teachers' and students' perspectives on the possibilities and challenges of student voice in teaching and learning. *Asia Pacific Journal of Education*, 42(3), pp. 542–555. https://doi.org/10.1080/02188791.2022.2037512

Feuerman, C. (2008) Listening as leadership. *Principal Leadership.*, 8(7), pp. 64–65.

Fielding, M. (2004) Transformative approaches to student voice: Theoretical underpinnings, recalcitrant realities. *British Educational Research Journal*, 30(2), pp. 295–311.

Flutter, J. and Rudduck, J. (2004) *Consulting pupils: What's in it for schools*. London: Routledge Falmer.

Freire, P. (1970) *Pedagogy of the Oppressed*. New York: Seabury Press.

Gilligan, C. (1982) *In a different voice: psychological theory and women's development*. Cambridge, MA: Harvard University Press.

Hajisoteriou, C. and Sorkos, G. (2023) Students as informal leaders in deliberate acts of inclusion. *Research Papers in Education*, 38(6), pp. 924–943.

Hallinger, P., and Truong, T. (2016) 'Above must be above, and below must be below': enactment of relational school leadership in Vietnam. *Asia Pacific Education Review*, 17, pp. 677–690.

Hatcher, R. (2005) The distribution of leadership and power in schools. *British Journal of Sociology of Education*. 26(2), pp. 253–267.

Hattie, J. (2009) *Visible Learning – A synthesis of over 800 meta-analyses relating to achievement*. Abingdon: Routledge.

Helstad, K. and Møller, J. (2013) Leadership as relational Work: Risks and opportunities. *International Journal Leadership in Education*, 6(3), pp. 245–262.

Himeles, D. (2016) Learning to be heard and learning to listen: A preservice teacher's reflections on consulting students during practice teaching. In Cook-Sather, A., Clarke, B., Condon, D., Cushman, K., Demetriou, H., and Easton, L. (2016) (Eds). *Learning from the Student's Perspective: A Sourcebook for Effective Teaching* Taylor & Francis Group. ProQuest eBook Central, pp. 116–130. Accessed from: https://ebookcentral.proquest.com/lib/worcester/detail.action?docID=4186024.

Hipolito-Delgado, C. P. (2024) Student voice and adult manipulation: Youth navigating adult agendas. *The Urban Review*, 56, pp. 122–149.

Jarrett, E., Wasonga, T. and Murphy, J. (2010) The practice of co-creating leadership in high- and low-performing high schools. *International Journal of Educational Management*, 24(7), pp. 637–654.

Johnson, S. D. and Bechler, C. (1997) Leadership and listening: Perceptions and behaviors. *Speech Communication Annual*, 11, pp. 57–70.

Johnson, S. D. and Bechler, C. (1998) Examining the relationship between listening effectiveness and leadership emergence: Perceptions, behaviors, and recall. *Small Group Research*, 29(4), pp. 542–571.

Jones, M. and Bubb, S. (2021) Student voice to improve schools: Perspectives from students, teachers and leaders in 'perfect' conditions. *Improving Schools*, 24(3), pp. 233–244.

Jones, M.A. and Hall, V. (2021) Redefining student voice: applying the lens of critical pragmatism. *Oxford Review of Education*, 48(5), pp. 570–586.

Kugelmas, J. W. (2003) *Inclusive Leadership: leadership for Inclusion*. National College for School Leadership. Nottingham.

Lac V. T. and Mansfield, K.C. (2018) What do students have to do with educational leadership? Making a case for centering student voice. *Journal of Research on Leadership Education*, 13(1), pp. 38–58.

Liggett, R. (2022) Democratic leadership in a study of school based professional leadership culture: policy implications. *International Journal of Leadership in Education*, pp. 1–16. https://doi.org/10.1080/13603124.2021.2009036

Louis, K.S. and Murphy, J. (2016) Trust, caring and organizational learning: The leader's role. *Journal of Educational Administration*, 55(1), pp. 103–126.

Mansfield, K. C. (2011) *Troubling Social Justice in a Single-Sex Public School: An Ethnography of an Emerging School Culture*. Unpublished dissertation: The University of Texas at Austin.

Mansfield, K.C. (2014) How listening to student voice informs and strengthens social justice research and practice. *Education Administration Quarterly*, 50(3), pp. 392–430.

Mansfield, K. C. (2015) The importance of safe space and student voice in schools that serve minoritized learners. *Journal of Educational Leadership, Policy & Practice*, 30(1), pp. 25–38.

Mansfield, K. C., Welton, A., and Halx, M. (2018) Listening to student voice: Toward a more holistic approach to school leadership. *Journal of Ethical Educational Leadership*, Special Issue 1, 5(2), p10–27.

Mayes, E., Finneran, R. and Black, R. (2019) The challenges of student voice in primary schools: Students 'having a voice' and 'speaking for' others. *Australian Journal of Education*, 63(2), pp. 157–172.

Mitra, D. (2018) Student voice in secondary schools: The possibility for deeper change. *Journal of Educational Administration*, 56(5), pp. 473–487.

Møller, J. (2006) Democratic schooling in Norway: Implications for leadership in practice. *Leadership and Policy in Schools*, 5, pp. 53–69.

Murphy, J. T., Hunt, D., and Wasonga, T. (2004) Cocreated leadership: Leadership from Within. *School Business Affairs*, 35(2), pp. 20–21.

Nelson, E. (2016) Re-thinking power in student voice as games of truth: Dealing/playing your hand. *Pedagogy, Culture & Society*, 25(2), pp. 181–194.

Noddings, N. (2013) *A relational Approach to ethics & Moral Education*. Los Angeles: University of California Press.

Noyes, A. (2005) Pupil voice: Purpose, power and the possibilities for democratic schooling. *British Educational Research Journal*, 31(4), pp. 533–540.

Quinn, S. and Owen, S. (2016) Digging deeper: Understanding the power of student voice. *Australian Journal of Education*, 60(1), pp. 60–72.

Safir, S. (2017) Learning to listen. *Educational Leadership*, 74(8), pp. 16–21.

Salisbury, J. (2021) Relinquishing power: Creating space for youth of color leaders. *Journal of Educational Administration*, 59(6), pp. 759–775.

Simmons, R. (2011) Leadership and listening: The reception of user voice in today's public services. *Social Policy and Administration*, 45(5), pp. 539–568.

Smith, S.C., and Piele, P.K. (2006) *School Leadership: The Handbook for excellence in Student Learning*. 4th Ed. Thousand Oaks, California: Corwin Press.

Spillane, J. P., Halverson, R. and Diamond, J.B. (2001) Investigating school leadership practice: A distributed perspective. *Educational Researcher*, 30(3), pp. 23–28.

Stephenson, M.E. (2017) Ethical Decision-making: Learning from Prominent leaders in not-for-profit organisations. PhD Thesis, University of Worcester. https://eprints.worc.ac.uk/8294/1/Ethical%20decision-making-%20Learning%20from%20prominent%20leaders%20in%20not-for-profit%20organisations.pdf

Tamadoni, A., Hosseingholizadeh, R. and Bellibas, M.S. (2024) A systematic review of key contextual challenges facing school principals: research-informed coping solutions. *Educational Management Administration & Leadership*, 52(1), pp. 116–150.

Tate, J. S. (2003) School leaders and the strategic impact of listening. *International Listening Association*, 32nd Annual Convention Stockholm, Sweden, July 17–20, 2003.

Taylor, C. and Robinson, C. (2009) Student voice: Theorising power and participation. *Pedagogy, Culture and Society*, 12(2), pp. 161–175.

Waks, L.J. (2011) John Dewey on listening and friendship in school and society. *Educational Theory*, 61(2), pp. 191–205.

Wang, F. (2018) Social justice leadership – theory and practice: A case of Ontario. *Educational Administration Quarterly*, 54(3), pp. 470–498.

Wasonga, T.A. and Murphy, J.F. (2007) Co-creating leadership dispositions. *ISEA*, 35 (2), pp. 20–32.

Watson, K.W. and Barker, L.L. (1984) Listening Behavior: Definition and measurement. In R.N. Bostrom (Ed), *Communication Yearbook 8, 178-197*. Beverly Hills: Sage.

Ward, S. C., Bagley, C., Lumby, J., Woods, P., Hamilton, T., and Roberts, A. (2014) School leadership for equity: lessons from the literature. *International Journal of Inclusive Education*, 19(4), 333–346. https://doi.org/10.1080/13603116.2014.930520

Welton, A. D., Mansfield, K.C., and Salisbury, J.D. (2022) The politics of student voice: The power and potential of students as policy actors. *Educational Policy*, 36(1), pp. 3–18.

Index

Note: Pages in *italics* refer to figures and pages in **bold** refer to tables.

academic self-concept 69–78; developing process 77
academics' experience, of teaching 7–9
ACEs *see* adverse childhood experiences
adaptation process 119; learner voice for 119–122
adult learner 3
adverse childhood experiences (ACEs) 38–40
advocacy 59–67; equity 63–65; project methodology 65–66; survivor 43–44
advocacy groups 17
agency 28–29; academic self-concept and 69–78; and empowerment 138–141; in nineteenth-century schools 29–30; in schools 30; in universal design for learning 130–142
Ahmad, F. 87
Åkerlind, G. S. 6, **6–8**, *8*
Altbach, P.G. 121
andragogical approach 3
anticipatory inclusive design 132
antiracism 94–96
anxiety 77
Appleton, L. 2
Ariès, Phillipe 29
assessment methods 49
authority 22
Azmitia, M. 77

Bain, J. D. 3
Bandura, A. 29, 33, 54, 77
Bandura elucidates 28
Barker, L.L. 146
Bechler, C. 146
belonging, concepts of 51–53
Bertrand, M. 146
Best, R. 52
Biesta, Gert 10–11
Biesta's functions of education 10–11
Bilimoria, D. 7

binary system 48
Black Lives Matter (BLM) movement 92
Black, R. 150
Bloom's Taxonomy 3
bodily chastisement 27
Bois, Du 92
Bovill, C. 22–23
Brasof, M. 145, 150
British Council funded project 130
Bronfenbrenner, U. 103, 106
Brooman, S. 1, 124
Brown report (2010) 48
Bubb, S. 147, 150–151
Budge, K. 63

CAI *see* Commonwealth Awareness Initiative
Cameron, David 85
Campbell-Stephens, R. 91
career teacher experience 1
caring educational spaces 148
caring in education, notion of 148
Carnell, E. 4–5
case/control design 7
case study: of education 47; Evesham Church of England School, 1883–1886 30–32
Caslin, M. 146
Chahboun, S. 122, 124
"cheerful obedience to duty" 30
childhood 29; experiences of neurodiversity 72–73
child's voice 27–28; agency and 28–29; Evesham Church of England School, 1883–1886 30–32; late nineteenth-century schools 26; in nineteenth-century schools 29–30; past 26–35; role of parents 32–33
Choudry, A. 54
Clandinin, D.J. 37
Coelen, R.J. 121
Coffey, M. 7
cognitive learning impairment 139

collective agency 28, 33
common ground: conflict avoidance as 20–21; listening to learners' voices as 21–22; polarisation as 21
Commonwealth 92–94
Commonwealth Awareness Initiative (CAI) 92, 96; methods and methodology 94–95
Commonwealth Games 93
communication style 123
community approach **5**
community building 136–137
conception of learning 2–3, *6*
conception of power 31
conceptions of teaching 3–5, *6*, **9**
conflict avoidance as common ground 20–21
confluence of conceptions 5–7
constructivist approach 94
construct knowledge 82
consumer-drive culture 3
contextual influences *104*, 106
Continuing Professional Development (CPD) training 77, 92
Cook-Sather, A. 121–122, 126, 145–147
corporal punishment 26–28
CPD training *see* Continuing Professional Development (CPD) training
Creely, E. 94
critical discourse analysis (CDA) 94
critical engagement 122
Critical Race Theory (CRT) 63
cross-system interactions 112–113
cultural differences 123
cultural distance 121
cultural intelligence 121
culture shock 53
curriculum development 136
Czerniawski, G. 148

Dale, K. 70
Dantley, M.E. 145
Darwent, S. 1, 124
data analysis processes 71–72
Davis, S.W. 103, 113
Dawkins, Richard 85
de Certeau, Michel 30–31
decision-making processes 28, 148–149
decolonisation 96
deep learning 2
depression 77
"design thinking" 62
developmental strategies **9**
Dewey. J. 146
Diangelo, R. 100
diary entries 38
direct models of democracy 81
disobedience 30–31
diverse needs 59–67
diverse students 48, 55

diversity 96
Dollinger, M. 126
Doscher, S. 63
double consciousness 92
Duncan, K. 145
dyslexia 65

Early Childhood Education 118
education; *see also* higher education (HE); common ground *see* common ground; egalitarian and humanising purpose of 103; experience of 15; lifelong learning 20–21; narrative story 72–76; prison *see* prison education; relationships in 42–43; secular normativity in 84; teach *see* teaching; transitions in *see* transitions, in education
educational leadership 145, 148–149, 151–152
education-based courses 102
Education Reform Act, 1988 48
education's purpose: academics' teaching experience 7–9; Biesta's functions of 10–11; conception of learning 2–3; conceptions of teaching 3–5; conceptualisation of teaching 9–10; confluence of conceptions 5–7; student voice 1; voice 11
Education Studies 17
Edwards-Groves, C. 148
Elliot, G. 60
embryonic plans 92
emotional and social well-being 148
Empireland (Sanghera) 93
empowerment 138–141; disabled learners' 130–142
Eng, C. L.K. 146
entanglement 22
epistemic injustice 80–88
Epistemic Injustice: Power and the ethics of knowing (Fricker) 82
Equality Act (2010) 61, 88
equity 63–65
equity, diversity and inclusion (EDI) 119
Ethical Global Issues Pedagogy Framework 98
ethical permission 72
ethnic minorities 91
Evesham Church of England School, 1883–1886 30–32
exosystems *107*

Fairclough, N. 94
"feedback loop" 124
Fernandez, L. 146
Feuerman, C. 146
Fielding, M. 148
Finneran, R. 150
Fitzgibbons, D. E. 9, **9**
flexibility, of teaching methods 136
Flutter, J. 149

fragmentation 49
Fraser, C. 24
Freire, P. 113, 119, 122–123, 125–126, 136
Fricker, M. 82
Fuller, F.F. 6, **6–8**
Further and Higher Education Act, 1992 48

Gale, T. 54
Garriy, L. 64
Gazeley, L. 52
GCSE see General Certificate of Secondary Education
gender-segregated spaces 86
General Certificate of Secondary Education (GCSE) 38, 48
Gibbs, G. 7
Giddens, Anthony 30–31
Gilligan, C. 148
Ginsberg R 111–112
Girma, H. 63
Glazzard, J. 70
Global Majority 91–92, 95, 99
global voices 118–128
governmental departments 50
grade inflation 50
Great Britain 29
Grootenboer, P. 148
Guha, Ranjit 28
GUIDE Project 64

Habermas, J. 84
Haigh, N. 8
Hajisoteriou, C. 150
Hallinger, P. 148
Hämäläinen, R. 3
Harris-Evans, J. 54
Harrison, N. 54–55
Hartman, D. 53
HEADSUP acronym 98–99
Heckman J.J. 54
HEIs see higher education institutions
Hendrick, Harry 27
Heng, M.A. 146
Her Majesty's Inspectors of Schools (HMIs) 33
Hesser, J. 77
higher education (HE) 37; adverse childhood experiences (ACEs) 38–40; assessment methods in 49; disaffection 38–40; Further and Higher Education Act and 48; gathering narrative data 38; learner's reflection on 49–51; learner voice in 40–42, 80; relationships in 42–43; for supporting learners with individual needs 61; survivor advocacy 43–44
higher education institutions (HEIs) 52–53, 55, 121
Hinton-Smith, T. 52
Hipolito-Delgado, C. P. 150

His Majesty's Prisons and Probation Service (HMPPS) 108
Houston, S. 28
Howells, K. 51–53
human agency 28
humanisation 123

idiographic approach 70
iERA see Islamic Education and Research Academy
inclusive education 139–141
inclusive practice 49
inclusivity 86
independent learning 10
independent thinking 33
individual-collective continuum 5
individual learners 64
information technologies 139
Initial Teacher Education (ITE) 99
Institute for Adult Continuing Education (NIACE) 60
Institute for Fiscal Studies 50
institutional barriers 137–138
institutional racism 122
"intentional act of development" 8
"intentional, insistent, deep collaboration" 113
intercultural interaction 53
international students, voices of 122–125
interviews 7, 71
intrinsic motivation 2
Islamic Education and Research Academy (iERA) 84–85

James, A. 28, 30, 35
James, A.L. 30, 35
Jansen, Y. 87
Johnson, S. D. 146
Jones, E. 121
Jones, M. 147, 150–151

Kahu, E. R. 52
Khalaila, R. 77
Kiili, C. 3
Knowles, M. 3
Krauss, Lawrence 85
Krieger, S. 71
Krishnamurti, Jiddu 103
Kugel, P. 6, **6–8**

Lackey, Jennifer 105
Lac V. T. 149
Landon, Joseph 27
Langton, R. 82
language 63
learner (student-) centred learning 7
learner participation 149
learners' needs 61–63

learner voice 34, 60, 119; for adaptation 119–122; and belonging 47; as common ground 21–22; concept of 80, 119; expressing 40–42; and placement experience 102–115; political dimensions of 81; reimagining 87–88; role of 145–153; threading 133–135; types of 81
learning: communities model 51; community approach **5**; concept of 2; needs of 61; self-advocacy 64
Lee, H. 24
legislation pertaining, reflection of 48–49
Lehane, T. 60
life-history approach 71
lifelong learning 20–21, 60
Liggett, R. 145
listening to learners' voices 21–22
lived realities 52
"locutionary silencing" 82, 86
Logbook 26, 31–32
looked-after child (LAC) 38
Louis, K.S. 148
Low, C. 60

Macpherson, W. 122
macrosystem *109*, 111, *114*
Malay, E.D. 121
Mallman, M. 24
Mansfield, K.C. 145, 147, 149–151
marketisation 55
Marton, F. 2
Matthews, K.E. 126
Mayes, E. 150
Meadows, S. 24
Meehan, C. 51–53
mental health 73–74, 77
mental health disorders 39
mesosystem 106
Michaels, B. 103
microsystems *107*, 108
Middleton, J. 35
Ministry of Justice (MoJ) 105, 108
Mitra, D. 149–151
Mkonto, N. 51–53
Modood, T. 87
Møller, J. 148
Moore, E. 62
Mullet, D. R. 94
multiculturalism 85–87
Murphy, J. 148, 151–152
Murphy, J.F. 148–152
Murphy, M.S. 37
mutual shaping 72
mutual trust 110

Nakkula, M. J. 9
national curriculum in England 16
National Student Engagement Survey (NSSE) 2–3
National Student Survey (NSS) 2, 37
National Student Survey and Teaching Evaluation Framework 48
Neal, J. 103, 105–106
Neal, Z. 103, 105–106
Nelson, K. 52
neoconservative approach 150
neoliberalism 83–84
neurodiversity, childhood experiences of 72–73
Noddings, N. 52, 148
nomothetic approach 69
non-cognitive psychological factors 54
non-cognitive skills 54
non-traditional students 37, 53
Noyes, A. 149
NSSE see National Student Engagement Survey
nurture democratic spaces 149

objective-subjective continuum 5
"occasional" truancy 32
"omnipresence of risk management" 108
"one-size-fits-all" approach 139
online questionnaires 65
organised truancy 32
Oswell, D. 35
Otten, S. 121
Owen, S. 147

Page, A.G. 122, 124
Palmer, P. J. 6
parents, role of 32–33
Parker, S. 54
Parrett, W. 63
Parsons, Talcott 29
participatory governance models 148
Pashby, K. 98
pastoral care 52
pedagogic models 55
"pedagogue of process" 103
pedagogy of hope 151
peer-facilitated learning (PFL) activities 51–52
peer support 136–137
"peer-to-peer educators" 113
persistent truancy 32
personal diary entries 38
"personal experiences of schooling" 69–70
PFL activities see peer-facilitated learning (PFL) activities
PGCE see Post Graduate Certificate of Education
physical violence 28
Piaget, Jean 29
Pierson, R. 64
Pimor, A. 1, 124
placement experience 102–115; cross-system interactions 108–112; filtering education ideologies and agendas 112–113; prison education 104–106; prison-education paradox 106–108; trade-off to pay-off 103–104

poetry 38
polarisation, as common ground 21
positive learning 44
possible selves 54–55
Post Graduate Certificate of Education (PGCE) 91, 93
"potential corruptor" 109
power, notion of 149
practitioner concludes 55
prison agendas 104
prison education 103–104, 113; macrosystem *114*; networked model of *107, 109–110*; paradox mapped onto ecological systems 106–108; prison exchange project 115; prison ideologies and agendas 108–111; punishment-security-freedom paradox 104–106
"Prison Education Paradox" 104
prison newspapers 115
professional reflections 95–97
project methodology 65–66
proxy agency 33
punishment-security-freedom paradox 104–106
punitive measures 31
pupils 32–33; voice 149
purposive sampling 70
Pythagoras's Theorem 15

qualification 10
Quality Assurance Agency for Higher Education's (QAA) 83
questioning approach 102
Quinn, S. 147
quotations 72

racism: and decolonisation 95; institutional 122; in Secondary Education 92; in teacher education 91–99
"radical secularism" 84
Ramsey, V. J. 9, **9**
readiness, concept of 48
"reading against the grain" 28
Reay, D. 87
reflection process 38
Regio Emelio Approach 132
relational leadership 148, 151
repressive punishment 28
resilience 55
resistance 48
Rico, N. 63
"rights-based" culture 3
"risk bureaucracy" 106
Robinson, C. 149, 151
Rodela, K. C. 146
Rogers, Carl 110
Rosen, M. 63
Ross, C.A. 43
Roy, E. 62

Rubinstein, Y. 54
Rudduck, J. 149

Said, E.W. 123
Salisbury, J.D. 147, 150
Säljö, R. 2
Salmon, David 27
Samuelowicz, K. 3
Sanghera, Satnam 93
SAR *see* student academic representation
SCALE Project team 64, 66
Schmidt, S. 53
schools, agency in 30
Scott, P. 49
scrutiny 18
Seale, J. 1
Seary, K. 52
secularism 84–87
self-advocacy 50, 59, 64
self-directed learning 10
self-efficacy theory 54
self-fulfilling prophecy 76
self, fundamental concept of 77
self-reflection questions 98
self-silence 82
semi-structured interviews 3–4, 94
seven-level framework 4
severe punishment 31–32
Sewell, Alexandra 70
Shakespeare 118–119
shared knowledge 51
silencing of student voices 80–88
Smith, B. E. 3
social, emotional, and mental health (SEMH) 38
social science research methods 71
Sorkos, G. 150
South African Boer War of 1899–1902 29
speaker 70–72
Special Educational Needs (SEN) 118
Special Educational Needs and Disability (SEND) 44; learner's identity 69–78
Specific Learning Differences (SpLDs) 69
Stake, R. 71
Statutory Assessment Tests (SATs) 48
Stephenson, M.E. 148
St Giles Trust Peer Advisor Programme 116
STIR magazine 115
structuration theory 31
student academic representation (SAR) 80, 84, 87–88
student-centred approach 4
students: of Education Studies 17–19; problems to environmental limitation **62**; voices 1, 11, 50, 80–88, 149
Students' Unions (SU) 81
subjectification 10
Sund, L. 98
supportive learning environment 128

"surrogate parents" 60
survivor advocacy 43–44
Sustainable Development Goal 140
Sutcliffe. J. 59–60
systematic enquiry (research) 8
systemic action 91–99; Commonwealth Awareness Initiative 92–95; participants' personal and professional reflections 95–97; pause for reflection 97; self-reflection questions 98

Tate, J. S. 146
Tavares, V. 119, 123, 126
Taylor, C. 149, 151
Taylor, C. A. 54
teacher-centred approach 4
teacher development models 6, **6**
teacher education, racism in 91–99
teacher-learner relationship 111
teaching: academics' experience 7–9; career experience 1; community approach **5**; conceptions of 3–5; conceptualisation of 9–10; education at school 15–24; scholarship 9
teaching assistants (TAs) 18, 60
teaching-oriented pedagogy 132
teach-to-test culture 52
Thomas, Aisha 92, 98
Thompson, D. W. 55
threading learner voice 133–135
three Rs (rules, reflection and research) 8
Tillman, L.C. 145
Timpson, James 105
Tinto, V. 51
Tomlinson, J. 59–60
tracing education 104
trade-off to pay-off 103–104
traditional governance models 148
traditional research methods 38
transformative educational leaders 152
transgender dysphoria 64
transitions, in education 47–56; belonging 51–53; learner concludes 55; learner's reflection of legislation pertaining 48–49; learner voice and belonging 47; practitioner concludes 55; types of 53–54
triple consciousness approach 92, 98
truancy 30, 32

Truong, T. 148
two-way continuum of teaching 5

UDL *see* Universal Design for Learning
UK: higher education system 120; prison system 105–106
Universal Design for Learning (UDL) 62, 130–142; implementation, collaborative praxis of 135; inclusivity and flexibility into curriculum design 136; learner voice and agency through 133–135; LV praxis and research on principles of 140; peer support and community building 136–137
university readiness 47

"Velcro" model of support 60
Vincent, C. 64
virtual and online platforms 52
voices 11; adult learner 3; child/children *see* child's voice; demands 16; development 1; empowering disabled learners' 130–142; global 118–128; of international students 121–125; of learners 60; notion of 146; and systemic action 91–99
Vygotsky, Lev 29

Waks, L.J. 146
Waller, R. 54–55
Ward, G. 63
Wasonga, T. 151–152
Wasonga, T.A. 148–152
Watson, K.W. 146
Weiner, I. A. 87
Welton, A. D. 147, 150
Wheeler, J. V. 7
widening participation strategies 48
Widnall, E. 24
Willans, J. 52
Wilson, D. 106
Wolf, T. 71
Woodgates, P. 125
Woolley, R. 63
world-class education 118–128

"you said, we did" approach 2

Zeller, N. 71–72

For Product Safety Concerns and Information please contact our EU
representative GPSR@taylorandfrancis.com
Taylor & Francis Verlag GmbH, Kaufingerstraße 24, 80331 München, Germany

www.ingramcontent.com/pod-product-compliance
Lightning Source LLC
Chambersburg PA
CBHW080119020526
44112CB00037B/2794